Flaming Prawns Tahitian

The Polynesian Cookbook

By Victor Bennett

GALAHAD BOOKS · NEW YORK

Dedicated to
Mama Rossi
and
Joan Rossi, Executive Secretary
and
Roland W. Force, Director of
The Bernice P. Bishop Museum
Honolulu, Hawaii
and
Ed Turner, Secretary-Treasurer,
of the Marine Cooks and Stewards Union,
San Francisco A.F.L.-C.I.O
*without whose respect and devotion
this volume would never have
been published*

Color photographs by Roy Carlson

Published by Galahad Books, 95 Madison Avenue, New York, N.Y. 10016, by arrangement with Prentice-Hall, Inc. Formerly titled *The South Pacific Cookbook*. Copyright under International and Pan American Copyright Conventions. All rights reserved. No part of this book may be reproduced in any form or by any means, except for the inclusion of brief quotations in a review, without permission in writing from the publisher.

Library of Congress Catalog Card Number: 73-85502. ISBN: 0-88365-071-1

Manufactured in the United States of America

Man Shall Not Live by Bread Alone

You may be thinking, "How odd for a pastor to be writing for a cookbook." But when Victor Bennett phoned from San Francisco and asked for an article on "the true story of Christian Missions in Hawaii," I saw an important connection to draw between providing bread for the stomach and Bread of Life for the soul of man, as well as a clue to peace on earth and goodwill among races and nations.

In both the culinary arts and the religious sciences, the food that men, women, and children prepare and provide should appeal to and satisfy the hunger of both body *and* soul. Every chef or cook has a ministry to perform. He or she seeks to delight not only the body but also the soul of the one who receives the gifts prepared by the heart and mind and hand. He aims to provide not just bread alone, but "every Word that proceeds out of the mouth of God"—food that has beauty, grace, joy, and love in it. The feeling of highest satisfaction comes to the one who receives food that *looks* good, *tastes* good, is prepared with *love*, and served with *grace*. Highest joy comes to the chef when the one who eats has the time and the wit to enjoy and appreciate what has been prepared.

The short-order cook at a busy street-corner stand and the chef in a fine restaurant are important people. Both try to feed the hungry. But there is a great difference between the sweating short-order cook, who, constantly pressured by four or five back orders, mechanically slaps pancake batter or hamburger meat on a scorching, greasy iron slab, and the chef at the Mauna Kea Beach Hotel who takes the time to add beauty, grace, and love to the food he prepares. There is also a big difference between the ulcer-developing man who in a hurry gulps down huge mouthfuls of carefully prepared nutriment, and the man who takes time to sit down and enjoy food that delights the eye, pleases the soul, and satisfies the palate. To the fine chef and grateful gourmet, God gives the rare gift of wonder and well-being—the sense of the Holy.

The missionaries who brought the Gospel to Hawaii were fine Chefs of the Lord. The Gospel they brought was not Bread of Life turned into Stone (as the movie "Hawaii" implied), but was a life-giving gift of God that brought joy to the poor and liberty to captives in dark caves of the heart, mind, and soul—until native Hawaiians and their brothers who came from the East and West over the next century-and-a-half could be called "trees of righteousness, the planting of the Lord" (Isaiah 61), the Aloha State.

There are those today who are quick to berate our missionaries for ruining Hawaii, and who call for a return to the good old days of pre-Christian Hawaii. These people do not know the cultural breakdown and sorrows that came upon our people after the arrival of Captain James Cook in 1778, nor do they remember the harsh realities of human sacrifices upon the altars of the ancient gods of Hawaii, or the killing of children born with any physical abnormality, or the constant warfare between the tribes of Hawaiian chiefs that continued to rob the race of its finest manhood. Those who ridicule the missionary and accuse him of robbing the Hawaiian confuse him with the unscrupulous trader, and commit a grave injustice upon these faithful servants of the Lord. But what's the true story?

Pre-Christian Hawaii was a Stone-Age Hawaii. Despite the barbarous customs cited above (modern foetus-deforming drugs and nation-destroying nuclear warheads make these ancient barbarities look civilized by comparison), my ancestors were far from being complete savages. They were a people of great nobility and dignity of life and thought. Except for their constant warfare, they had achieved a fair balance with their environment. They had an exacting and intricate religious system that was the foundation of their society.

Religion, what a person or people believe about God and Man and Nature and Self, is the source of a man's or nation's stability and order. Like the Ten Commandments of the Hebrews, the Code of my ancestors identified their gods and spelled out the right things for the people to do, as well as the wrong things they were not to do. It was called the Kapu. By this Kapu System their life found order, direction, stability. But the influence of Western life and culture upon the life of my forbears after Captain Cook happened upon these islands in 1778 was devastating. By the year 1819 the meticulous and detailed Kapu System was overthrown.

It is important to note here that the overthrow of the Kapu by my people occurred *before*, and not after, our missionaries arrived in these islands. This means that when they arrived, the atmosphere in which these men and women of God had to do their work was one of cultural chaos and lawlessness.

But how do you build an Aloha State or a peaceful world out of a despairing, bitter, proud, fallen people and shattered culture? How is the need for a new civilization and a stabilizing code met in every age?

In the process of God's Creation, unless a saving force appears to provide new foundations for a broken people and culture, they die. Arnold Toynbee's monumental history of civilizations tells that story most vividly. Firewater, new diseases, rioting and brawling, licentiousness, threats from foreign citizens and powers were all brutal and bewildering problems to our Hawaiian rulers. Their greatest need at that moment of history was the appearance of a special kind of help—a help consisting of a people of unconditional compassion for them, a people who were familiar with the best teachings and tools of the culture of the West, who would not turn tail and run from the slightest discomfort or danger, who would not try to cheat them, who could be trusted. But where was such a people to be found?

Man Shall Not Live by Bread Alone

In the year 1808 a despairing and disappointed teenager dove into the ocean at Kealakekua, Kona, and swam out to a trusted trader's vessel anchored there—swam toward the Light, for himself and Hawaii.

Opukahaia is the Hawaiian singled out by the *Encyclopaedia Brittanica* as the one who "altered the course of Hawaii's history." Opukahaia had survived tribal warfare that took his father, mother, and brother—to become the inspirer of the Christian Mission to Hawaii. After sensing the creative meaning and redemptive power of the Christian faith at Yale College in New Haven and the Cornwall School in Connecticut, he pleaded with great fervor and eloquence throughout the New England states for a Christian Mission to Hawaii. The memoirs of this remarkable Hawaiian, first published in 1818, have been reprinted and are available at Kawaiahao Church, Honolulu, Hawaii.

What kind of profound love for God and deep courageous concern for the well-being of one's fellow man was called for? Who would leave his home and dear ones for the sake of unknown people and places? Yet in answer to Opukahaia's plea, Holy Vows were taken and many lives were committed to the taking of the Bread of Life to Hawaii. These volunteers had answered the call sent forth by the newly formed American Board of Commissioners for Foreign Missions.

The first torchbearers who left Boston Harbor for Hawaii on the brig "Thaddeus" (not "Thetis" as in the novel *Hawaii* by Michener) on October 23, 1819 were:

> The Rev. and Mrs. Hiram Bingham
> The Rev. and Mrs. Asa Thurston
> Farmer Daniel Chamberlain, Mrs. Chamberlain, and their
>   five children
> Medical doctor Thomas Holman and Mrs. Holman
> Printer Elisha Loomis and Mrs. Loomis
> Teacher Samuel Ruggles and Mrs. Ruggles
> Teacher and Mechanic Samuel Whitney and Mrs. Whitney
> Thomas Hopu, Willian Kanui, John Honolii—fellow students of
>   Opukahaia from the Cornwall School in Connecticut

When Opukahaia died of typhus fever on February 17, 1818, in Cornwall, it was thought that the idea of the Mission to Hawaii had died with him. Instead, his death increased the efforts made for the Mission. Over the years spanning 1819–1848, a total of 184 ordained ministers, physicians, teachers, printers, farmers, bookbinders, and secular agents were to give their lives for the cause of Christ in Hawaii.

The aim of these Chefs of the Lord was to feed not only the soul but also the body of the Hawaiian. For the nourishment of the heart and soul there were preachers; for developing the mind there were teachers and printers; for maintaining the health of the body (foreign diseases were decimating the population) there were doctors; for introducing new methods of planting food there were farmers; for giving Hawaiians the skill to use the tools of western civilization there were mechanics.

The Charter under which our missionaries came can well serve as modern man's chart for peace on earth:

> To cover these islands [we might say "continents"] with fruitful fields and pleasant dwellings and schools and churches; To raise up the whole people to an elevated state of Christian civilization; To make them acquainted with letters; To bring them the Bible with the skill to read it; To turn them from barbarous customs and habits; . . . To convert them to the living and redeeming God.

The Hollywood missionary stereotypes (hard-nose, hell-fire and damnation preachers) do not at all resemble the members of this Mission to Hawaii. Had our missionaries been the pitiful cinema characters portrayed in that unfortunate movie "Hawaii," these islands would have turned out far differently from the Aloha State it now is. Had the rulers of Hawaii not been properly advised by the missionaries in the handling of the island's kingdom affairs, and had the purveyors of foreign power and economic greed won their way, Hawaii today would be the property of a nation other than the United States of America.

It was providential that at the very moment in its history when the Kapu was destroyed and Hawaii was open to any new system of government, religion, economics, and society—there appeared the forces that would save life, stipulate new growth, and point new directions for Hawaii. I am thankful as a Hawaiian that these forces were Christian and American in the highest and best sense of that faith and nationality.

Our Protestant missionaries were welcomed to Hawaii in April 1820. With great love and grace they prepared the Bread of Life for my people. True to their purpose, they translated the Bible into Hawaiian, reduced the language to writing, and printed it, taught my kupunas (ancestors) to read and write this new language, built the first schools and churches, laid foundations for agricultural and commercial development, taught principles of social intercourse that led to constitutional government, and exerted a profound moral influence. The climax of this giant effort was focused and felt when statehood was granted to Hawaii in 1959.

I remember March 13, 1959, very well. Prior to that date, Hawaii had gone through a period of hopeful, watchful, and prayerful waiting. Statehood would mean moving up from the status of a territory to that of a full-fledged state of the American Union. We would be grownup enough to vote for the next President of the United States. We would have two senators and two representatives in the Congress instead of one voteless delegate. We would feel like the youngster who had long yearned for the freedom of graduating from the restricted teenage years to the magic age of maturity and greater independence.

But unlike the inevitability of chronological age for the teenager, the gift of Statehood for Hawaii could not be an automatic bestowal by calendar. In the eyes of Congress and the United States, Hawaii had to be qualified for statehood on many counts before she could be included as an equal in the company of great states. Politically, economically, educationally—in every way—she had to be more ready and qualified than any state previously admitted.

On the morning of March 13, 1959, I had gone to my office early. I was chaplain of the Senate of the Territory of Hawaii and was preparing my prayer for the day's session when the phone rang. Mayor Neal Blaisdell said: "I have a feeling it's going to happen today. Could you open the doors of Kawaiahao now? I want to come across the street to say my prayer of thanksgiving."

I walked the long half-block to Iolani Palace (Hawaii is the only state with an authentic palace) where the Senate would meet. As I was offering the Invocation for that morning, the whistles of the ships in Honolulu Harbor began to blow. The sirens atop Aloha Tower had *joy* in their wailing. The horns of the automobiles and buses and trucks on the streets of Honolulu joined in a loud and grateful chorus. The heart of Hawaii overflowed with thanksgiving and praise and celebration. I paused in my prayer at the podium and the sounds of Hawaii spoke to God in my stead. *E mililani aku ia Iehova*—"Give praise to God ye people."

Like the rest of Hawaii, I walked back to the church on clouds. People of all ages and races were filing into the church. I saw the mayor waving me on. "Let's have a service," he said. I looked in, and the great sanctuary of Kawaiahao that holds 2,000 people was already well filled. I asked Mayor Blaisdell if he would help by reading the Scripture: "Blessed is the nation whose God is the Lord." I asked the people to sing "America, the Beautiful." Never was it sung more beautifully, loudly, meaningfully, tearfully. I thought the roof of the Hawaiian cathedral would cave in. The next day, at the Statehood Service planned by the Honolulu Council of Churches at Kawaiahao, I gave the sermon that was later placed in the *Congressional Record* by our delegate to Congress at that time, presently the Governor of Hawaii John A. Burns. In that sermon I recalled the first Christian service conducted in Honolulu on April 25, 1820. The text of the sermon by The Rev. Hiram Bingham was from the Christmas story: "Fear not, for behold I bring you good tidings of great Joy which shall be to all people." Although our grandfathers did not fully realize it then, all their hopes and fears for the next century and more were to be met in the meaning and power of those words, for from that beginning a new Hawaii was born. Our missionaries and those following them under God became the greatest single creative influence in Hawaii's whole development—politically, economically, educationally, socially, religiously. Hawaii's real preparation for statehood can be said to have been truly begun on that day 148 years ago.

New Chefs for the Lord are needed for every new age. When Hawaii shifted from the Stone Age to the Machine Age, the diet for the body and soul of the nation had to be revised. Our Protestant missionaries proved to be the needed Chefs for Hawaii. We are moving now from the Machine Age into the Space Age. In a world facing cultural chaos and the peril of extinction, missions must begin all over again. New diets must be prepared by new culinary artists who can adequately nourish the bodies and souls of space-age men and nations. Can you help prepare the Cookbook?

The prayers and faith of men like Borman, Lovell, and Anders brought a feeling of the holy to an awed and delirious world when from the moon orbit they read: "In the beginning God created the heaven and the earth." With the same prayers and faith, Armstrong, Aldrin, and Collins accomplished the Apollo X1 mission enabling Armstrong to say from the surface of the moon "One small step for a man, one giant step for mankind." For this new morning of the Space Age, mankind is asking: "I'd like my egg sunny side up." Let's *not* scramble or scorch it. Add your page to the Great Cookbook, your recipe for doing justly, being merciful, and walking humbly before God in the Space Age.

The Rev. Abraham K. Akaka
Pastor, Kawaiahao Church

Acknowledgments

University of Hawaii's Committee for the preservation and study of Hawaiian Language, Art and Culture, for their permission to use the authentic photographs.

Joan Rossi, Executive Secretary of University of Hawaii's Committee for the preservation and study of Hawaiian Language, Art and Culture, for selecting the black and white photographs from the Baker and Donald Angus Collections of the Bishop Museum, Honolulu.

The Coopers (Allen, Vickie, Vee Gee, and Viti), Honolulu, Hawaii, for the "essential" material to start this book.

The Braults—my chef on many South Pacific voyages, Guy Brault, his mother, Mama Francine Brault, and Papa Leon Brault of Papeete, Tahiti—for their hospitality during my enjoyable stay at their home situated on a beautiful lagoon. It was here that the idea for this volume was born.

Mrs. James Norman Hall, Papeete, Tahiti, for allowing me to kitchen-test some of the recipes on her children and grandchildren.

Alexander MacDonald, Journalist Club; Sid Jones; Chef Jerry Kearny; Ern Gomer, owner of Seppelt Winery; Johnny Walker, restaurateur, and all my other mates "down under" in Sidney, Australia.

My gratitude to my shipmates over the years from 1937 to 1969, with Ed Turner at the helm of the Marine Cooks and Steward's Union, San Francisco, for their suggestions, endorsements, and understanding of my exuberance while formulating and writing this book.

To Don and Ruth Scheley of San Francisco for their most loyal encouragement.

Richard F. Guggenhiem, President, Guggenheim International, San Francisco, for his friendship, assistance, and excellent suggestions.

Contents

	Man Shall Not Live by Bread Alone	5
	Acknowledgments	10
	Ethnic Origins of Polynesia and Hawaii—An Album	13
	Ethnic Origins and Food Customs in Polynesia and Hawaii	35
	A Hawaiian Luau	45
1	Hors d'Oeuvres, Hot and Cold	47
2	Soups	61
3	Salads and Salad Dressings	73
4	Fish and Shellfish Entrees	87
5	Fowl Entrees	107
6	Meat Entrees	119
7	Special Barbecue Recipes	141
8	Garnishes, Chutneys, Pickles, Fruits, and Vegetables	155
9	Curries, Rice, and Eggs	169
10	Breads, Fritters, and Pancakes	185
11	Desserts	193
12	Flaming Coffees and Tropical Drinks	203
	Purchasing Guide	210
	Index	211

Ethnic Origins of Polynesia and Hawaii - An Album

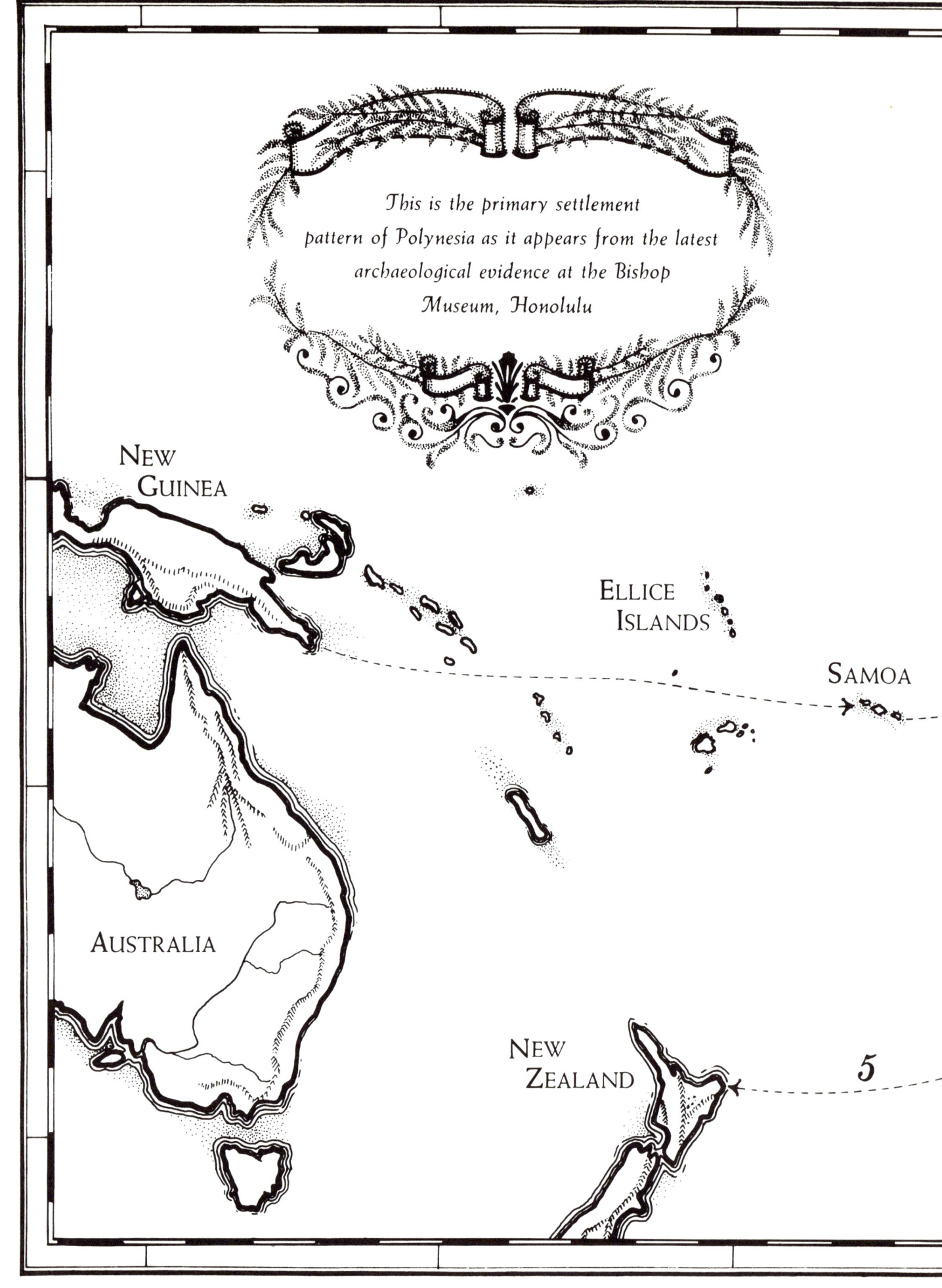

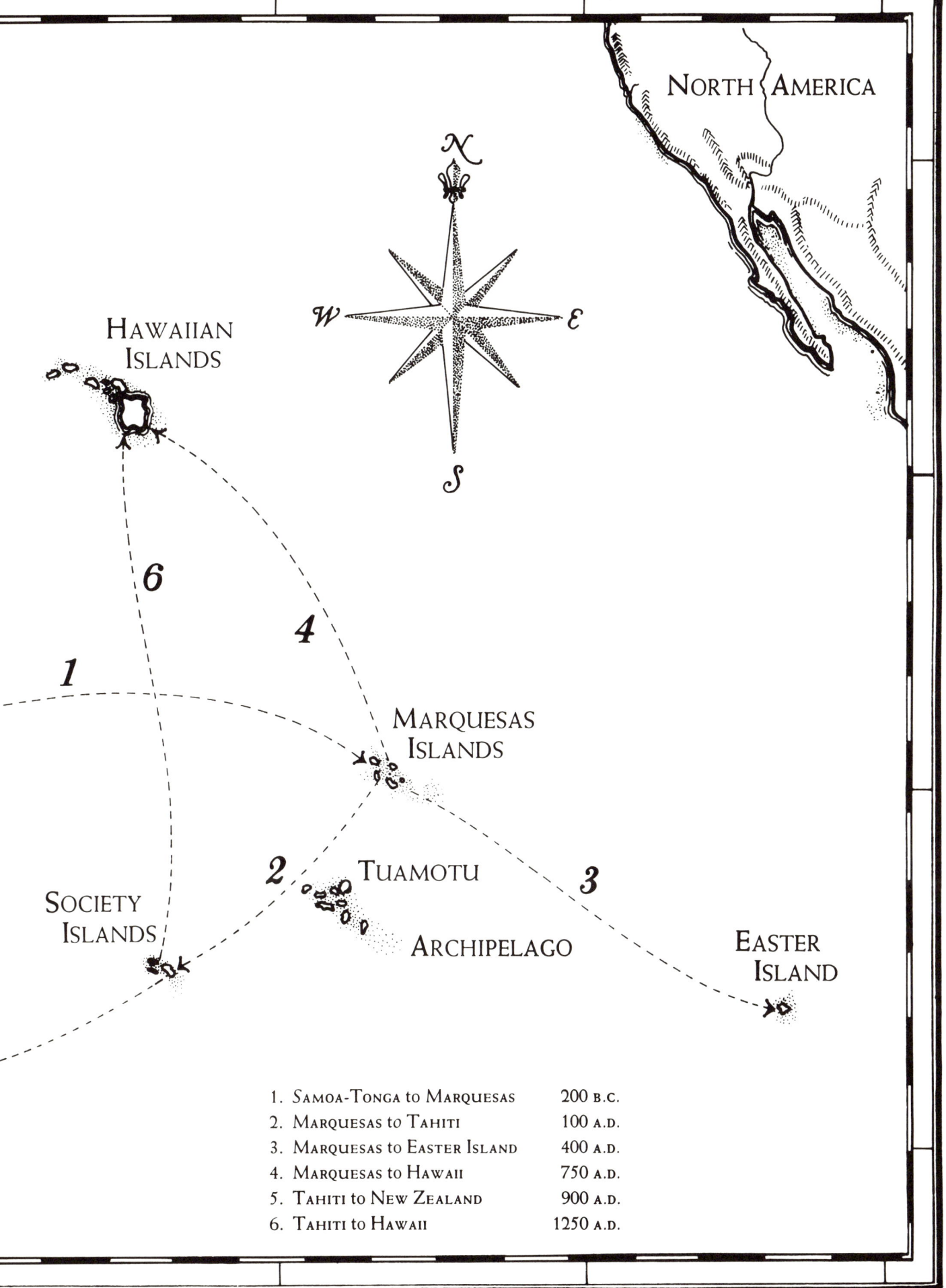

KING KAMEHAMEHA I   Twenty years after Captain Cook's landing, King Kamehameha I consolidated a kingdom in the Hawaiian Islands that lasted a century.

Kamehameha towered 6 feet 6 inches and was a tremendously powerful man. Adept in warrior sports, he delighted in having javelins flung at him while he plucked them from mid-air and side-stepped them—at the same time.

Born in a stone-age society of breechcloths and outrigger canoes, he lived to negotiate with the western world. At his death, he left among his vast properties a 175-ton flagship and several resplendent uniforms of Napoleonic cut.

Islanders celebrate June 11 as Kamehameha Day, honoring the noble man who united Hawaii's jealously guarded tribal kingdoms under one scepter. A four-day festival follows, featuring parades, dancing and singing pageants and aquacades. The bronze statue in Honolulu's Civic Center wears fresh garlands of scented blossoms day and night!

Engraving taken from Dampier's drawing done in 1825.

PRINCESS NAHIENAENA   Daughter of Kamehameha I and his most chiefly wife, Keopuolani.

KEALAKEKUA BAY, HAWAII
King Kalaniopuu of Hawaii
paid an official visit to Captain
Cook's ships in Kealakekua Bay.
He set out in a large double
canoe accompanied by two other
similar canoes.

Engraving from John Webber drawing.

Engraving from the original drawing by John Webber.

VILLAGE ON KAUAI Captain James Cook anchored his two ships in Waimea Bay, Kauai, on January 20, 1778. In this interesting view of the village, the Polynesian-Hawaiians, in their native dress, are seen as they help to fill water casks and barter with Captain Cook's men. The different shapes of the grass houses are also noticed in this scene.

KEALAKEKUA, HAWAII Multitudes of canoes put off from shore when Captain James Cook anchored off Kealakekua, Hawaii, on January 17, 1779. The monument to his memory was erected here.

Engraving from original drawing by John Webber.

CHIEF KAIANA Chief Kaiana shown here in feathered cloak and helmet. He was described by Captain James King as "one of the finest men I ever saw. He was about six feet tall, had regular and expressive features, with lively, dark eyes; his carriage was easy, firm and graceful."

Engraving from John Webber drawing.

Engraving from a drawing by Robert Dampier.

LAHAINA, MAUI Lahaina, Maui, as it looked in 1825. The houses and the dress of the natives reflect the days of Hawaii's past. Just six years later in 1831, the oldest school west of the Rocky Mountains opened—Lahainaluna High School. Famous Hawaiian kings and queens are buried in the cemetery at Wainee Church.

Copy of a painting by George Burgess.

DIAMOND HEAD—1887 Diamond Head as seen from Honolulu Beach. The mingling of foreign influences with ancient Hawaiian ways can be seen in the houses and the dress of the natives. The extinct volcano Diamond Head was called "Leahi" by the Hawaiians; it was the home of the Fire Goddess Pele. British sailors found some shining crystals (Pele's tears) early in the 19th century and believed they had found diamonds, hence the name—Diamond Head.

KING KAMEHAMEHA I (1758-1819) It took twenty years, from 1790 to 1810, for King Kamehameha I to realize his ambition to become master of the entire group of the Hawaiian Islands. He began his conquest on the island of Hawaii in an attempt to consolidate the entire island, a feat he accomplished after a fierce battle and victory over the warriors of Keoua. Five years later, Kamehameha directed his attentions and army to the Leeward Islands and conquered Maui, Molokai and Oahu. With the cession of Kauai in 1810, Kamehameha the Great's Hawaiian kingdom was complete. As he had fought in battle, he now fought for organization and centralization of his government. The sandalwood trade with China came into prominence and flourished; industry and agriculture were stimulated and encouraged by King Kamehameha I. Thus the island's government and economy, as the world would later know it, began under King Kamehameha I.

Engraving taken from the painting of King Kamehameha I by artist Choris in 1816.

Engraving from original drawing by Louis Choris made in 1816.

AHUNEA HEIAU, AT KAILUA KONA, HAWAII The Ahunea heiau (temple) stood next to Kamakahonu, Kamehameha's residence.

QUEEN KAMAMALU. QUEEN OF THE HAWAIIAN ISLANDS AND WIFE OF KAMEHAMEHA II. The Queen accompanied the King to England where both succumbed to the measles, a disease unknown to Hawaii in 1824. The bodies were brought back to the Islands aboard the H.M.S. Blonde, captained by Lord Byron, cousin of the poet.

Engraving made from Robert Dampier's drawing.

HILO BAY, HAWAII   The grass house which housed Lord Byron on his visits to Hilo Bay, Hawaii.

PRINCE KAUIKEAOULI, SON OF
KAMEHAMEHA I BECAME
KAMEHAMEHA III (1814-1854)
On June 6, 1825, the young
prince Kauikeaouli, son of
Kamehameha I, became King
with the title of Kamehameha
III. As a lad of six or seven, at
his mother's (the queen mother
Keopuolani) request he ate his
evening meal with her, and thus
the strict tabu which prohibited
men and women from eating
together had been violated.
During King Kamehameha III's
reign, the island's first census
was taken in 1832——population
130,313. During his reign the
first sugar plantation was started
 (in 1835) on the island of Kauai,
a silk plantation was started, and
the first newspapers were
published in the islands. The
government was reorganized,
creating a supreme court with a
king, a premier, and four judges
to be appointed by the legislative
body—the legislative body to
consist of fifteen nobles and
seven representatives, the latter
to be elected by the people.
Freedom of religious worship
was guaranteed. The Punahou
School was founded in 1840.

Engraving from the original painting by Dampier, artist with Lord Byron, made in 1825.

Engraving from the original drawing by artist J. Arago made in 1819.

A young officer in a typical costume of malo, feather cloak, and helmet. The tattooing on the arm of the officer is: "Kamehameha died May 8, 1819."

All of the preceding photographs are courtesy of the Bernice P. Bishop Museum of Honolulu, Hawaii.

The Bernice P. Bishop Museum is a memorial to Princess Bernice Pauahi Bishop, last of the Kamehameha family of Chiefs of Hawaii. It was founded in 1889 by her husband, Charles Reed Bishop, who for nearly fifty years took a prominent part in business and public affairs in Hawaii. The museum operates under a deed of trust dating from 1896 and emphasizes "Polynesian and kindred antiquities, ethnology and natural history."

None of the income from the Bishop estate is available to the museum. The Kamehameha schools are the sole beneficiary of a separate trust established by Mrs. Bishop; these schools have given preference to students of Hawaiian ancestry. The Bishop Museum, however, serves as an official depository for the State of Hawaii. The scientific program and collections of the museum emphasize anthropology, botany, entomology, geology, zoology, and Hawaiian and Pacific history. The museum's scientific contributions at an international level are matched by its role in providing public service to Hawaii and its visitors.

Annually on December 19 Princess Bernice Pauahi Bishop's birthday is observed by Hawaiian societies and the Kamehameha schools with stately ceremonies at the Royal Mausoleum, Nuuanu Valley.

Victor's Flaming Spinach Salad

Honolulu Trout

Ethnic Origins and Food Customs in Polynesia and Hawaii

The history of the early Polynesians and their settlements is based on water and pursuit of land. If a diary had been kept, those courageous people could have told of an authentic adventure as exciting as the travels of the Vikings. A true diary does exist, though not in writing; it has been passed along orally from mothers to daughters and from fathers to sons. From these teachings, we can learn how the Polynesians first came from Southeast Asia in outrigger canoes by "short voyages and numerous haltings that spanned generations, along island-studded routes that led them to the eastern Pacific." Legend tells us that the canoes were known as "the seven canoes of the great fleet"—the *Aotea, Arawa, Horout, Mataatia, Tainui, Takitimi,* and *Tokomaru*. Gradually the new arrivals settled in the islands now known collectively as Polynesia, "many islands."

The latest linguistic and archaeological evidence suggests that the ancestors of the present-day Polynesians and their ethnic cousins throughout the entire South Pacific area had settled in the Marquesas as early as 200 B.C. From the Marquesas they spread to Tahiti and Easter Island and later to Hawaii and from Tahiti to New Zealand. Around A.D. 1250, there was another migration from Tahiti to Hawaii.

It is interesting to note here the three general regions of the South Pacific: Polynesia, Melanesia, and Micronesia. "Nesia" means black islands, and hence, Micronesia, tiny or small black islands.

The Polynesians dwell in the vast archipelagoes of the Polynesian triangle. The points of the triangle are Hawaii and New Zealand in the north and south and Easter Island in the east. Within the watery boundaries are the Samoas, Tonga, Tahiti, Ellice, Cook Islands, and Niue. The Polynesians are brown-skinned, have straight hair, and are usually quite handsome—as the voyagers and poets of the past have testified. Today most of the Polynesians of Hawaii and Tahiti are an admixture of European and other races.

The Melanesians are oceanic Negroids and occupy the islands of the western fringe of the South Pacific—Papua, New Guinea, New Caledonia, Fiji, New Hebrides, the Solomons, and the Bismarck archipelago. The Melanesians are dark-skinned, have fuzzy hair, and are the most artistically creative. The Papuan Melanesian found in New Guinea and New Caledonia is smaller than the Melanisian of Fiji and shows Australoid strains similar to those of the Australian aborigines.

Finally there are the peoples and islands of Micronesia. These include the Marianas (Guam, Rota, Saipan, and Tinian), the Caroline Island archipelagoes (Palau, Yop, Truk, Ponape and Kusaie in the east), the northern atolls, the Marshall Islands, and the Gilbert Islands. Some scholars believe that the Polynesians passed through Melanesia, others that they came through Micronesia; they may have used both routes. These accounts of Polynesian origins were dramatically challenged by the *Kon Tiki* expedition, but the preponderant scholarly opinion is that its leader, Thor Heyerdahl, has failed to establish his controversial hypothesis that Polynesia was populated by westward migrations from the Americas.

The aura of mystery surrounding the Polynesians, who faced and conquered the South Pacific, is enhanced by the joy expressed in their music and poetry. They found their own pleasures, in fishing, planting, and sharing food. But their compassion for one another—welded in their fight for survival—was predominant, as can be seen in their legends, language, and musical conversations. Their music reflects the sounds of the sea washing against land and the inner rumblings of volcanic earth accompanied by wind. The mystery is not that they survived the onslaughts of nature but how they maintained their carefree attitude toward life and their feeling for their fellow man. Their philosophy is difficult for us to understand in a world torn by violence, war, and unrest—yet are we not seeking a life similar to that of the Polynesians, survival on land and sea with freedom for all?

Statistics show that the youngest of the fifty states and the gateway to the South Pacific, Hawaii, received more than 1 million visitors in 1967. The Hawaiian islands, with a resident population of 792,444, are a notable example of how people with varied ethnic backgrounds can live together in small areas without conflict. Statistics reveal this interesting breakdown of the ethnic origins of the islands' population: 39 percent Caucasian, 28 percent Japanese, 14 percent part Hawaiian (combinations of Japanese, Chinese, and Polynesian), 10 percent Filipino, 5 percent Chinese, 1 percent pure Hawaiian (Polynesians who come from Tahiti), 1 percent Negro, and 2 percent other (including Korean, Samoan, Indian, Puerto Rican, Cuban, and other Pacific extractions).

Knowing that land, water, and food are essential to human life, it naturally follows that food is an essential part of any people's history. According to Sir Peter Buck, "The early true settlers of the Hawaiian Islands brought no cultivable food plants or domestic animals. Thus they had to depend entirely upon native plants for their vegetable foods and upon local birds and fishes for their proteins. As in the rest of the Polynesian islands, the indigenous plants that could be used for food were poor in quality and none of them were of a sufficient nutritional value to warrant their cultivation."

The arrival in Hawaii of later settlers from Tahiti, in the Society islands, changed conditions materially, for they brought a number of cultivable food plants. All these plants, with the exception of the sweet potato, came originally from the Indo-Malayan region. Botanical evidence establishes that the ancestors of the Polynesians came from there. The sweet potato is believed by botanists to have originated in South America. Its presence in Polynesia in pre-Columbian times is generally explained by the theory that some early Polynesian navigator actually reached the western coast of South America and brought the sweet potato back to Polynesia.

Pigs and domesticated fowl were also carried by the early Polynesians to central Polynesia and thence to Hawaii. As such animals also belonged to the Indo-Malayan region, the zoological evidence supports the theory that the Polynesians came from the west, rather than the east.

The presence of the breadfruit and banana in widely separated islands of Polynesia, shows that the voyages were carefully planned for settlement and that the old-time voyagers had a shrewd idea of where they were going to settle. They planned for provisioning the future in a new land. Since the breadfruit and banana are propagated by suckers, for the long sea voyage from Tahiti to Hawaii the suckers had to be dug up with the earth surrounding the roots and securely wrapped to keep the soil intact.

In Hawaii the fertile soil, the congenial climate, and the industry of the people produced a rich and abundant food supply. The people became well nourished, robust, and healthy; in physique, stamina, and intelligence they became one of the most advanced branches of the widespread Polynesians. A detailed outline of the sources of Hawaii's (and Polynesia's) abundant food supply and their methods of preparation follows here to give the reader a more thorough knowledge of the customs and food history of this South Pacific people.

Mammals

No indigenous land mammals were present in Hawaii, except for the bat (*ope ape a*), which was not edible. The Polynesians introduced the pig, the dog—and man. The rat (*iole*) probably accompanied the voyagers as a stowaway, for it was not eaten.

MAN

Man (*kanaka*) was the highest form of offering to the gods in certain important ceremonies, but unlike other animal offerings human beings were not eaten after the ritual was concluded. In some rites, however, the priest would extract an eye and swallow it. This custom also prevailed among the Tahitians, who, like the Hawaiians, were not eaters of human flesh. Human sacrifices were cast into the refuse pits of the religious temples, or *heiaus*, and not used.

PIGS

Pigs (*pua a; puaka* in Polynesian) were evidently bred in large numbers for food. They also served as offerings in religious ceremonies but were usually eaten after the gods had received their "immaterial" share. They were bred by tenant farmers, not only for their own use, but also for payment of rent to overlords. The kings and chiefs made great demands on the people for pigs to be used in religious ceremonies and official feasts. During religious observances over a five-day period more than 2,200 pigs were used. Probably more pigs were bred in Hawaii than elsewhere in Polynesia. Furthermore, the Hawaiian pig was credited with more intelligence than is usually attributed to the animal. It was used by priests to identify the sorcerer or his employer after a death ascribed to sorcery (*ana ana*). The priest made his diagnosis from the movements of the pig; perhaps it was the priest who was intelligent and not the pig. Pigs also had an uncanny gift for identifying people of high rank who were living unrecognized in exile. From some instinct of respect they would raise their snouts in obeisance, and their recognition was said to be infallible. The pig thus had important functions other than providing food for the hungry.

Birds

The domesticated fowl (*moa*) was introduced to Hawaii from central Polynesia long before Europeans reached the Pacific. The ornithological evidence collected on various expeditions indicates that the *moa* is a descendant of the jungle fowl (*Gallus gallus*) of the Malaysian region. Although it has undergone much evolution, there can be no doubt that it was brought from that area by the early ancestors of the Polynesians. In Hawaii some cocks were trained for fighting, but fowl were principally used for food. They were also appropriate offerings to the gods. All the native birds, large or small, from land or sea, were edible, though some species were hunted primarily for their feathers. Yellow, red, black, or green feathers were used for capes and cloaks. The birds were caught during the moulting season by professional fowlers, who used bird lime made from breadfruit gum (*kepau*) or *kukui* gum (*pilali*). The Hawaiians did not believe in killing the birds that grew golden feathers; the golden feathers of the *'o 'o* (*Acrulocerus nobilis*) and the *mamo* (*Drepanis pacifica*) were plucked without harming the birds, which were then liberated to grow more feathers. Some *'o 'o* (pronounced "oo oo") were killed for their black body feathers. The *'i ieve* (*Vestiara coccinea*) and the *apapane* (*Himatione sanguine*), which could not survive the plucking of their red feathers, were killed, skinned, and eaten.

Fish

All fish were eaten in Hawaii, for there were no poisonous ones as in some parts of Polynesia. An exception was the porcupine fish; but if its poisonous gall was removed without spilling, the flesh could safely be eaten. In fact it was—and still is—delicious.

Crustaceans and Shellfish

All crustaceans and shellfish large enough to repay the work of extracting the meat were considered good eating, except for the poisonous *kumimi* crab.

Plants

The food plants introduced to Hawaii from central Polynesia thrived in a climate similar to that from which they came. Taro was the favorite, and the sweet potato and breadfruit were next in importance. Other plants introduced were the coconut, banana, yam, Polynesian arrowroot, and sugar cane.

TARO

Taro, still an important staple today, was the most important food in Hawaii and throughout the uplands of Polynesia, with the exception of the Marquesas and Mangareva, where fermented breadfruit took precedence. The taro corn was made into poi, and the young leaves and peeled stalks of some varieties were cooked as greens.

SWEET POTATOES

The sweet potato was the principal crop of the dry lands that were unsuitable for taro. The tubers were cooked in earth ovens, and the tender tips of the vines made excellent greens.

YAMS

Yams (*uhi*) were not as important in the Hawaiian islands as in western Polynesia, where large crops of them were grown. Large quantities were, however, grown in Niihau, where Captain James Cook noted their abundance in the eighteenth century. They keep better than do taro roots or sweet potatoes and therefore they were preferred by sea captains. Yams were cooked in earth ovens, but unlike taro roots and sweet potatoes they were too meaty to mash into poi.

ARROWROOT

Polynesian arrowroot grew wild; it was also cultivated along the edges of wet taro patches and in damp uplands. It grows from tubers that are planted in holes in the ground. When mature, raw tubers were grated on rough stone surfaces. The gratings were placed in a bowl of water to stand until the starch had settled; the starch was then decanted, and fresh water was added to it. After several washings the starch lost its bitterness. A preparation called *haupia* was made of *pia* starch (arrowroot blended with coconut milk) mixed with coconut cream, wrapped in ti leaves, and cooked in an earth oven. Today *pia* mixed with coconut cream is boiled in a pot.

TI

The ti plant (*ki*) grew wild at first, but later it was also planted near dwellings. A piece of stalk was stuck in the ground and grew downward to form a swollen underground stem containing saccharine material. The underground stem was formerly cooked in earth ovens, then chewed like sugarcane. In times of famine large ovens of ti root were prepared by the community. The Honolulu suburb of Kaimuki (*ka-imu-ki*) is said to have taken its name from such an oven (*imu*). From the first European visitors the Hawaiians learned to distill an alcoholic liquor (*okolehao*) from a mash of cooked ti root.

GOURDS

Gourds (*hue*, or *ipu*) were grown intensively for containers for cooked food and other articles. Their use as containers completely overshadowed their use as food.

TURMERIC

Turmeric (*‘olena*) grew wild and was also cultivated domestically. The thick underground stems, which grow horizontally, furnish a yellow dye. They were also eaten in times of famine.

Cooking

Food was cooked by three methods: broiling, boiling, and a combination of steaming and roasting with hot lava stones in an earth oven.

MAKING FIRES

Fire was started by the Polynesian method of rubbing a pointed piece of wood along a groove in the upper surface of a piece of dry wood like *hau*. The pointed piece was held in a forward slant, with the fingers of both hands clasped over the front and the thumbs to the back. The grooved piece was anchored by placing its front end against a fixed object or under an assistant's foot. The stick was rubbed in successive forward movements to deepen the groove and push particles of detached wood to the forward end. When sufficient wood dust had collected, the movements were quickened until the friction caused the wood dust to smoulder and smoke. Some flammable material like dry tapa, coconut husk, or coconut stipules, was placed on the ground; strips of dry tapa were often plaited in loose three-ply braids, each with a frayed end for easy ignition. The grooved wood was inverted and given a sharp tap on the back with the upper stick to dislodge the smouldering dust onto the dry material, which was waved in the air or blown gently until it burst into flame.

BROILING

Out in the fields or at home when the quantity of food did not warrant the trouble of preparing an earth oven, broiling (*ko ala*, or *pulehu*) was used. The term *ko ala* means "hot coals," whereas *pulehu* means "hot ashes." The term *pulaha* was used when food was warmed near the fire and turned from time to time. The general word for broiling, *tunu*, in the dialectical form *kunu*, applies to broiling of meat on coals. Breadfruit and unripe bananas were broiled in their skins, which protected the flesh from burning. Other foods were protected from burning by ti-leaf wrappings (*lau lau*). A leaf package of fish was called *lawalu*, but fish and other foods could also be cooked on the coals without wrapping.

BOILING

Boiling (*ha kui*, *puholo*) was somewhat primitive in Polynesia, owing to the absence of fireproof utensils. Whatever knowledge the Polynesian ancestors may have had of pottery in their Asian homes, their descendants had lost it, for suitable clay was lacking in the islands that they occupied. In Melanesia, where the islands belong to an older continental formation, suitable clay is abundant. The Melanesians thus made pottery, not because their culture was superior, but because they had the raw material that the Polynesians lacked. To boil food, throughout Polynesia heat was applied from the inside instead of from the outside. The food was placed in wooden bowls containing water, and red-hot stones were dropped into the bowls. Heated stones called *'eho* were also placed inside fowls. Alternate layers of stones and food were put in the bowl, and water was added; fish cooked this way are delicious. Greens, including indigenous plants, the tops of young taro leaves (*lu au*), and the tender ends of sweet-potato vines (*palula*) were also boiled.

ROASTING AND STEAMING

The earth oven (*imu*) used for the third type of cooking was a shallow hole in the ground under a shelter forming a permanent kitchen (*hale imu*); it could also be made in the open for special occasions if the weather permitted. Cooking in an earth oven was called *kalua* (*ka* means "the"; *lua* means "hole"). The wide spread Polynesian term *tao* was dropped in Hawaii and replaced with the name *imu*. Kindling wood was put in the middle of the hollow, larger pieces of wood were placed around and over the kindling, a layer of lava stones was placed over the wood, and then the kindling was lighted. The cook blew through a length of bamboo, the "bamboo fire blower," to fan the fire. The lava stones were the size of a closed fist; once heated they were spread out with a stick to make an oven floor, over which grass (*honohono*) or leaves were spread to prevent the food from being scorched. After taro, breadfruit, sweet potatoes, and other foods had been packed in and covered with layers of leaves, preferably ti leaves, an outside layer of old mats and tapa strips was applied. A final cover of earth was generally used in Polynesia but apparently not in Hawaii. Sweet potatoes took about two hours to cook in the earth oven; taro was cooked three to four hours, in order to break down the calcium chloride crystals, which irritated the mouth and tongue. Pigs were cooked whole with red-hot lava stones in the abdominal and thoracic cavities. Special cone-shaped stones were used in fowls, which, like fish, could also be wrapped in ti-leaf *laulau*. When the *kalua* had continued long enough the coverings were removed from the oven, and the cooked food was placed on receptacles to cool. It was served cold. In parts of Polynesia tongs made of doubled pieces of coconut-leaf midrib were used to handle hot lava stones and food. The Hawaiians, however, appear to have dispensed with tongs; they picked up the hot stones or cooked food with their bare hands after dipping their hands into cold water. Large hogs were never cooked in the earth oven. After a hog was dressed, the inside was salted, and hot stones were placed inside. The carcass was then wrapped in old tapa strips and mats, placed on a poi board (a board generally used to pound taro in preparing poi), and left for forty-eight hours. The meat was then cut from the inside, which was better cooked. Thanks to the salting, the cooked hog lasted for some time; the parts that had not been sufficiently cooked were recooked in the earth oven.

PREPARING POI

Poi preparations were made by mashing breadfruit, sweet potato, banana, or taro. Cooked breadfruit, sweet potato, and ripe bananas were soft enough to mash with the fingers, but cooked taro, because its of firmness, had to be mashed with considerable force. In ancient times a stone pounder and a pounder board were used. Today poi is available in cans in most gourmet stores throughout the world.

PREPARING HAUPIA

Haupia consisted of arrowroot mixed with coconut cream wrapped in ti leaves and cooked in an earth oven. It is a popular dessert at modern Hawaiian feasts.

PREPARING KAVA OR 'AWA

"Kava" is the Polynesian name for both *Piper methysticum* (a kind of pepper plant) and a drink prepared from its roots. The plant was carried by the Polynesians to their new settlements and later cultivated. Kava, as it is called in Fiji and Samoa, or 'awa, as it is called in Hawaii, was a refreshing drink for the aristocracy and for farmers, fishermen, and other commoners when they could get it. It was also used as medicine, an offering to the gods, and in various other ways. The roots from a three-to-five-year-old plant were dug up, washed, scraped, and dried. In Hawaii the drying was not as thorough as in Samoa, for the Hawaiians preferred to make the more potent drink made from fairly fresh roots. The roots were pounded into small pieces with a stone, and men and women with good teeth were given the pieces to chew. The fibers, thus broken down and mixed with saliva, formed a pulpy bolus.

(It has been claimed by some informants that the chewers could reduce the root to a soft bolus without adding saliva; although that is impossible, the root does have an astringent quality that probably stimulates less saliva than other foods do.) The chemical ingredients of kava root (isolated in Tahiti in 1857) include an essential oil combined with a balsamic resin, a large amount of starch in small round grains, and a special neutral principal to which are credited the stupefying and intoxicating properties of kava. The superiority of the chewed root resulted from the ptyalin in saliva, which rendered the starch grains more easily absorbed in the stomach. Though the Polynesians knew nothing of chemical theory, they learned from experience that chewed root was superior to pounded root, and chewing thus became the recognized method of pulverizing the root throughout Polynesia. Missionaries and other foreign critics, however, persuaded Polynesians to abandon chewing for the more sanitary pounding method. The process of chewing without swallowing was called *mama*, and the bolus of chewed roots was called *mana*. Chewing the woody roots was tiring. Portlock (in 1789) described the amusing quandary of an old priest who often visited his ship. The priest was an inveterate ʻawa drinker, and he was accompanied by two attendants who chewed ʻawa root for him. He worked his chewers so frequently that at times their chewing muscles became exhausted, and he had to hire outside labor at the price of one trade bead per bolus of chewed root. To prepare ʻawa for a number of people the chewers sat around a bowl and deposited the results of their labors in the bowl. It took two boluses to a cup of water to make an ordinary drink. After the quantity required for the company had been chewed, the necessary amount of water was added to make an infusion. Mixing bowls, strainers, and serving cups were then required. In Samoa the highest-ranking chief received the first cup, but in Hawaii a chief of very superior rank received the last cup. Before drinking, the chief "poured a little on the ground" as a libation to the gods, a routine procedure in Samoa. Kava is not alcoholic, but it has a slightly diuretic effect when consumed in large quantities.

Condiments

The condiments used by the Hawaiians were salt (*paʻakai*), *kukui* nut (*ʻinamona*), and seaweed. All three were often blended together and placed in gourd containers. They are used in the same manner we use salt and pepper today, pinched to flavor according to individual taste.

SALT

Hawaiians were the only Polynesians who extracted salt from sea water in properly constructed salt pans made of earth and lined with clay (there were also gourd pans, wood pans, and containers made of stone), each six or eight feet square and about eight inches deep. The pans were raised on a bank of stones near the high-water mark; the salt water was conducted in small trenches to fill the pans. The sun quickly evaporated the water.

KUKUI NUT

The *kukui* tree grows abundantly in the Hawaiian islands; the island of Molokai uses the *kukui* flower in its official lei. The sap that runs from the branch when the nut is picked is used for medicinal purposes. A much relished condiment called '*inamona* has long been prepared from *kukui*. The hard-shelled nuts were roasted in embers or on hot stones; care was taken to turn them from time to time to prevent the shells from burning. When the kernel was brown, it was cracked and ground in a small stone mortar (*poho 'inamona*) with a stone muller; salt was then added. Today some people add pepper. The *'inamona* was served in the stone mortar or in small wooden or gourd receptacles or simply placed on a freshly plucked ti leaf. A small pinch was taken with the fingers as a relish for food. Caution had to be exercised, however, as too much *kukui* oil had purgative properties.

SEAWEED

Many varieties of seaweed (*limu*) were eaten by Hawaiians as an ordinary food, but one kind, *limu kohu*, was used in small quantities as a relish. The seaweed was washed and then pounded with a pestle in a mortar, to reduce it to small pieces. As with *'inamona*, the seaweed was picked up in small pinches between finger and thumb and eaten with other food. Nowadays, *limu* relishes, like *'inamona*, are enjoyed as much by the younger generation as by older people and are considered necessary items for proper Hawaiian feasts (*luau*).

A Hawaiian Luau

In old Hawaii feasts were held on many occasions, each with its own religious significance. An important accomplishment like laying the foundation of a house, completing a house, or building a canoe was celebrated by a luau.

A pig was consecrated to Lono (Hawaiian god) at the birth or weaning of a child. Portions of the cooked pig were offered as a sacrifice to the god, and the remainder was eaten by the guests. In modern times the first birthday of a child of Hawaiian ancestry may be celebrated with a large luau. Marriages are also occasions for luaus.

Aside from an abundance of food, the most important aspect of a luau is its relaxed atmosphere, created by decorations and costumes in the Hawaiian manner: aloha shirts for the men and casual shifts or muumuus for the women. If possible, fresh-, plastic-, or paper-flower leis ordered from a specialty shop should be offered to guests to make them look and feel festive.

At an authentic Hawaiian luau the featured meat dish is a pig that has been cooked in an *imu*, or underground oven. The salad is *lomi* salmon, a mixture of salted salmon, fresh tomatoes, green onions, *kukui*-flavored salt, and ice. Chicken luau, a combination of chicken and taro leaves cooked in coconut milk, is included in most luaus, and baked or boiled sweet potatoes or breadfruit serve as vegetables. Poi is probably the most discussed dish at a luau table. It is a staple food that Hawaiians use not only in luaus but also eat as a cereal, plain or with milk and sugar. Its place in the Hawaiian diet is equivalent to that of rice or potatoes in mainland diets. Its strange texture and flavor are strange to mainlanders, however, and it is seldom enjoyed by visitors.

On the mainland luaus are adapted to the available foods, the menu being only similar to those of the Hawaiian islands. Rather than the luau pig, a suckling pig or, more often, pork loin is the main meat. Barbecued spareribs are marinated in a sweet-

and-sour sauce that is typical of Hawaiian food. Polynesian chicken adds an island flavor to the menu. Baked yams with pineapple substitute for sweet potatoes or breadfruit, and rice takes the place of poi. Spinach or other greens may be used in place of cooked taro leaves, and heavy-duty aluminum wrap is used in place of banana, ti, or taro leaves to wrap foods before cooking them. Fish fillets with macadamia butter replace the delicious *mahi mahi* that is so popular in Hawaii, although this fish is becoming more readily available in markets on the mainland.

This book contains many wonderful and simple recipes to be used for your next luau. Increase amounts in the recipes according to the number of guests. The table for a luau should be set with a bamboo or tatami mat and ti leaves, if available; otherwise any colorful mats, large, fresh green leaves from the yard; and vivid fresh or artificial flowers brighten the table. The fresh leaves are used as bases for the various dishes served. If a florist cannot provide ti leaves, ask for long, flat leaves as a substitute. Green plants or foliage massed at the back of the buffet table or in corners of the room will help to create a Polynesian atmosphere. The atmosphere should be warm, friendly, and above all relaxing. Flowers can be combined with fruits and vegetables to give a feeling of lush abundance.

Plan a menu that is manageable. Try to serve one dish that is typical of the islands or include a traditional island food like bananas, pineapples, coconuts, sweet potatoes, pork, chicken, salmon, coconut pudding or other dessert, or beverages served in coconut shells. The food is generally set out all at once, rather than served in courses. Paper plates may be substituted for ti leaves, or pottery and wooden dishes may be used. Each place setting must have a punch cup, a small relish plate, a medium salad plate, and a large plate for the entrée. As most of the food is to be eaten with the fingers, provide plenty of napkins and individual finger bowls with thin lemon slices floating in water scented with your favorite cologne.

Fresh or artifical leis are available through Orchids of Hawaii, 305 Seventh Avenue, New York City; Paradise Products, P.O. Box 415, El Cerrito, California; and Hirose Nurseries, Inc., P.O. Box 51, 2212 Kanoelehua Avenue, Hilo, Hawaii. The first two companies will send catalogues listing decorations and costumes available; prices are determined by the quantities ordered. The Hirose Nurseries will fly fresh flowers to you at unbelievably low prices. Just mail your name and address, specifying the type of flowers, leaves, or leis desired.

The dishes and recipes in this book are the same as those served in Hawaii and throughout the entire South Pacific. Baked bananas and pineapple combine two island fruits. *Shrimp tempura* was a dish brought to the islands by the Japanese. Beef teriyaki is flavored with Kikkoman soy sauce, a very popular flavoring in Hawaii. Have a lot of fun with your next luau.

Hors D'Oeuvres, Hot and Cold

1

HORS D'OEUVRES, HOT AND COLD

Hawaiian Banana–Bacon Pupus

MAKES 20

Ready Tray
1/3 cup Kikkoman Hawaiian teriyaki sauce
1 tablespoon coconut honey
4 medium-sized slightly underripe bananas, peeled and cut in 1-inch cubes
10 slices bacon, halved

Combine teriyaki sauce and honey in shallow baking dish, and marinate bananas 30 minutes. Drain, reserving marinade, wrap each banana cube with bacon, and fasten with toothpick. Brush with sauce, and arrange on rack in shallow pan. Broil 4 inches from heat 7–8 minutes, or until bacon is crisp, turning occasionally.

Hawaiian Beef Jerky Pipikalua

SERVES 6–8

Ready Tray
1 1/2 pounds round steak, well marbled with fat
3/4 cup Kikkoman soy sauce
1 1/2 tablespoons Hawaiian salt or ice-cream salt
1 teaspoon sugar
1 clove garlic, chopped fine
1 teaspoon lemon juice
1/4 teaspoon monosodium glutamate
1/4 teaspoon pepper

Slice meat 1/4-inch thick; then cut into 1/2-inch strips. Pound lightly to break up tough tissue. Blend remaining ingredients, and pour over meat; marinate 1 hour. Dry in hot sun one full day, turning meat occasionally. Brown over charcoal or in broiler.

Uncooked meat keeps well in refrigerator for later use.

Australian Lamb's Brains Piquant

SERVES 6

Ready Tray
2 pairs lamb's brains
  water
2 tablespoons grated cheese
1 1/2 tablespoons sweet cream
1 egg, well beaten
1/2 teaspoon salt
1/8 teaspoon pepper
3 capers, chopped fine
2 tablespoons sherry
  crackers or toasted bread triangles
  stuffed olives, sliced
  whole capers

Clean and skin brains. Simmer in water to cover until tender; drain, and mash thoroughly with fork. Add cheese, cream, egg, salt, pepper, chopped capers, and sherry. Cook over medium heat, stirring until mixture is thick enough to mound on crackers. Garnish with olives and capers. This dish is good hot or chilled.

Flaming-Volcano Sesame Clams

SERVES 8

Ready Tray
24	cherrystone clams and shells
4	water chestnuts
1/4	cup bean sprouts, chopped
4	scallions, chopped fine
2	teaspoons Kikkoman soy sauce
1/2	teaspoon fresh ginger, chopped fine
2	tablespoons butter
2	tablespoons flour
1/2	teaspoon salt
1/8	teaspoon pepper
1	cup light cream
1/4	cup grated Parmesan cheese
1/2	cup sesame seeds
	rock salt
4	tablespoons lemon extract

Remove clams from shells, and reserve shells. Dice clams and water chestnuts; mix with bean sprouts and scallions. Add soy sauce and ginger. Spoon mixture into shells. Melt butter in saucepan, and gradually add flour and seasonings. Add cream slowly, stirring constantly until thickened. Add cheese to sauce, and spoon over clam mixture. Sprinkle generously with sesame seeds. Place filled shells on bed of rock salt (or half rock salt and half sand) in baking pan, and bake at 450° F. 5–6 minutes. Place pan in center of table, dribble lemon extract between clam shells onto sand and rock salt, turn lights low, and ignite for a beautiful effect. Allow guests to help themselves.

Suva Curry Dip

MAKES 3 1/2 cups

Ready Tray
1/4	cup butter
1/4	cup fine-chopped onion
2	tablespoons flour
3	tablespoons chopped crystallized ginger
2	tablespoons curry powder
2	teaspoons salt
1	teaspoon sugar
1/4	teaspoon crushed dried mint leaves
4	whole cloves
dash	cayenne
2	cups milk
1/2	cup fresh-shredded coconut
1/2	cup fresh lime juice
1/2	cup heavy cream

Melt butter in blazer pan of chafing dish over direct medium heat. Sauté onion until transparent. Blend in flour until mixture bubbles. Add ginger, curry powder, salt, sugar, mint leaves, cloves, and cayenne, and mix thoroughly. Remove from heat and gradually stir in milk until smooth. Replace on heat, and cook rapidly, stirring, until sauce thickens. Place over pan of simmering water, cover, and cook 30 minutes, stirring occasionally. Add coconut, and cook 10 minutes. Stir in lime juice. Gradually add cream, stirring constantly until thoroughly heated.

Escargots New Caledonia Style

SERVES 2–3

Ready Tray
1	can snails
1	jar snail shells
3/4	cup butter
2	tablespoons fine-chopped shallots
2	cloves garlic, crushed
2	tablespoons fine-chopped fresh parsley
	salt and fresh-ground black pepper to taste

Drain snails, rinse in cold water, and drain again thoroughly. Combine butter, shallots, garlic, parsley, salt, and pepper. Place 1/2 teaspoon seasoned butter in each shell; then place snail on top. Seal with a little more seasoned butter. Arrange shells in snail pan, open sides up. Bake at 375° F. 10–15 minutes, or until butter is bubbly. Serve at once in pan.

The accepted way to eat a snail is to hold shell with snail tongs, spear the snail with snail fork, and to eat it. Expert snail eaters usually tip the shell into their mouths to savor the last drop of the pungent butter sauce. Snails and shells are available in gourmet shops everywhere. Snail pans, tongs, and forks can be bought, but a flat pie pan filled with rock salt can be used for heating snails, and cocktail forks substitute for snail forks.

Flaming Sweet-and-Sour Ham Tidbits

SERVES 12

Ready Tray
1/4	cup brown sugar
1 1/2	tablespoons cornstarch
3/4	cup juice from canned pineapple
1	tablespoon Kikkoman Hawaiian teriyaki sauce
1/3	cup white vinegar
2	pounds cooked ham, cut in 3/4-inch cubes
2	cups canned pineapple chunks, drained
1/2	cup light rum, slightly warmed

Combine sugar and cornstarch in saucepan, stir in 1/4 cup pineapple juice, and stir until sugar is dissolved. Place over low heat, and stir in remaining juice, teriyaki sauce, and vinegar, and cook, stirring constantly until slightly thickened. Just before serving add ham and pineapple, and heat through. Add rum, and ignite. Spoon sauce through and around ham and fruit while still burning.

This dish is a good appetizer to prepare in a chafing dish while guests look on. Serve with cocktail picks.

Laulau Hawaiian

SERVES 6–8

Ready Tray
1	pound butterfish or salted salmon, cleaned, boned, and cut in 1/2-inch pieces
	water
2	pounds pork loin, cut in 1/2-inch pieces
	salt to taste
2	bunches taro, spinach, or chard leaves, with center ribs removed
	ti, grape, or cabbage leaves or corn husks

Soak butterfish 1 hour (soak salmon overnight) in water to cover; run fresh cool water over fish before using. Season pork with salt. Clean leaves. Wrap fish and meat in 3 taro leaves. Arrange 2 ti leaves in cross shape, place meat and fish in center, and tie leaves together near top. Steam 3–4 hours. After steaming, it is good to let packets cool until next day; then reheat and serve. Cooling allows grease to run off taro and congeal. Serve cut or opened in artistic manner, with baked sweet potatoes.

Do not use smoked salmon. Fresh salmon soaked in salted water overnight may be used if salted salmon is unavailable. Beef, shrimp, *mahi mahi*, or any white fish can be substituted in this recipe. Aluminum foil can be used instead of ti leaves.

Teriyaki Meatballs Hawaiian

MAKES ABOUT 100

Ready Tray
1	cup Kikkoman teriyaki Hawaiian sauce
1/2	cup water
2	teaspoons fine-chopped fresh ginger root or powdered ginger
2	cloves garlic, chopped fine
3	pounds ground chuck

Combine all ingredients except meat, and set aside. Form meat into balls about 1 inch in diameter. Place in large, flat roasting pan, and cover with sauce. Bake uncovered at 275° F. 1 hour. Serve warm with toothpicks, or keep warm in chafing dish during cocktail hour.

Nectarines on a Stick

SERVES 6–8

Ready Tray
1/2	cup brown sugar
1	teaspoon fine-chopped fresh green ginger
18	fresh nectarines or 12 medium peaches, halved and peeled
1/2	cup clarified sweet butter

Combine sugar and ginger. Dip fruit in butter, and roll in mixture. Thread on skewers, and grill over hot coals 5–6 minutes. Serve with barbecued pork or chicken.

Chinese–Hawaiian Oyster Roll

SERVES 6–8

Ready Tray
16	dried oysters
	hot water
10	water chestnuts, chopped fine
1	pound ground pork
4	fresh small green onions, chopped fine
1/4	dry onion, chopped fine
1/2	teaspoon salt
1/4	teaspoon monosodium glutamate
2	eggs, 1 well beaten
	cracker crumbs
	fat

Soak oysters overnight in hot water. Clean by removing muscle and all bits of shell and sand. Chop fine. Combine oysters, water chestnuts, pork, onions, salt, monosodium glutamate, and unbeaten egg. Mix thoroughly, and form into rolls 1/2 inch in diameter and 2 inches long. Dip in beaten egg, roll in cracker crumbs, and fry in deep fat. Do not brown too rapidly, as pork must be sufficiently cooked. Drain, and serve hot.

Dried oysters are available in all Chinese grocery stores.

Boiled Shrimp

SERVES 4–6

Ready Tray
2	pounds medium shrimp in shells
	water
3 or 4	dried hot red chili peppers, crushed
1	lemon, sliced
2	cloves garlic, crushed

Wash shrimp, leaving shells intact, and put in large kettle with water to cover; add peppers, lemon, and garlic, and cook, covered, over medium heat 30–40 minutes, or until tender. Drain, and serve, allowing each guest to shell his own and dip into *Avocado Dip*, or, for large group, shell shrimp before placing on attractive platter.

Shrimp are good hot or cold. If served cold, arrange on crushed ice, with one end of each shrimp hanging over side of bowl and *Avocado Dip* in center.

Avocado Dip

MAKES 3 CUPS

Ready Tray
2 or 3 very ripe medium avocados, peeled
2 or 3 medium, fresh tomatoes, peeled and chopped
1 medium onion or 1 bunch scallions, chopped fine
 salsa jalapeña or green chili peppers, peeled and chopped, to taste
 wine vinegar or fresh lemon juice to taste
 salt to taste

Mash avocados with fork, not too smooth, add remaining ingredients, and blend. Add avocado seed to keep mixture from turning dark.

If dip is not to be served immediately, cover with Saran wrap or foil, for it darkens quickly when exposed to air. It is best not to make it too far in advance. Salsa jalapeña and chili peppers, are very hot, so add sparingly. Vary this dish by adding pomegranate seeds; fresh coriander or fresh Chinese parsley, chopped fine; chopped peanuts or macadamia nuts; or bits of crisp bacon or fine-chopped roasted rind from *Hawaiian Barbecued Pig*.

Flaming Prawns Tahitian

SERVES 2–4

Ready Tray
6 tablespoons sweet butter, clarified
1 cup fine-chopped Bermuda onions
3 cloves garlic, chopped fine
12 whole raw prawns, washed, shelled, and butterflied, with tails on
1/2 teaspoon curry powder
1 teaspoon grated fresh ginger root
1/2 teaspoon paprika
2 tablespoons Kikkoman Hawaiian teriyaki sauce
 salt and fresh-ground black pepper to taste
1 cup cognac
1 tablespoon fine-chopped fresh parsley
2–4 slices crusty French bread

Heat crepe pan over high Sterno flame, electric frying pan set at high temperature, or large frying pan on stove over high heat. When pan is very hot, add butter; when it simmers add onions and garlic, and sauté until onions are transparent, stirring constantly to prevent scorching. Add prawns and cook, turning constantly, until they turn red. Add curry powder, ginger, paprika, teriyaki sauce, salt, and pepper; cover, reduce heat, and simmer gently a few minutes. Add cognac, and ignite; then cover quickly to keep flavor in, and cook 2–3 minutes longer. Remove cover, and sprinkle with parsley. Serve 3 prawns on a bread slice to each person as an appetizer.

Double servings, with saffron rice, make a first course or light luncheon course. Place 1/2 cup rice on each plate, and push downward in circular motion with bowl of tablespoon to make ring. Fill hollow with prawns, and sprinkle pan juices over top. Give each guest a finger bowl with floating rose petals and a steaming perfumed terrycloth hand towel rolled on a small plate to the upper left of the serving. A fine Moselle, chilled, enhances this dish. Invite guests to pick up prawns by the tails to eat. This most popular dish always commands attention when prepared in the presence of guests. Notice how guests, after enjoying prawns, go for the bread slice.

Suva Curry Puffs

MAKES 24

Ready Tray
2 cloves garlic, chopped fine
1 slice ginger root, mashed
1 1/2 tablespoons fine-chopped onion
1 tablespoon curry powder
2 tablespoons butter
1/2 pound ground beef
1 tablespoon lime juice
1/2 teaspoon salt
1 recipe plain pie pastry, made with half butter and half lard

Sauté garlic, ginger root, onion, and curry powder in butter 5 minutes. Add meat, stirring until brown. Add lime juice and salt, and mix thoroughly. Roll out pastry, and cut in 2-inch rounds. Place bit of meat mixture on each round, and cover with another round, pinching edges together well. Place on cookie sheet, and bake at 450° F. 15 minutes, or until nicely browned.

Beer is an excellent accompaniment for these appetizers.

Hors D'Oeuvres, Hot and Cold

Lobster Rumaki

SERVES 6

Ready Tray
- 10 slices bacon, halved
- 2 lobster tails, boiled and sliced 1/4-inch thick
- 1/2 cup Kikkoman Hawaiian teriyaki sauce
- 6 water chestnuts or fresh pineapple, sliced thin

Partially cook bacon in oven to render some of fat. Dip lobster meat in teriyaki sauce, and sandwich each slice between 2 thin slices water chestnut. Wrap each in half-slice bacon, and fasten with toothpick. Broil in oven or over charcoal in hibachi until bacon is crisp.

Polynesian Rumaki

SERVES 8

Ready Tray
- 12 chicken livers
- 36 water chestnuts
- 18 bacon strips, halved
- 18 scallions, halved lengthwise
- 1 cup Kikkoman soy sauce
- 1/2 teaspoon ground ginger
- 1/2 teaspoon curry powder

Cut each chicken liver into three pieces, and fold each piece over 1 water chestnut. Wrap 1/2 strip bacon and scallion half around liver, securing each with toothpick. Combine soy sauce, ginger, and curry powder, and marinate livers 1 hour. Broil until bacon is thoroughly cooked, 5–7 minutes.

Barbecued Spareribs

SERVES 8

Ready Tray
- 3 cloves garlic, minced
- 1 cup *Bean Sauce*
- 1/2 cup *Plum Sauce*
- 1/4 cup sugar
- 1 teaspoon salt
- 5 pounds spareribs, separated
- 1 cup fresh pineapple chunks

Combine all ingredients except ribs and pineapple, and brush on ribs. Place ribs on rack in roasting pan, and bake at 350° F. 1 hour, turning occasionally and basting with remaining sauce. Pour off excess fat. Broil 5 inches from heat about 5 minutes on each side, or until ribs are brown and crusty. To serve, skewer pineapple chunks on ends of ribs.

Plum Sauce

MAKES 1 2/3 CUPS

Ready Tray
- 1 1/2 cups plum jam
- 3 tablespoons vinegar
- 1 tablespoon Kikkoman plum wine
- 1/8 teaspoon allspice
- 1/2 teaspoon dry mustard

Combine all ingredients in saucepan; stir over low heat until jam is melted and sauce is smooth.

Bean Sauce Hawaiian

MAKES 2 CUPS

Ready Tray
- 1 can red kidney beans
- 1/3 cup water
- 1 clove garlic, minced
- 1 cup apricot jam
- 1 teaspoon kitchen bouquet
- 1 tablespoon chili powder
- 1/2 teaspoon cinnamon
- 1/2 teaspoon ground cloves
- 1/8 teaspoon pepper
- 1/2 teaspoon salt
- pinch ground anise or fennel

Rub beans through sieve, or put through blender until smooth. Combine remaining ingredients in sauce pan; bring to boil. Cook, stirring constantly, 5 minutes. Add beans, and simmer gently 10 minutes.

Filipino–Hawaiian Squid

SERVES 8

Ready Tray
- 1 pound fresh squid, cleaned and cut in 1-inch pieces
- 2 cloves garlic, chopped fine
- 1 small piece ginger root, mashed
- 2 tablespoons vinegar
- 1/2 cup water
- 1 1/2 teaspoons salt
- 1 tablespoon sesame oil

Put squid, garlic, ginger, vinegar, water, and salt, in saucepan, and simmer until dry, stirring occasionally. Add oil, and cook until browned. Serve with toothpicks.

Portuguese-Hawaiian Anchovy Spread

MAKES 2/3 CUP

Ready Tray
- 1 2-ounce can anchovy fillets
- 1 3-ounce package cream cheese
- 1 level tablespoon butter
- 1 level teaspoon prepared mustard
- crackers or small trimmed bread rounds, lightly toasted

Empty anchovies and oil into small mixing bowl. Break up anchovies well with fork. Add remaining ingredients, except crackers, and blend thoroughly. Serve on crackers.

Shrimp Tempura

SERVES 6

Ready Tray
1 1/2   cups sifted flour
1   teaspoon salt
3   dozen large shrimp, shelled, devined, with tails on
1   cup fresh pineapple chunks
1/2   cup water
1/2   cup pineapple juice
1   egg, beaten
1   tablespoon grated fresh ginger root
        peanut oil

Combine 1/2 cup flour and 1/2 tesapoon salt. Skewer 1 shrimp and 1 pineapple chunk on cocktail pick, or hold shrimp by tail; roll in flour mixture. Beat remaining flour and salt with water, juice, egg, and ginger to smooth batter. Dip floured shrimp and pineapple into batter, drain slightly, and drop into 350° F. oil 2 inches deep. Fry untill golden brown, turning once. Drain on absorbent paper, and keep hot. Serve plain or with sauce or dip or with *Hot Soy Sauce*.

Carrot sticks or strips, whole or julienne string beans, and zucchini sticks can be dipped in batter and fried in same way to accompany shrimp and fried rice.

Tempura, deep-fried seafood and vegetables, is thought to have been introduced to Japan by Jesuit missionaries in the late 1500s. The name derives from the Portuguese word for Lenten Ember Days, when meat and poultry were proscribed for Christians.

Hot Soy Sauce

MAKES 1 2/3 CUPS

Ready Tray
1   cup Kikkoman soy sauce
2/3   cup water
1/2   cup brown sugar
1   teaspoon grated onion
2   teapsoons grated horseradish
2   teaspoons cornstarch

Blend all ingredients, and bring to light boil. Serve as dip for *Shrimp Tempura* or other *pupus* or as sauce for fish or chicken.

Cold Soy Sauce

MAKES 1 CUP

Ready Tray
1   cup Kikkoman soy sauce
6   tablespoons brown sugar
4   tablespoons wine vinegar

Blend ingredients well. Serve in small bowls with hot fried foods or cold meat and fish *pupus*. This sauce is excellent with *Shrimp Tempura*.

Chinese Mustard

MAKES 1/2 CUP

Ready Tray
1/3   cup dry mustard
1   tablespoon salad oil
1   teaspoon sugar
1/2   teaspoon salt
2   tablespoons water, flat beer, or sake
1   teaspoon lemon juice

Mix all ingredients until smooth, and serve in small bowl.

Abalone Bites

SERVES 6

Ready Tray
1   can abalone
1/4   cup water
1/2   teaspoon onion juice
1/2   cup Kikkoman soy sauce
1/2   teaspoon prepared mustard
        pepper to taste

Cut abalone in 1/2-inch squares. Combine other ingredients. Using toothpicks, dip abalone pieces into sauce.

Avocados Stuffed with Seafood

SERVES 6

Ready Tray
1/2   pound fresh cooked shrimp, cut in small pieces
1/4   pound cooked lobster, cut in small pieces
1/4   pound cooked crabmeat, cut in small pieces
1/2   cup thin-sliced celery
2   small green onions, chopped fine
4   stuffed olives, sliced thin
1/2   cup yogurt
3   tablespoons French dressing
        salt and pepper to taste
3   ripe avocados, halved, pitted, but not peeled
        crisp lettuce leaves

Combine seafood, celery, onions, and olives. Blend yogurt and French dressing, and add to seafood mixture. Season with salt and pepper, toss lightly, and spoon into avocado halves. Refrigerate 2 hours. Serve on lettuce leaves.

Poor Man's Caviar Australian

MAKES 2 CUPS

Ready Tray
- 1 medium eggplant
- water
- 4 medium tomatoes, peeled and chopped
- 2 tablespoons light salad oil or olive oil
- 1 medium onion, chopped fine
- 1 clove garlic, chopped fine
- salt and pepper to taste

Remove green stem from eggplant. Place eggplant in medium saucepan, and add water to cover. Cover loosely, and cook over medium heat until soft, turning once during cooking period. Drain thoroughly, and peel. Chop pulp, and cook in medium skillet over medium heat 10 minutes, mashing and stirring until smooth. Add tomatoes and 1 tablespoon oil, and cook, stirring, until smooth and well blended. Remove from heat, and turn into bowl. Cool at room temperature. When cool, add onion and garlic, remaining oil, and salt and pepper. Chill thoroughly before using. Spread on brown bread, toasted bread, or crackers.

Avocado Cocktail

SERVES 6

Ready Tray
- 3 firm ripe avocados, seeded, peeled, and diced
- 1 cup catsup
- 2 teaspoons Kikkoman Hawaiian teriyaki sauce
- salt to taste
- 6 drops (or more) Tabasco
- 1 tablespoon chutney
- 1/2 dill pickle, chopped fine

Combine all ingredients, and serve in chilled cocktail glasses.

South Pacific Fruit Cocktail

SERVES 6–8

Ready Tray
- 1 grapefruit
- 1 tangerine
- 1 orange
- 2 guavas
- 1 banana
- 1 papaya
- 1 mango
- 1 fresh pineapple
- 4 fresh litchis
- 6–8 teaspoons grenadine or maraschino syrup
- 6–8 teaspoons Triple Sec, Cointreau, or Curaçao

Separate grapefruit, tangerines, and orange into segments, and cubes if pieces are large. Cube guavas, banana, papaya, and mango. Hollow out pineapple, and cube flesh. Combine fruits, and serve in chilled cocktail glasses; pour 1 teaspoon grenadine and 1 teaspoon Triple Sec over each dish of fruit.

The litchi is an exotic fruit with a rough, leathery red skin that is easily removed, and a delicate white flesh. It is fresh during the months of July and August and may be purchased in most Chinese and Japanese grocery stores. Canned litchis are also available.

Litchi Cocktail

SERVES 4–6

Ready Tray
- 1 cup fresh litchis, seeded and halved or quartered, or 1 cup canned litchis
- 1 cup diced fresh pineapple
- 1 cup diced orange sections
- 1 tablespoon sugar
- 2 teaspoons lemon juice

Combine fruits, and chill 1 hour. Add sugar and lemon juice. Serve in chilled cocktail glasses or coconut shells.

Papaya Cocktail

SERVES 4

Ready Tray
- 2 papayas, peeled, seeded, and scooped out in balls
- 1 cup fresh cherries, pitted
- 1/2 cup port wine
- mint leaves

Put papaya balls in cocktail glasses. Place 4–6 cherries on top of each dish. Pour a little wine over fruit, and chill thoroughly before serving. Garnish with mint leaves.

"Down Under" Watermelon

SERVES 6

Ready Tray
- 1 medium, ripe watermelon
- 1 cup gin
- fresh mint leaves, slightly crushed

Halve watermelon lengthwise, and scoop out easily edible portions with melon-ball cutter; remove seeds. Scoop out remainder of 1 melon half, leaving at least 1-inch rind. To make more attractive cut 1/2-inch diagonal slits with sharp paring knife, making picot edge. Place melon balls in scooped-out half, pour gin over, and chill thoroughly. Place on attractive platter, garnish with mint leaves, and let guests help themselves, or serve melon balls in individual cocktail glasses, with gin and mint leaves over each.

Filipino-Hawaiian Pickled Eggs

MAKES 12

Ready Tray

1	dozen chicken or duck eggs
1	cup vinegar
1/2–3/4	cup sugar
1	teaspoon whole allspice, tied loosely in clean cheesecloth
1	teaspoon salt

Boil eggs, in enamel pan if possible, until hard, stirring while cooking. Cool in running water, and remove shells. Put vinegar, sugar, allspice, and salt in saucepan, and boil 10 minutes, or until sugar is dissolved and blended with seasonings. Add eggs, and simmer 5 minutes. Put eggs in jars, cover with syrup, and seal.

The longer eggs remain in spiced syrup the better. They are very good in salads, eaten whole, or sliced for garnish on other dishes.

Raw Fish Hawaiian

SERVES 4

Ready Tray

1	whole fresh mackerel or blue runner
1	cup Kikkoman soy sauce
1/2	cup fine-chopped dulce seaweed
2	cloves garlic, chopped fine
1	tablespoon brown sugar

Clean fish thoroughly. Remove skin with very sharp knife. Cut enough fish into 1/4-inch cubes to make 1 cup, and place in medium bowl. Blend soy sauce, seaweed, garlic, and sugar, stirring until sugar is dissolved. Pour over fish, and marinate in refrigerator 6 hours.

This dish has a nut-like flavor and no fishy taste or texture. Dulce seaweed is available in many health-food stores or Oriental food stores. It has the texture of moist tobacco leaves and is dark brown to dark purple in color. It may be eaten as purchased or cooked and has a slightly sweet-and-sour flavor.

Tahitian Fish

SERVES 6

Ready Tray

1	cup water
1 1/2	teaspoons salt
1 1/2	pounds halibut or any white fish, boned, skinned, and cut in 1/2-inch (or smaller) cubes
	juice of 4 limes
1	teaspoon fresh-grated ginger
2	tablespoons white rum

Combine water and salt, pour over fish, and soak 1 hour. Drain, and rinse fish in fresh water. Arrange fish on large platter, and cover with lime juice, ginger, and white rum.

The Tahitian maidens of Papeete feed raw fish to their men to make them more loving.

Nouméa Raw Fish

SERVES 6

Ready Tray

2	pounds boneless fillet of red snapper, cut in 1-inch squares
	juice of 3 lemons
2	medium onions, sliced thin
1	large clove garlic, sliced thin
12	shallots, chopped fine
2	sprigs fresh parsley, chopped fine
	salt and pepper to taste
	meat of 1 fresh coconut, grated
1	cup hot water
	chopped parsley

Place fish in deep casserole, and add lemon juice, onions, garlic, shallots, and 2 parsley sprigs. Season with salt and pepper. Marinate 3 hours. Soak coconut meat in hot water 30 minutes. Then squeeze coconut through cheesecloth thoroughly. Discard pulp, cool liquid, and pour over fish. Sprinkle with chopped parsley before serving.

Papeete Lomi Salmon

SERVES 6

Ready Tray

1	pound salted salmon
	water
6	small green onions, chopped fine, then mashed to paste with fingers
6	medium tomatoes, peeled and chopped fine
1	small chili pepper, chopped fine
	lemon wedges

Soak salmon in water to cover overnight. Drain, and wash thoroughly in clear water. Remove bones and skin, and shred meat fine. Combine salmon, onions, tomatoes, and chili pepper, and mash, preferably with fingertips or fork, until mixture is soft and thoroughly blended. If too thick, add a little cold water. Chill thoroughly, garnish with lemon wedges and serve with *Poi*.

Pearl Harbor Pineapple Sticks

SERVES 6

Ready Tray

1	fresh pineapple
1	cup rum

Hors D'Oeuvres, Hot and Cold

Remove top and bottom from pineapple, and set aside. Insert sharp knife near edge of pineapple, and remove fruit, leaving shell intact. Cut fruit into sticks, and soak overnight in rum. Fill shell with pineapple sticks, and pour rum marinade over. Set on decorative plate, and replace top.

Poi

MAKES 5 CUPS

>Ready Tray
>2 1/2 pounds taro root
>2 1/2 cups water or milk

Boil taro until mealy. Peel, and cut into small pieces. Place in wooden bowl, and pound with wooden potato masher until smooth, heavy paste is formed, adding a little water or milk while pounding. Strain through several thicknesses of cheesecloth to remove fiber and lumps. Add more liquid, and knead to thick paste. Serve immediately, or allow to ferment 2–3 days until sour flavor develops.

Poi is made in different thicknesses: One-finger poi is firm paste, whereas five-finger poi is very soft, thin paste. To eat thinner poi, hold fingers of one hand tightly together, and dip into mass. The early Hawaiians are said to have eaten 10–15 pounds a day each.

Before refrigerating poi be sure to mix with water; otherwise keep at room temperature in bowl covered with a damp cloth several days. Taro flour may be purchased at drugstores, or canned poi may be substituted. Commercially prepared poi should be mixed with water to desired consistency.

To prepare canned poi, open can, and place can in pan of water, or put contents in double boiler. Steam until soft, smooth, and sticky, stirring occasionally. Place in bowl, and pour enough water on surface of poi to prevent crust from forming. Cover, chill, and serve cold. For bottled poi loosen top, and follow instructions for canned poi. Or remove frozen from bag. Place in double boiler, and proceed as for canned poi.

Sashimi

In feudal Japan the preparation of *sashimi*, or sliced raw fish, was an elaborate ritual. After sharpening his knife, the deft *sashimi* master would keep it in water overnight so that the smell of the whetstone would not affect the delicate flavor of tuna or bream. The paper-thin strips were arranged symmetrically, garnished with seaweed and *daikon* (white radishes), and served with soy sauce.

Look long and searchingly at the deep-red raw flesh of raw tuna, for example. Spear a thin slice with a pick, and dip into hot mustard, then into clear Kikkoman soy sauce, and into your mouth! Savor its sweet tenderness. Suddenly the paradox is clear; this fish does not taste like fish. Your first bite tells you that there are, indeed, more things in heaven and earth than you had dreamed of. You remember that fish, direct from river or sea, nourished primitive man, himself a later stage in an evolution that began in the sea. You are, perhaps for the first time in your life, feeding an instinctive hunger that you have never recognized before. Each bite renews your desire. *Sashimi* is the perfect *pupu* or appetizer, and your delight spreads and deepens, as you realize the importance of this long-forgotten secret, that has been revealed to you.

Japanese-Hawaiian Sashimi

SERVES 6

>Ready Tray
>1   pound white meat of fresh sea bass or any white fish, skinned and boned
>3/4 cup Kikkoman soy sauce
>1 1/2 teaspoons grated ginger root or 1/4 teaspoon ground ginger
>2   teaspoons dry mustard
>   shredded lettuce or cabbage
>   crushed ice

Cut fish into 1 1/2-inch strips; then slice diagonally 1/8 inch thick. Chill thoroughly. Combine soy sauce, ginger, and mustard to make smooth sauce. Arrange fish on lettuce and crushed ice. Using toothpicks, dip fish into sauce.

A little sour cream or mayonnaise may be added to sauce for creamy, milder flavor.

Soups

2
SOUPS

The Japanese-Hawaiians classify soups, *shirumono*, in two main groups: *suimono*, clear broths to which various garnishes are added, and *miso*, broths thickened with mashed, fermented soy-bean paste, which may also be garnished. At a formal or festive holiday dinner both types may appear, the clear *suimono* at the beginning and the *miso* during the main part of the meal. *Miso* soups are also standard breakfast fare.

Dashi, a fish-flavored stock, is also frequently used in Japanese-Hawaiian and other cooking in Hawaii and throughout the South Pacific. *Dashi* combined with chicken broth is served as a soup.

Chinese-Hawaiian Abalone Soup

SERVES 8

Ready Tray
6	Chinese dried mushrooms
	cold water
2	tablespoons Kikkoman soy sauce
2	teaspoons cornstarch
1/2	teaspoon sugar
1/4	teaspoon white pepper
2	tablespoons salad oil
1/4	pound lean, raw pork tenderloin, sliced 1/2 inch thick
2	teaspoons thin-sliced ginger root
8	cups boiling water
5	stalks celery, sliced 1/4 inch thick
1/4	pound smoked ham, julienned
	salt to taste
1/2	teaspoon monosodium glutamate
1	can abalone, julienned

Wash mushrooms, and soak in cold water to cover 10 minutes. Drain, and slice thin. Combine soy sauce, cornstarch, sugar, pepper, and 1 tablespoon oil. Toss pork strips in this mixture. Heat remaining oil in large saucepan, add ginger, and sauté 1 minute. Add boiling water, and bring to boil over medium heat. Add pork mixture, mushrooms, celery, ham, salt (sparingly), and monosodium glutamate. Cover, and cook over low heat 15 minutes. Add abalone, and cook 5 minutes to heat through; overcooking will toughen abalone.

Clear Abalone Soup

SERVES 4

Ready Tray
1	can abalone and juice
4	cups water
1/4	teaspoon monosodium glutamate
1	teaspoon Kikkoman soy sauce
4	slices lemon

Combine abalone juice and water in large saucepan, and bring to boil. Add monosodium glutamate and soy sauce. Just before serving, slice abalone thin, add to stock, and cook over medium heat 2 minutes. Pour soup into bowls, and place lemon slice in each.

Swiss chard, watercress, or green onions may also be added. Slice vegetables thin, and add to broth 1 minute before it is done.

Chinese-Hawaiian Almond Soup

SERVES 6

Ready Tray
- 1 tablespoon cornstarch
- 1 quart cold chicken broth
- 1 teaspoon grated lemon rind
- 1 tablespoon lemon juice
- 2/3 cup ground browned almonds
- 1 tablespoon simple syrup
- 1 cup heavy cream
- 3 tablespoons Kikkoman plum wine
- whole browned almonds

Blend cornstarch with a little cold broth. Heat remaining broth; then add cornstarch paste, stirring until slightly thickened. Add lemon rind, juice, ground almonds, syrup, and cream, and heat thoroughly. Add wine, place 3 whole almonds in each soup plate, and ladle soup in.

Simple syrup:

Blend 1/2 cup water with 1 cup granulated sugar. Boil mixture until slightly thickened, and a syrup-like consistency is achieved.

Breadfruit or Green-Papaya Chowder Tahitian

SERVES 6

Ready Tray
- 2 strips bacon, cut in small pieces
- 1/3 cup thin-sliced onion
- 2 cups diced breadfruit or green papaya
- 1/2 cup diced carrots
- 2 teaspoons salt
- 3 cups boiling water
- 1 1/3 cups coconut milk

Fry bacon until light brown, and remove from pan. Sauté onion in bacon grease until delicately browned. Place bacon and onions in soup kettle, and add other vegetables, salt, and water. Boil until vegetables are tender. Add milk, and serve hot.

If papaya is used, choose one whose flesh is still green. See Chapter 8 for how to obtain milk.

Korean-Hawaiian Beef and Sweet-Potato Soup

SERVES 6

Ready Tray
- 2 pounds lean whole beef brisket
- 2 pounds thick seaweed, cut in 1-inch pieces
- black pepper to taste
- water
- 2 pounds small whole sweet potatoes, peeled
- 1 teaspoon Kikkoman soy sauce

Cook beef and seaweed with pepper and water to cover in soup kettle over medium heat 4 hours. Add sweet potatoes, and cook until tender. Add soy sauce. Remove beef, slice thin, and return to soup. Serve in soup plates with few slices of beef and sweet potatoes in each.

This soup is for holidays.

Bird's-Nest Soup

SERVES 8

Ready Tray
- 4 ounces bird's nest
- water
- 6 cups chicken broth
- 1 tablespoon salt
- 4 slices cooked chicken breast, shredded
- 4 slices boiled ham, shredded
- 6 Chinese peas, shredded
- 1/2 teaspoon monosodium glutamate

Cover bird's nest with water, and soak overnight until expanded. Drain, and rinse in colander, removing feathers if necessary. Bring broth to boil in large soup kettle, add salt and bird's nest, and simmer 20 minutes. Add chicken, ham, peas, and monosodium glutamate, and heat thoroughly.

Bird's nest is available in oriental food stores.

Coconut Soup

SERVES 6

Ready Tray
- 2 teaspoons curry powder
- 1 1/2 tablespoons cornstarch
- 3 cups chicken broth
- 3 cups coconut cream

Blend curry powder and cornstarch with a little broth, and add to remaining broth. Cook over low heat, stirring constantly, to boiling. Reduce heat, and simmer 10 minutes. Stir in coconut cream, heat thoroughly, but do not boil.

To make coconut cream, for each 2 cups grated coconut, and 1 cup hot water. Let stand 30 minutes; then squeeze through cheesecloth to extract all liquid.

Soups

Coconut Soup Bora Bora

SERVES 4

Ready Tray
- 3 tablespoons butter
- 3 tablespoons flour
- 1 whole coconut
- 3 eggs
- 1 cup hot heavy cream
  salt and fresh-ground black pepper to taste
- 1/4 teaspoon monosodium glutamate
- 2 tablespoons fresh-grated coconut

Melt butter over medium heat, blend in flour, and stir until smooth. Open coconut, and heat liquid. Add liquid to flour paste, and stir until smooth. Chop coconut meat, add to soup, and cook over low heat 20 minutes, stirring frequently. Strain soup, and discard coconut meat. Beat eggs until light, and blend with cream; season with salt and pepper, and add monosodium glutamate. Add to soup, and blend thoroughly. Serve immediately garnished with grated coconut.

Champagne–Almond Soup

SERVES 6

Ready Tray
- 1 cup diced cooked chicken
- 1/2 cup blanched almonds, chopped
- 1/8 teaspoon almond extract
- 3 cups chicken broth
- 1 tablespoon fine-chopped onion
- 3 tablespoons flour
- 4 tablespoons butter, melted
- 1 1/2 cups light cream
- 1 cup champagne
  salt and fresh-ground black pepper to taste
- 1 cup avocado cubes
- 1 tablespoon fine-chopped fresh parsley

Put chicken, almonds, almond extract, broth, and onion in soup kettle, cover, and simmer 15 minutes. Blend flour and butter until smooth, and add to broth, stirring until mixture boils. Reduce heat, add cream, champagne, salt, and pepper, and heat through. Garnish each serving with avocado cubes, and sprinkle lightly with parsley.

Japanese-Hawaiian Chicken Soup

SERVES 4

Ready Tray
- 1 chicken, skinned, boned, cooked tender, and sliced very thin
- 4 cups chicken broth
- 3/4 cup sliced fresh mushrooms
- 2 teaspoons Kikkoman soy sauce
- 1 cup cooked Japanese noodles or fine egg noodles
- 4 thin slices lemon peel

Place chicken in broth in saucepan, bring to boil over medium heat, and cook 5 minutes. Add mushrooms, stir in soy sauce and noodles, and cook 4 minutes. Serve with slice of lemon peel in each soup plate.

Korean-Hawaiian Clam Soup

SERVES 6

Ready Tray
- 3 dozen clams in shells
- 1/2 pound beef tenderloin 1/2-inch thick, sliced paper-thin
- 2 tablespoons safflower oil
- 2 tablespoons ground sesame seeds
- 1 clove garlic, chopped fine
- 3 tablespoons Kikkoman soy sauce
- 5 cups water
- 1/4 teaspoon ground dried chili pepper

Scrub clams thoroughly. Brown beef in oil. Add sesame seeds, garlic, soy sauce, water, and chili pepper. Place in large soup kettle, and bring to boil over medium heat. Reduce heat, and cook 30 minutes. Add clams, and cook until shells open.

Canned minced clams (3 cups) can be substituted for clams in shells. Add to hot broth, and cook 7 minutes to heat through. To grind sesame seeds, first brown seeds in skillet. Sprinkle with a little salt, and pound very fine with mortar and pestle, or put through blender a few seconds. Store in tightly sealed jar.

Haddock Soup New Zealand

SERVES 4

Ready Tray
- 1 1/2 pounds boned haddock, cut in small pieces
- 1/2 onion, chopped fine
- 2 tablespoons fine-chopped parsley
- 1/4 teaspoon dried thyme
- 1 bay leaf
  dash fresh-ground nutmeg
  fresh-ground black pepper to taste
- 5 cups boiling water
- 1/4 cup butter
- 1/4 pound lean salt pork or smoked ham, cut in 1-inch cubes
- 2 tablespoons flour
  croutons

Place fish in large kettle with onion, herbs, and seasonings. Pour water over, and cook slowly 10 minutes. Melt butter in saucepan, brown pork, and add to soup. Cook, covered, 30 minutes. Add flour and a little soup to remaining fat in saucepan, stir until smooth, and add soup. Simmer 10 minutes. Serve with croutons.

Toheroa Clam Soup New Zealand

SERVES 4

Ready Tray
1	tablespoon butter
1	tablespoon flour
2	cups milk
	salt and pepper to taste
1	can whole Toheroa clams, minced fine
1	cup heavy cream, whipped
1	teaspoon fine-chopped fresh parsley

In large saucepan, blend butter and flour until smooth. Slowly stir in milk, and cook, stirring until smooth. Season with salt and pepper, add clams, and heat. Just before serving fold in cream, heat through, but do not boil. Garnish with chopped parsley.

The variety of green clam called Toheroa is undoubtedly the giant of all edible clams. It forms the basis of many fine dishes, which unfortunately cannot often be enjoyed, for the Toheroa is not readily available, and there is no adequate substitute. Canned Toheroa clams are exported in only small quantities but may be available in gourmet food stores.

Australian Kangaroo-Tail Soup

SERVES 6

Ready Tray
3	pounds kangaroo tail, cleaned and cut in 2-inch pieces
1/2	pound kangaroo steak, cut in 1-inch pieces
1	large onion, chopped coarse
1	celery stalk, sliced 1/4-inch thick
1	carrot, sliced coarse
1	whole leek, sliced thin
1	bay leaf
1	small sprig fresh rosemary, chopped fine
1	sprig fresh parsley, chopped fine
1/2	cup sherry
	salt and fresh-ground black pepper to taste
	water
1/2	cup barley
2	tablespoons fine-chopped chives

Place kangaroo tail and steak in large kettle. Add onion, celery, carrot, leek, bay leaf, rosemary, parsley, wine, salt, and pepper. Cover with water to 1 inch above ingredients. Cover, and simmer slowly 2–3 hours or until meat is tender. Add barley during last hour of cooking. Add more water if soup is too thick. Soup may be served thick or strained as a heavy broth. Garnish with chives.

Ox joints may be substituted for kangaroo tail and round steak for kangaroo steak. See Purchasing Guide for places where kangaroo is sold.

Cock-a-Leekie Sydney

SERVES 6

Ready Tray
12	sweet prunes
4	large leeks, sliced 1/4-inch thick
3	tablespoons butter
	water
6	cups hot veal or chicken broth
2	tablespoons cornstarch
3	tablespoons cold water
	paprika

Soak prunes in water to cover, and steam a few minutes. Sauté leeks quickly in butter, and add to hot broth; simmer 15 minutes. Blend cornstarch with 3 tablespoons cold water, add to soup, and cook until clear, stirring. Drain prunes, and add to soup. Place two prunes in each soup plate, pour soup over, and sprinkle with paprika before serving.

According to Scottish tradition, this soup was associated with cockfighting. The loser was tossed into the pot, with leeks for flavor, and spectators all shared in the soup. Some say that cock-a-leekie is simply an adaptation of fourteenth-century English dish called "ma-leachi," "ma" meaning fowl.

Filipino-Hawaiian Fish Soup

SERVES 4

Ready Tray
1	pound fresh croakers or porgies, cleaned and cut in 1-inch cubes
1	teaspoon thin-sliced fresh ginger, mashed, or 2 teaspoons powdered ginger
2	medium tomatoes, quartered
1	teaspoon monosodium glutamate
4	cups water
	salt and pepper to taste
	juice of 1 lemon
1	scallion stalk, chopped fine

Put all ingredients except lemon juice and scallion stalk in soup kettle, cover, and simmer slowly 45 minutes. Before serving, add lemon juice and scallion stalk.

Tahitian Green Soup

SERVES 4–6

Ready Tray
1	tablespoon sesame seeds
1	pound short ribs
6	cups water
1/4	cup Kikkoman soy sauce
3/4	teaspoon salt
3	cups 1-inch pieces scallions
	fresh-ground black pepper to taste

Heat sesame seeds in small skillet until golden. Wipe ribs with damp cloth, and place in soup kettle with water, soy sauce, salt, and sesame seeds. Cover, and simmer 1 1/2 hours. Remove meat, discard bones and fat. Cut meat in 1-inch pieces. Skim excess fat from surface of soup, and return meat to kettle. Add onions, cover, and cook 10 minutes. Sprinkle pepper over soup before serving.

Egg-Flower Soup with Cucumbers

SERVES 10–12

Ready Tray
2	tablespoons Kikkoman plum wine
2	tablespoons Kikkoman soy sauce
2	tablespoons cornstarch
1/2	pound fresh pork tenderloin, cut in 1/2" × 1 1/2" strips
4	tablespoons light salad oil
1	leek stalk, cut in 1/4-inch pieces
12	cups beef or chicken broth or water
2	medium cucumbers, peeled and sliced thin
	salt to taste
1/4	teaspoon monosodium glutamate
2	eggs, lightly beaten

Combine wine, soy sauce, and cornstarch, and dredge pork strips in mixture. Heat oil in deep kettle, and brown strips with leek stalk, stirring constantly. Add broth, and bring to boil. Add cucumbers, salt, and monosodium glutamate. Slowly stir in beaten egg.

Chicken or beef may be substituted for pork.

Mutton Soup New Zealand

SERVES 4

Ready Tray
2	pounds lean mutton with bone
1	quart water
	salt and pepper to taste
1/4	cup pearl barley
1/2	onion, sliced thin
1	leek, sliced thin
1	carrot, diced
1	turnip, diced
2	stalks celery, diced
2	tablespoons minced parsley

Remove fat, skin, and bone from meat, and cut meat in 1-inch pieces. Place meat and bone in soup kettle, and add water, seasonings, and barley. Cover, and simmer 2 hours. Add vegetables, except parsley, and simmer 1/2 hour, or until tender. Add more water if necessary. Remove bones, and skim off surface fat. Sprinkle with parsley before serving.

South Pacific Cold Fruit Soup

SERVES 6

Ready Tray
1	pound fresh black cherries, pitted
2	fresh peaches, peeled, seeded, and sliced thin
1	stick cinnamon
4	whole cloves
	juice of 1 lime
4	cups water
3	tablespoons honey
2	tablespoons cornstarch
3	tablespoons cold water
1/2	teaspoon almond extract
1	cup claret
1/2	cup sour cream
1/4	cup slivered browned almonds

Place fruit, spices, juice, 4 cups water, and honey in large kettle; cover, and simmer 15 minutes. Remove spices. Blend cornstarch with 3 tablespoons water, and stir into soup until clear. Stir in almond extract and wine, and chill thoroughly. Place a few cherries and peach slices in each chilled soup plate, pour soup over, and garnish with teaspoon of sour cream (or more, if desired) and sprinkle with almond slivers.

Lentil Soup New Zealand

SERVES 6

Ready Tray
1/2	cup dried lentils or split peas
2	strips bacon, cut in small pieces
2	medium onions, chopped fine
2	carrots, chopped fine
3	stalks celery, chopped fine
2	tablespoons butter
1	quart water
2	tablespoons flour
2	cups milk
	salt and pepper to taste

Wash lentils thoroughly. Fry bacon until crisp. Sauté other vegetables in butter 3 minutes. Place lentils in soup kettle with water. Add bacon and drippings and other vegetables. Cover, and simmer 1 1/2 hours. Blend flour with a little milk until smooth, stir into soup, and cook 10 minutes. Add remaining milk, season, and slowly bring to boil. Serve hot in tureen with ladle.

If desired, puree by putting all ingredients through sieve before adding flour. For exceptional flavor chop fine 4 large cloves garlic, sauté in 2 tablespoons sweet butter until golden brown, and add to hot soup at very last minute, stirring gently down to bottom. Do not cook further.

Famous Korean-Hawaiian Wedding Soup

SERVES 6–8

Ready Tray
- 1 1/2 pounds whole raw boiling beef
- 6 cups water
- 6 cloves garlic, chopped fine
- 4 large green onions, sliced 1/4 inch thick
- 1 medium, dry onion, sliced thin
- 3 tablespoons peanut oil
- 6 large tomatoes, chopped coarse
- 2 teaspoons pine nuts
- 1/4 teaspoon black pepper
- 1/4 pound Chinese thin noodles or vermicelli
- 3 tablespoons Kikkoman soy sauce
- 1 recipe *Wedding-Soup Meat Balls*
- 1 egg white
- 1/8 teaspoon Kikkoman soy sauce
- 1 teaspoon water
- 2 tablespoons fine-chopped parsley

Put beef and 6 cups water into soup kettle, cover, and cook over medium heat. Sauté garlic and onions in oil. Add tomatoes, pine nuts, and pepper. Simmer 5 minutes; then add to soup kettle, and cook 1–1 1/2 hours, or until meat is tender. Remove meat, and save for some other purpose. Add noodles to boiling soup, and cook until tender. Add 3 tablespoons soy sauce and meat balls. Beat egg white, 1/8 teaspoon soy sauce, and 1 teaspoon water together but not stiff. Pour by tablespoonfuls into oiled frying pan, to make very thin pancakes. Remove from pan, roll up, and cut into thin threads with sharp knife. Place a few meat balls in center of each soup plate, pour soup over, sprinkle egg white shreds on top, garnish with parsley, and serve.

Wedding-Soup Meat Balls

SERVES 6–8

Ready Tray
- 1 pound coarse-ground raw beef, pork, chicken, or duck
- 2 eggs
- 2 tablespoons Kikkoman soy sauce
- 2 teaspoons fine-chopped onion
- salt and pepper to taste
- 1/4 teaspoon ground fresh ginger or 1/8 teaspoon powdered ginger
- 1 tablespoon sesame seeds, ground or pounded fine
- 2 tablespoons flour
- 1/4 cup hot peanut oil

Combine meat thoroughly with 1 egg, soy sauce, onion, salt (use sparingly), pepper, ginger, and sesame seeds. Shape into 1/2-inch balls. Beat remaining egg. Roll meat balls in flour, then in egg, and fry slowly in heated oil until egg is brown and meat well done.

Turtle Soup Fiji

SERVES 6–8

Ready Tray
- 1 6-pound turtle, shelled, cleaned, and cut in small pieces, or 5 (1 pound) cans turtle meat
- 1 pound whole lean beef brisket
- water
- 1/2 teaspoon fine-chopped fresh basil
- 1/2 teaspoon fine-chopped fresh marjoram
- 1/2 teaspoon fine-chopped fresh fennel
- 1/2 teaspoon fine-chopped fresh mint leaves
- 1/2 teaspoon fine-chopped fresh sage
- 1/2 teaspoon ground allspice
- 1 cup Kikkoman plum wine
- 1 1/2 teaspoons Kikkoman soy sauce
- fresh-ground black pepper to taste
- chopped hard-cooked turtle eggs

Place turtle meat and beef in large kettle, and cover with water. Add remaining ingredients, except turtle eggs. Cover, and cook slowly 2 1/2–3 hours, or until meat is tender and broth strong and clear. Remove beef, cut into thin strips, and return to soup. Garnish with hard-cooked turtle eggs. Serve in scrubbed turtle shell or tureen.

The women of Fiji wade into the water in the nude to call the turtles.

Shrimp-and-Oyster Bisque

SERVES 3–4

Ready Tray
- 1 cup fine-chopped shrimp meat
- 1 cup fine-chopped oysters, and liquid
- 3 cups milk
- 1/4 cup chopped celery
- 1 1/2 tablespoons fine-chopped onion
- 1 teaspoon fine-chopped fresh parsley
- pinch ground mace
- salt and pepper to taste
- 2 1/2 tablespoons butter
- 2 1/2 tablespoons flour
- 3 or 4 whole medium shrimps, shelled, devined, and cooked
- paprika to taste

In top of double boiler over boiling water cook chopped shrimp and oysters, oyster liquid, milk, celery, onion, parsley, mace, salt, and pepper 30 minutes. Strain bisque. In saucepan melt butter, and stir in flour. Gradually add strained bisque, stirring constantly. Heat thoroughly, but do not boil. Serve in heated soup plates, garnish each plate with 1 whole shrimp, and sprinkle lightly with paprika.

Famous Korean-Hawaiian Wedding Soup

Chicken Momi

Soups

Polynesian Cold Melon Soup

SERVES 6

Ready Tray
- juice of 2 limes
- 1/4 teaspoon fresh-grated nutmeg
- 3 cups pureed ripe, sweet cantaloupe, mango, or papaya
- juice of 1 grapefruit
- 1/2 cup dry white wine
- 1 cup melon balls
- 1/2 cup whipped cream or sour cream

In large bowl mix lime juice and nutmeg with melon puree. Blend in grapefruit juice and wine. Chill thoroughly. Put 2 or 3 melon balls in each chilled soup plate, pour soup over, and garnish with 1 teaspoon of whipped or sour cream.

Add 2 tablespoons honey dissolved in 1/2 cup boiling water to lime juice for sweeter soup.

Macadamia-Nut Soup

SERVES 4

Ready Tray
- 1/2 cup butter blended with 1/4 cup fine-grated macadamia nuts
- 4 cups chicken broth
- dash cayenne
- salt and pepper to taste
- 1/2 cup heavy sweet cream
- 1/2 cup coarse-chopped macadamia nuts

Blend nut butter with broth, a little at a time, until smooth. Add cayenne, salt, pepper, and cream. Heat thoroughly. Serve hot, garnished with chopped nuts.

Macadamia nuts are available in various-sized cans in all major gourmet stores.

Oyster Soup New Zealand

SERVES 6

Ready Tray
- 2 dozen fresh oysters, shelled, and liquid
- 2 tablespoons butter
- 2 tablespoons flour
- 1/2 teaspoon salt
- dash cayenne
- 4 cups milk
- 1/2 cup whipped cream
- 1 tablespoon fine-chopped fresh parsley

Pick over oysters to be sure all shell pieces are removed. Chop oysters, reserving liquid. Melt butter in heavy-bottomed saucepan, gradually add flour and seasonings, and stir until smooth. Add milk and oyster liquid a little at a time, and stir until mixture boils. Add oysters, and simmer 5 minutes. If soup is too thick, and more milk. Adjust seasoning, and pour into heated tureen. Top with 1 teaspoon whipped cream (pass the remaining whipped cream), and sprinkle lightly with parsley.

Dried-Pea Soup Pago Pago

SERVES 6

Ready Tray
- 1 (4-ounce) package dried green-pea soup mix
- 2 tablespoons fine-grated orange peel
- 1/3 cup orange juice
- 1 1/2 cups milk
- 1/2 teaspoon ground mace
- 4 cups water
- 1 cup popcorn, popped

Combine all ingredients, except popcorn, in 2-quart saucepan, and mix well. Cook, uncovered, over medium heat 15 minutes, stirring occasionally. Serve at once in mugs, and top with several kernels of popcorn.

Pumpkin Banana Soup

SERVES 4

Ready Tray
- 1 1/2 cups mashed cooked pumpkin
- salt and pepper to taste
- 1/4 teaspoon fresh-grated nutmeg
- 2 tablespoons sweet butter, melted
- 3 tablespoons honey
- 1 cup milk
- 1 cup light cream
- 1 cup mashed banana
- 4 tablespoons light rum

In large saucepan combine pumpkin, salt, pepper, nutmeg, butter, and honey. Stir in milk, cream, and bananas until smooth, and heat thoroughly. Put 1 tablespoon rum in each soup plate, and ladle soup over.

Seaweed Soup Hawaiian

- 2 oz *dashi konbu*
- 2 oz *hana katsuo*
- 6 cups water
- 2 oz *shiro miso*
- 1 lemon slice

Boil *dashi konbu* and *hana katsuo* in water 45 minutes. Strain, and add *shiro miso* to liquid. Pour into tureen, add lemon slice, and serve.

The strained stock is used as a bouillon or a base for sauces. *Dashi konbu*, a seaweed used as a base for soup stock, is dried giant kelp; its leaves may be 8 inches wide by 6 feet long. *Hana katsuo* is dried bonito flakes, and *shiro miso* is fermented rice paste. All three are available at Oriental food stores and at many health-food stores.

Vichyssoise New Caledonian

SERVES 6

Ready Tray
1	medium onion, chopped fine
1	bunch scallions, white part only, chopped fine
1/4	cup butter
4	cups chicken broth
3	medium potatoes, peeled, boiled, and mashed
1	cup sour cream
1/2	cup light cream
1/2	cup vodka or Chablis
	salt and pepper to taste
2	tablespoons fine-chopped chives

In large saucepan, sauté onion and scallions in butter until soft, but do not brown. Add all other ingredients, except chives, and bring to boil over medium heat. Chill thoroughly 4 hours. Serve in chilled bowls, and sprinkle chives lightly over top.

Pass pepper mill, and allow each guest to grind additional fresh pepper to taste.

Cold Tomato Soup Australian

SERVES 6

Ready Tray
2	pounds ripe tomatoes
2	ice cubes
1	tablespoon sugar
2	teaspoons salt
1	teaspoon onion juice
	juice and rind of 1 lemon
1/2	cup sour cream
4	slices cooked ham, cut in thin strips
1	cup melon balls
1	cup cucumber balls
2	teaspoons celery seed

Press tomatoes through sieve to make 3 cups puree. Chill thoroughly until serving time. Then add ice cubes, sugar, salt, onion juice, lemon juice, and lemon rind. Beat in sour cream until smooth. Add ham. Place a few melon and cucumber balls in pyramid in center of each soup plate, and gently pour soup over. Sprinkle celery seeds lightly over each portion.

Shark's-Fin Soup

SERVES 6

Ready Tray
1/4	pound refined shark's fins
	water
2	leek stalks
10	thin slices ginger root
1/2	chicken
2	quarts water
1/2	cup shredded bamboo shoots
2	tablespoons dry white wine
1	tablespoon salt
1/2	teaspoon monosodium glutamate

Soak shark's fins overnight in water to cover. Rinse in cold water three times. Boil with 1 leek stalk and 5 slices ginger in 2 quarts water 1 hour. Drain, rinse shark's fins, and set aside. Boil chicken 1 1/2 hours with remaining leek stalk and ginger slices in enough water to make 10 cups broth after boiling. Remove chicken from broth, bone, and shred meat. Boil shark's fins again in chicken broth (add wine to broth), 30 minutes. Add shredded chicken and bamboo shoots. Add salt and monosodium glutamate, and serve hot.

Shark fins are available in Oriental sections of leading food stores and in Chinese grocery stores.

Salads and Salad Dressings

3

SALADS AND SALAD DRESSINGS

Cherry-Blossom Salad

SERVES 8

Ready Tray
2	packages apple gelatin
1	cup hot water
1	7-ounce bottle ginger ale
2	cups canned dark, sweet cherries, pitted, with syrup
	gin
1 1/4	cups canned mandarin-orange sections, drained, with syrup
	orange Curaçao
1/2	cup chopped macadamia nuts
12	marshmallows
2	tablespoons milk
1	8-ounce package cream cheese
2	tablespoons Grand Marnier
1	cup sour cream
	nasturtium leaves and parsley sprigs
	maraschino cherries

Dissolve 1 package gelatin in hot water, and cool. Add ginger ale, and refrigerate until mixture begins to set. Combine cherry syrup and gin to make 1 cup, heat to boiling, and dissolve second package of gelatin. Combine orange syrup and Curaçao to make 1 cup, add to cherry gelatin, and chill until mixture begins to set. Pour half the ginger-ale gelatin into bottom of 1 1/2-quart ring mold. Chill until it begins to thicken; then arrange half the cherries and half the orange sections on top. Cover with remaining ginger-ale gelatin, and chill until firm. Mix remaining fruit and nuts into fruit-gelatin mixture, and pour into mold on top of ginger-ale mixture. Chill until very firm. In the meantime, melt marshmallows with milk in top of double boiler, stirring constantly. Soften cheese, and cream with fork; add to marshmallow mixture. Add Grand Marnier; then fold in sour cream. Chill thoroughly. Unmold salad on large round platter and arrange leaves and parsley sprigs around it in wreath; dot with maraschino cherries. Place chilled cheese dressing in bowl, and set in the center of ring.

This exciting salad is good to serve during the Christmas holidays. If nasturtium leaves are unavailable, use lettuce leaves or sprigs of fresh mint or English holly.

Tahitian Fish Salad (I'a Ota)

SERVES 4

Ready Tray
1	3-pound raw fish
1	cup fresh lime or lemon juice
2	medium Bermuda onions, sliced thin
6	tablespoons olive oil
3	tablespoons wine vinegar
	salt and fresh-ground black pepper to taste

Bone fish, and cut into pieces about 1 inch square and 1/2 inch thick. Put in large casserole, and add juice; let stand approximately 1 1/2 hours. Drain off juice, and put fish on large platter with onions. Blend olive oil, vinegar, salt, and pepper. Pour over fish and onions. Toss lightly, and serve on individual cold plates.

Another way to make dressing is to grate a coconut kernel into its own milk, press through cloth to extract cream, and add salt and white pepper to taste, thin-sliced raw onions, and a little garlic.

The fish is actually anything but raw, for it is completely "cooked" in the acid of the lime juice. It can also be served as an hors d'oeuvre. In Tahiti it is widely known and appreciated as a specific for the man who has drunk too long from the flowing bowl the night before.

Chinese-Hawaiian Cabbage Salad

SERVES 4

Ready Tray
1	head Chinese cabbage, shredded fine
1	fresh unpeeled cucumber, diced
1	green bell pepper, diced
1	tablespoon fine-chopped Bermuda onion
1	tablespoon sesame seeds, toasted
	salt and fresh-ground black pepper to taste
1/3	cup French dressing
1	tablespoon Kikkoman Hawaiian teriyaki sauce

In wooden salad bowl combine cabbage, cucumber, green pepper, onion, sesame seeds, salt (use sparingly), and pepper. Combine dressing and sauce, add to salad, and toss lightly. Serve on chilled salad plates with chilled salad forks.

Leave salad plates and salad forks in freezing compartment of refrigerator at least 2 hours before serving. Watch the surprised faces of your guests when they pick up their frozen forks.

Korean-Hawaiian Bean-Sprout Salad

SERVES 6

Ready Tray
1/4	cup peanut oil
2	tablespoons wine vinegar
2	tablespoons Kikkoman Hawaiian teriyaki sauce
	salt and fresh-ground black pepper to taste
1/4	cup fine-chopped scallions
1/4	cup thin-sliced pimiento
2	tablespoons ground sesame seeds
1	clove garlic, chopped fine
2	cups bean sprouts

In small bowl blend throughly oil, vinegar, sause, salt (use sparingly), pepper, scallions, pimiento, sesame seeds, and garlic. Place bean sprouts in large wooden salad bowl. Pour dressing over bean sprouts, and toss gently. Chill thoroughly approximately 1 hour. Serve on chilled salad plates.

Hawaiian Salad Japanesque

SERVES 6

Ready Tray
2	medium carrots
2	medium cucumbers
1	tablespoon salt
	ice water
1/2	cup salad oil
1/2	cup white-wine vinegar
1/4	cup sugar
1/4	cup dark-toasted sesame seeds
1	teaspoon salt
1	teaspoon ground ginger
1/2	cup minced green onions and greens
1	cup fresh pineapple chunks
	crisp lettuce leaves

Peel carrots and cucumbers. Slice carrots very thin diagonally. Slice cucumbers 1/4 inch thick. Then use cutter to scallop edges. Sprinkle cucumber and carrot slices with 1 tablespoon salt. Let stand 5 minutes; then rinse with ice water, and drain well. Blend salad oil, vinegar, sugar, sesame seeds, 1 teaspoon salt, ginger, and onions. Toss vegetables with pineapple, and serve on lettuce leaves. Pour a little dressing over each portion; more dressing may be used if so desired.

If a scalloped cutter is unavailable, slice cucumbers diagonally.

Salade Coeur de Cocotier à la Tahitienne

SERVES 4

Ready Tray
1	fresh or canned heart of coconut palm
5	green onions, sliced thin
1/2	teaspoon salt
2	tablespoons wine vinegar
1/4	teaspoon Worcestershire sauce
2	tablespoons catsup
1	teaspoon prepared mustard
3	tablespoons pure olive oil
	dash pressed fresh garlic (optional)
1	teaspoon fine-chopped fresh parsley

Slice palm heart very thin, and place in wooden bowl; add onions, salt, vinegar, Worcestershire sauce, catsup, mustard, olive oil, and garlic. Toss lightly. Garnish with parsley, and serve on chilled salad plates.

Salads and Salad Dressings

Australian Fruit Salad

SERVES 6–8

Ready Tray
1	small fresh pineapple, peeled and cut into 1/2-inch cubes
4	bananas, peeled and diced
4	tablespoons fresh lemon juice
4	oranges, peeled, with membrane removed, and diced
1/4	teaspoon salt
1	unpeeled apple, cored and diced
1	pear, peeled and diced
2	passion fruits, peeled and diced
4	tablespoons confectioner's sugar
1/2	cup heavy cream, whipped and sweetened
	sprigs fresh mint

In large salad bowl combine pineapple and bananas, and sprinkle with lemon juice. Add oranges, salt, apple, pear, and passion fruits. Toss lightly, and sprinkle with confectioner's sugar. Refrigerate at least 1 hour. Serve in sherbet glasses. Garnish each with whipped cream and a sprig of fresh mint.

Lemon juice keeps discoloration of peeled bananas to a minimum. If passion fruit is unobtainable, payapa may be substituted. Any soft fresh fruit in season—peaches, small white grapes, or very small melon balls, for example—may be added, but pineapple, bananas, oranges, and passion fruit or papaya are essential.

Lobster Salad South Pacific

SERVES 4–6

Ready Tray
1	cup coarse-diced fresh mango
1	cup coarse-diced fresh papaya
2	cups coarse-diced cooked fresh lobster, chilled
1	cup thin-sliced celery
1/4	cup heavy cream (baker's cream)
1/2	teaspoon grated lime rind
2	teaspoons fresh lime juice
2	teaspoons Kikkoman soy sauce
1	teaspoon grated onion
1/2	teaspoon fresh-grated ginger
1	teaspoon coconut honey
	fresh-ground black pepper to taste
	crisp lettuce leaves
1/2	bunch watercress, tough stems removed
2	tablespoons toasted slivered almonds

Combine fruit, lobster, and celery in large wooden salad bowl. Toss lightly. Combine cream, lime rind and juice, soy sauce, onion, ginger, honey, and pepper. Stir until smooth. Pour over lobster and fruit, and toss lightly. Chill thoroughly. Serve on lettuce leaves, and garnish with watercress and almonds.

Hawaiian Fruit Bowl

SERVES 6

Ready Tray
1	cup fresh orange sections
1	cup 1/2-inch cubes fresh pineapple
1	cup 1/4-inch banana slices
1	cup seedless grapes
1	cup 1/2-inch mango cubes
1	cup 1/2-inch cubes papaya
1	cup fresh strawberry halves
1	cup miniature marshmallows
1/2	cup fresh-grated coconut
1	pint plain yogurt
	juice of 6 limes
1/2	cup peppermint schnapps
1	large sprig fresh mint leaves, chopped fine
	crisp lettuce levaes
	few whole strawberries

In large wooden salad bowl place orange, pineapple, banana, grapes, mango, papaya, strawberries, marshmallows, and coconut. In another bowl blend yogurt, lime juice, mint leaves, and schnapps until smooth. Add dressing to fruits, and mix gently. Chill thoroughly until serving time. Serve on lettuce leaves, and garnish with whole strawberries.

Macadamia Island Salad

SERVES 6

Ready Tray
1	unpeeled apple, cored and chopped coarse
2	cups coarse-chopped macadamia nuts
3	dried figs, quartered
6	dates, quartered
1/4	cup fresh-shredded coconut
2	tablespoons raisins
1	tablespoon melted butter
6	crisp lettuce leaves
3	large tomatoes, peeled and sliced 1/2-inch thick
1/2	cup salad dressing
	watercress

Combine apple, nuts, figs, dates, coconut, and raisins with butter, and set aside. Place lettuce leaves on chilled individual salad plates, or arrange on large platter. Place 2 or 3 tomato slices on each plate, or arrange tomatoes on large platter. Pour dressing over. Mound fruit-nut mixture in center, and garnish with watercress.

Flaming Orange Salad Bora Bora

SERVES 4

Ready Tray
4	medium oranges
3/4	cup granulated sugar
1/2	cup rum, warmed

Peel oranges, remove white membranes, quarter, and place in wooden salad bowl. Sprinkle sugar over oranges, and toss well. Add rum, ignite, and toss gently until rum is burned out. Oranges will be syrupy. Serve immediately on individual salad plates.

This salad is served during Christmas-New Year holidays.

Spanish-Hawaiian Lobster Salad

SERVES 6–8

Ready Tray
4	cups beer
2	cups water
2	teaspoons salt
1	bay leaf
1	medium Bermuda onion, chopped coarse
2	live lobsters or 4 lobster tails
2	cups diced cooked potatoes
2	cups cooked fresh-shelled peas
2	cups shredded Manoa, limestone, or Boston lettuce
	salt and fresh-ground black pepper to taste
1/4	teaspoon saffron powder
1	tablespoon lemon juice
1 1/2	cups mayonnaise

Combine beer, water, salt, bay leaf, and onion. Bring liquid to boil, and plunge lobsters in. Cover, and cook over medium heat 20 minutes. Cool in liquid 30 minutes. Split lobsters, and dice meat. In large salad bowl combine lobster, potatoes, peas, and lettuce. Season with salt and pepper. Chill thoroughly. Dissolve saffron in lemon juice, add to mayonnaise, and blend until smooth. Pour over salad, and toss lightly. Serve on chilled salad plates.

Niuafo'ou, Oyster Salad Tin Can Isle

SERVES 4–6

Ready Tray
2	cups fresh oysters and liquid
1	cup thin-sliced celery
1	pickled cucumber, sliced thin
	salt and fresh-ground black pepper to taste
2	hard-cooked eggs, sliced
3	tablespoons mayonaise
1	teaspoon fine-chopped fresh parsley
1	teaspoon fine-chopped gherkins
1	teaspoon fine-chopped chives
1	teaspoon fine-chopped capers
1	teaspoon fine-chopped shallots
	crisp lettuce leaves

Scald oysters in their own liquid until plump and frilled. Drain, and chill thoroughly. In salad bowl combine oysters with celery, cucumber, salt, and pepper. Add eggs, and toss lightly. Blend mayonnaise, parsley, gherkins, chives, capers, and shallots until smooth. Add to salad, and toss gently. Serve on lettuce leaves on chilled salad plates.

Tin Can Isle, Niuafo'ou, is a volcanic isle located between Fiji and Samoa. It takes its name from the peculiar manner in which the mails have been sent out by and delivered to its isolated inhabitants. The villagers used to send mail in tightly sealed tin cans in hopes that passing ships would pick them up and deliver the mail to the proper destinations or that the cans would drift to some other shore and be picked up by villagers and delivered or sent on its way. Today modern passenger liners and airplanes are able to deliver the mail to the waiting villagers, of whom there are approximately 600 or more.

Filipino-Hawaiian Papaya Salad

SERVES 4–6

Ready Tray
1	large, firm, ripe papaya, peeled, seeded, and coarsely grated
1/2	teaspoon grated green ginger or 1 teaspoon fine-chopped crystallized ginger rinsed of sugar
1/2	teaspoon salt
2	tablespoons fresh lemon juice
1	can peeled green chilis, chopped fine
	crisp lettuce leaves

Combine first five ingredients, and serve on lettuce leaves.

This salad may also be served as a condiment or relish. It is very good with broiled meats and curry dishes.

Water-Chestnut Salad

SERVES 4

Ready Tray
1	Small head manoa, butter, or limestone lettuce, sliced thin
	salt and pepper to taste
2	tablespoons lemon juice
1	tablespoon minced chives
2	medium tomatoes, peeled and halved
3	teaspoons light salad oil
1	teaspoon lemon juice
1	cup fine-chopped watercress
2	tablespoons fine-chopped water chestnuts

Arrange lettuce on chilled salad plates. Sprinkle with salt, pepper, 2 tablespoons lemon juice, and chives. Top each serving with tomato half. Blend oil, 1 teaspoon lemon juice, salt, and pepper with watercress and water chestnuts. Mound 1/4 cup of this mixture on top of each tomato half, and serve.

Salads and Salad Dressings

Mango Salad

SERVES 6

Ready Tray
2	hot red peppers, seeded and crushed
	salt to taste
1/4	cup wine vinegar
5	large 1/2-inch-thick slices fresh pineapple, cut in 1-inch pieces
3	medium, ripe mangoes, peeled, seeded, and cut in 1-inch pieces
3	medium bananas, peeled and cut in 1-inch pieces

In salad bowl mix peppers with salt and vinegar. Add fruit, and stir to moisten. Chill several hours. Remove pepper 30 minutes before serving time.

This salad is excellent with hot roasts, cold meat, or fowl.

Orange-and-Onion Salad Australian

SERVES 4

Ready Tray
2	large oranges
6	large lettuce leaves, torn into bite-size pieces
6	thin slices sweet red onion, separated into rings
1/3	cup French dressing
	juice of 1/2 lemon

Remove skin and white membrane from oranges. Slice whole oranges wafer-thin horizontally; then quarter slices. Place in salad bowl with lettuce and onion. Pour dressing and lemon juice over salad, and toss lightly.

Filipino-Hawaiian Sweet-Potato Leaf Salad

SERVES 6

Ready Tray
1 1/2	pounds young sweet-potato leaves or spinach leaves
1/2	teaspoon salt
2	medium tomatoes, peeled and sliced 1/4-inch thick
3	hard-cooked eggs, sliced 1/4-inch thick
6	tablespoons French dressing, *bagoong*, or *patis*

Remove stems from sweet-potato leaves, and wash thoroughly. Place in large kettle without water. Cover, and cook until leaves begin to wilt. Add salt, and cook, uncovered, until leaves are tender. Drain, and chill thoroughly.

Arrange tomato and egg slices alternately around edge of large platter. Place greens in center. Add French dressing, and allow to stand 15 minutes before serving.

A large onion, sliced thin, may be substituted for eggs. *Bagoong* is a mixture of small shrimp or various kinds of small fish and salt, fermented several days, pressed, and drained. It is used uncooked as a seasoning for meat, fish, and vegetable dishes. *Patis* is the clear liquid drained from *bagoong*. The fish are pounded, and more salt is added: Colored rice may also be added. The mixture is then allowed to stand 1–2 days longer.

Pineapple-Rum Salad

SERVES 8

Ready Tray
2	tablespoons plain gelatin
1/4	cup cold juice from canned pineapple
3/4	cup boiling juice from canned pineapple
1/4	cup lime juice
1/2	cup light rum
1	cup canned crushed pineapple, drained
1/2	cup candied lemon peel, chopped fine
2	cups heavy cream, whipped
	crisp lettuce leaves
	frosted grapes

Soften gelatin in cold pineapple juice. Dissolve in hot juice. Add lime juice and rum. Chill until partly set, then beat in electric mixer until light and fluffy. Add pineapple and lemon peel, and mix well. Fold in whipped cream. Pour into lightly oiled individual molds, and chill until firm. Line salad plates with lettuce leaves, umold salad, and garnish with grapes.

If lemon peel is too hard, let it stand in small bowl covered with light rum a couple of hours.

Korean-Hawaiian Sesame-Seed Salad

SERVES 4

Ready Tray
1	medium cucumber, peeled and sliced thin
1/2	teaspoon salt
1/4	cake bean curd, drained
	oil
	hot water
2	teaspoons ground toasted sesame seeds
2	tablespoons lemon juice
1	teaspoon Kikkoman soy sauce
2	teaspoons sugar
1	large tomato, cut in 12 wedges and drained

Combine cucumber and salt, and set aside. Fry bean curd in oil until brown on all sides. After frying, dip in hot water, dry, and julienne. Mix sesame seeds with lemon juice, soy sauce, and sugar. Drain cucumber, and press out excess liquid well. Add tomato wedges. Pour dressing over, and mix well. Chill before serving.

Ready-made fried bean curd can be used.

Victor's Flaming Spinach Salad

SERVES 4–6

Ready Tray
- 1 juicy lemon, halved
- 2 (10-ounce) packages tender fresh spinach
- 1/2 pound lean bacon, diced
- 1/2 cup red-wine vinegar
- 4 tablespoons Kikkoman Hawaiian teriyaki sauce
- 1/2 cup sugar
- 1/4 cup cognac or brandy

Squeeze lemon through napkin to hold back seeds and pulp. Remove and discard stems from spinach leaves Wash leaves thoroughly, and pat dry with clean cloth. Chill in refrigerator. Sauté bacon in blazer pan of chafing dish directly over high Sterno flame until it begins to brown. Add vinegar, teriyaki sauce, lemon juice, and sugar. Stir until sugar is dissolved. When sauce begins to simmer, pour sauce over spinach leaves, holding back bacon pieces. Toss salad hard. Divide spinach evenly among salad plates, and set aside. Continue to brown remaining bacon pieces. Add cognac with left hand; with right hand pull blazer pan 3–8 inches toward you over flame and ignite, holding hand back. While bacon is still flaming, ladle it evenly over spinach mounds, and serve immediately. Under no circumstances is salt or pepper to be added either during the creation of this salad or while you are enjoying the full-bodied sweet-and-sour flavor. So warn your guests! This salad can also be prepared in a regular frying pan in the kitchen. In tossing, do not be afraid to bruise leaves; breaking main spines of the leaves permits dressing to penetrate each.

This salad is one of the great recipes that was born in Sydney, Australia, one night as I was trading yarns with a friend at his home. It has been the most famous and popular salad that I have ever served, during many years of traveling the South Pacific on board the *S.S. Mariposa*.

Boiled Dressing

MAKES 1 1/2 CUPS

Ready Tray
- 1/4 cup butter
- 1 tablespoon flour
- 1/2 cup cider vinegar
- 1/2 cup dry white wine
- 1/2 cup granulated sugar
- 2 teaspoons prepared mustard
- salt and fresh-ground black pepper to taste

Melt butter in saucepan. Blend in flour, and stir until smooth. Combine vinegar, wine, sugar, mustard, salt, and pepper. Stir into butter-flour mixture. Simmer until thickened, stirring constantly. Cook, but do not chill.

This dressing is ideal for fruit salads. If sugar is omitted, dressing may be used for other salads.

Beer-boiled Salad Dressing

MAKES 2 CUPS

Ready Tray
- 1/2 cup wine vinegar
- 1/2 cup beer
- 1/4 cup sugar
- 1 tablespoon butter
- 1 teaspoon salt
- 1 teaspoon dry mustard
- 1/4 teaspoon fresh-ground black pepper
- 1 cup undiluted, evaporated canned milk
- 3 tablespoons flour
- 2 eggs

Combine vinegar, beer, sugar, butter, and seasonings in saucepan, and bring to boil over medium heat. Beat together milk, flour, and eggs. Add to hot mixture slowly, beating constantly. Cook over medium heat, stirring constantly, 5 minutes, or until mixture thickens.

This dressing is excellent on hot or cold boiled new potatoes.

Green-Goddess Dressing

MAKES 1 3/4 CUPS

Ready Tray
- 1 clove garlic, chopped fine
- 1/2 teaspoon salt
- 1/2 teaspoon celery salt
- 1 teaspoon sugar
- 2 tablespoons anchovies, chopped fine
- 2 tablespoons tarragon vinegar
- 2 tablespoons fine-chopped chives
- 1/4 cup fine-chopped parsley
- 3/4 cup *Beer-boiled Salad Dressing*
- 3 tablespoons gin
- 1/2 cup sour cream
- 1 tablespoon lemon juice

Beat all ingredients together well, or mix in electric blender until smooth.

Serve on salad greens or as dressing for shellfish.

This dressing was created by George Arliss while he was starring in *The Green Goddess* in San Francisco; Chef Philip Roemer of the old San Francisco Palace Hotel; and Adolph Steinoff, with whom I worked in later years in the dining rooms of that hotel. Since then this dressing has become popular on hotel menus in Hawaii and Australia.

Salads and Salad Dressings

Papeete Salad

SERVES 4

Ready Tray
1	medium head Manoa, butter, or Bibb lettuce, chilled and torn into bite-size pieces
4	medium, ripe tomatoes, peeled and quartered
1	cup julienned fresh pineapple
1	cup thin-sliced celery
1/3	cup sour cream
1	tablespoon whipped cream
	juice of 1/2 lemon
	dash beet juice

In wooden salad bowl combine lettuce, tomatoes, pineapple, and celery. Blend sour cream, whipped cream, lemon juice, and beet juice. Add to salad, and toss gently. Serve immediately.

Japanese-Hawaiian Potato–Mussel Salad

SERVES 6–8

Ready Tray
2	pounds potatoes, peeled and boiled in beef broth
	salt and fresh-ground black pepper to taste
2	tablespoons safflower oil
1	tablespoon wine vinegar
1	cup white wine
1	teaspoon fine-chopped fresh chervil
1	teaspoon fine-chopped fresh chives
1	teaspoon fine-chopped fresh tarragon
1	shallot, chopped fine
1	teaspoon fine-chopped fresh parsley
1	teaspoon fine-chopped fresh burnet
2	dozen mussels or very small clams
1/2	cup water
1	medium Bermuda onion, chopped fine
1	teaspoon fine-chopped fresh mignonette
1	teaspoon cider vinegar
1	truffle, sliced thin and cooked in sake

Slice potatoes into large salad bowl while still warm, and add salt, pepper, oil, vinegar, wine, chervil, chives, tarragon, shallot, parsley, and burnet. Toss gently but thoroughly, and set aside. In large kettle cook mussels in water with onion, mignonette, and vinegar over high heat, tossing frequently. When shells open remove mussel meat, and cut away "feet" (the black appendages). Add mussels to potatoes, toss lightly, and cover surface with truffle. Chill 1 hour; when serving, mix truffles into salad.

Japanese-Hawaiian Sunomono Salad

SERVES 4

Ready Tray
2	medium cucumbers
1 1/2	teaspoons salt
1/4	pound fresh shrimp or 1 (4-ounce) can cooked shrimp
	water
1	tablespoon sugar
4	tablespoons vinegar
2	tablespoons sesame seeds
1	teaspoon Kikkoman soy sauce

Peel cucumbers, and halve lengthwise. Scoop out seeds. Slice each cucumber half into crescents. Cover with salt, and set aside 20 minutes, or until soft. Drain off liquid; then squeeze cucumbers gently in white cotton cloth to extract remaining liquid. Devein shrimp, and boil in water to cover 15 minutes, or until tender. (No cooking is necessary if canned shrimp are used.) Slice shrimp 1/2-inch thick. Combine with cucumbers in salad bowl. Blend sugar, vinegar, 1 1/2 tablespoons sesame seeds, and soy sauce, and pour over cucumbers and shrimps. Toss lightly, and serve in small chilled salad bowls. Sprinkle remaining sesame seeds over top.

Canberra Ale 'n Oil Dressing

MAKES 2 1/2 CUPS

Ready Tray
1/3	cup flour
3	tablespoons butter
1	cup ale, heated
3	raw egg yolks
2	tablespoons fresh lemon juice
1	cup safflower oil
1/2	teaspoon dry mustard
1	teaspoon celery salt
3	tablespoons light-brown sugar

Blend flour and butter in saucepan, and add ale. Cook over medium heat, stirring constantly, until mixture thickens. Combine remaining ingredients in bowl of electric mixer. Add ale mixture, and beat until smooth. Chill before using.

This dressing will keep indefinitely in refrigerator. If electric mixer is unavailable, beat with rotary egg beater until smooth.

Banana–Cream Dressing

MAKES 2 CUPS

Ready Tray
3	medium, fully ripe bananas, peeled
2	tablespoons brown sugar
2	tablespoons honey
1	cup heavy cream, whipped

Mash bananas thoroughly, and blend with brown sugar and syrup until smooth. Force through sieve. Fold whipped cream into banana mixture.

Serve over melon, pineapple, or fruit salad.

Chutney–Cream Dressing

MAKES 1 CUP

    Ready Tray
- 1/3 cup chutney
- 1/3 cup sour cream
- 1/3 cup mayonnaise
- dash curry powder

Combine all ingredients thoroughly.

This dressing is good on shrimp salad, fruit salad, or fresh pineapple. Any kind of chutney can be used.

Curry Dressing

MAKES 1 CUP

    Ready Tray
- 1/2 teaspoon garlic salt
- 1 teaspoon fresh-ground black pepper
- 1 teaspoon sugar
- 1 teaspoon dry mustard
- 1 teaspoon curry powder
- 1/4 cup red-wine vinegar
- 1/2 teaspoon Kikkoman soy sauce
- 2/3 cup salad oil

Combine all ingredients in glass jar with tight-fitting cover. Shake well until blended thoroughly. Chill several hours before using.

This dressing is excellent on hearts of palm, chilled artichoke hearts, cold boiled celery, chilled celery root, and chilled Belgian endive.

Imperial Dressing

MAKES 2 3/4 CUPS

    Ready Tray
- 1/4 cup brown sugar
- 1 1/2 teaspoons salt
- 1/8 teaspoon fresh-ground black pepper
- 1 teaspoon onion salt
- 1/2 teaspoon celery seed
- 3 drops Tabasco
- 1 teaspoon paprika
- 1/2 teaspoon fresh dill
- 1/2 cup red-wine vinegar
- 1 cup catsup
- 1 cup olive oil
- 3 tablespoons capers
- 1 teaspoon juice from capers
- 2 teaspoons Kikkoman Hawaiian teriyaki sauce
- 1 or 2 cloves garlic on toothpick

In saucepan simmer sugar, salt, pepper, onion salt, celery seed, Tabasco, paprika, dill, and vinegar until thoroughly heated and blended. Cool 10 minutes. Blend in catsup, olive oil, capers and juice, and teriyaki sauce. Add garlic. Cool dressing at room temperature 1 hour. Refrigerate until ready to use. Shake well before using each time.

Fruit-Salad Dressing

MAKES 1/3 CUP

    Ready Tray
- 6 tablespoons peanut oil
- 2 tablespoons fresh lemon or lime juice
- 1/3 teaspoon salt
- dash fresh-ground black pepper
- 1 tablespoon honey

Blend all ingredients thoroughly. Chill, and mix thoroughly before using.

Ginger Dressing

MAKES 1 1/4 CUPS

    Ready Tray
- 1/2 cup mayonnaise
- 1/2 cup sour cream
- 2 1/2 tablespoons confectioner's sugar
- 1 1/2 tablespoons fresh lime juice
- 1/2 teaspoon powdered ginger

Blend all ingredients until smooth. Chill thoroughly.

This dressing is excellent on pineapple salad.

Roquefort Dressing

MAKES 1 1/2 CUPS

    Ready Tray
- 1 clove garlic
- 1/2 teaspoon salt
- 2 tablespoons Roquefort
- 2 teaspoons Kikkoman Hawaiian teriyaki sauce
- juice of 1 lemon
- 1/2 teaspoon paprika
- 1/2 teaspoon dry mustard
- 3 drops Tabasco
- 1 tablespoon olive oil
- 1 teaspoon wine vinegar
- 1 cup sour cream

Mash garlic in bowl with salt. Add cheese, and mash thoroughly. Add teriyaki sauce, lemon juice, paprika, mustard, Tabasco, olive oil, and vinegar, and blend thoroughly until mixture is fine paste. Add sour cream, blend until smooth, and chill.

Lemon–Cream Salad Dressing

MAKES 1 1/4 CUPS

    Ready Tray
- 1/2 tablespoon fresh lemon juice
- 2 egg yolks
- 1/2 tablespoon honey
- 1 cup sour cream

Beat lemon juice into egg yolks. Stir in honey, and add sour cream. Blend until smooth.

This dressing is recommended for fruit salads.

Salads and Salad Dressings

Orange Dressing

MAKES 1 1/2 CUPS

Ready Tray
- 3/4 cup salad oil
- 2 tablespoons tarragon vinegar
- 1 (6-ounce) can frozen orange-juice concentrate
- 1/2 teaspoon dry mustard
- 1/4 teaspoon salt

Combine all ingredients in a jar. Cover, and shake thoroughly. Chill. Shake well before serving.

Orange dressing is delicious on avocados or chilled fruits.

Vinaigrette Dressing

MAKES 1/3 CUP

Ready Tray
- 1 teaspoon salt
- 1/4 teaspoon fresh-ground black pepper
- 1 tablespoon wine vinegar
- 3 tablespoons vegetable oil or olive oil
- 1 teaspoon fine-chopped shallots
- 1 teaspoon fine-chopped fresh parsley

Combine salt, pepper, and vinegar in bowl, and stir until salt is dissolved. Blend in oil thoroughly. Add shallots and parsley, and mix well.

This dressing is excellent on all green salads and on cold meats.

Plum-Wine Fruit Dressing

MAKES 1/2 CUP

Ready Tray
- 2 tablespoons butter
- 1 teaspoon flour
- 3 tablespoons cider vinegar
- 3 tablespoons Kikkoman plum wine
- 1 tablespoon granulated sugar
- 1/2 teaspoon prepared mustard
- salt and fresh-ground black pepper to taste

Melt butter in small saucepan. Stir in flour, and blend until smooth. Combine vinegar, wine, sugar, mustard, salt, and pepper. Stir into butter-flour mixture. Simmer until thickened, stirring constantly. Cool, but do not chill.

Serve over fresh fruits.

Sweet-Sour Sesame-Seed Dressing

MAKES 2 1/3 CUPS

Ready Tray
- 1/4 cup sesame seeds
- 1 1/3 cups light salad oil
- 2/3 cup tarragon vinegar
- 2 teaspoons salt
- 1 teaspoon dry mustard
- 1/2 teaspoon garlic powder
- 1/2 teaspoon white pepper
- 1/4 cup sugar
- 1/4 cup grated Parmesan cheese

Toast sesame seeds on ungreased cookie sheet in oven at 275° F. 10–15 minutes, or until seeds are light brown. Cool. Combine oil, vinegar, salt, mustard, garlic powder, pepper, and sugar in glass jar. Shake until thoroughly blended. Add sesame seeds and cheese. Chill.

This dressing is very good when tossed with plain greens. Add just enough to coat leaves. It is also excellent with hot or cold fish.

Fish and Shellfish Entrées

4

FISH AND SHELLFISH ENTREES

The Polynesians eat small fish raw. Mullet is the most popular fish of the South Pacific islands. It is baked in ti leaves, boiled, or steamed. Old chiefs used to have special ponds built and walled in so that they could breed mullet for their exclusive use. Many of these pounds are still in commercial use today.

The Samoans like to cook the fish whole without removing scales or entrails. Before cooking, coconut cream is added; then the fish is wrapped in a banana leaf, then in a braided coconut leaf.

The Chinese eat fish both raw and cooked, often at the same meal. Ginger root and soy sauce are popular seasonings for all fish and shellfish dishes.

Fish is more economical than meat; therefore it has been used widely in Japan, but the Japanese also eat it because they really like it, raw or cooked. Fresh fish is broiled or cooked in *shoyu* (soy sauce). Shrimp is the most popular of the dried seafoods; it is used for flavor as well as substance in soup, stews, and vegetable and rice dishes.

Throughout the South Pacific, fresh fish is usually broiled or fried and served with a red-pepper sauce that accompanies or is used on almost everything.

The Portuguese are very fond of salt codfish, and, prepared in various ways, it seems to be most important in their diet. They are also fond of octopus and squid, which they cook in wine, pickle in vinegar, or stew with vegetables.

The Filipinos like most fish fried, even when it is later to go into stew. Shrimp and lobster are the most popular shellfish. But the most widely used fish product is a salty fermented fish paste called *bagoong*, which is used for flavoring pork, vegetable, and rice dishes, as well as eaten by itself.

The Tahitians are fond of and eat all fish, preparing it in a manner similar to that of the Hawaiians, but they generally use more coconut.

The fish and shellfish dishes prepared in Australia and New Zealand reflect American, English, Scottish, Irish, Oriental, and Continental European influence, thanks to the influx of settlers from all nations to these two countries. There is an abundance of all types of fish there, as well as many that are not found any place else in the world.

Fish

Fresh fish has firm, elastic flesh and does not pull away from the bones easily. It has no strong odor, and the eyes are bright and bulging. If the fish has been out of the water too long, its eyes are cloudy and sunken in the sockets. The gills of fresh fish are red and free of slime, and the skin has a shiny, iridescent quality and the characteristic color.

Fish are commercially available in several forms. Which you select depends upon your preference and how it is to be cooked and served. For whole fresh fish the size and type of scales determine whether or not it should be scaled and eviscerated before cooking. Small fish like smelt need only the entrails removed. Trout are often not scaled before cooking if the scales are small. Removing the outer skin before eating is a matter of individual taste.

A drawn fish is a whole fish with its entrails removed. A dressed or pan-dressed fish has been both eviscerated and scaled, and the tail, head, and fins have been removed. Fish steaks are cross-section slices of a large dressed fish, from 3/4 to 1 inch thick. Fillets are the practically boneless halves of a fish cut lengthwise from the backbone. In a butterfly fillet the two halves of the fish are connected by the flesh and skin of the belly. Fish sticks are fillets cut into long boneless pieces.

The amount of fish to purchase per serving depends upon how it is to be cooked: fried, baked, stuffed, or combined with other foods, as in curries or casseroles. This guide will serve when fish is to be the entrée, with vegetables and rice or potatoes:

whole or drawn—1/2–3/4 pound per serving
dressed   —1/3–1/2 pound per serving
steaks or fillets —1/3 pound per serving

Always purchase the freshest fish possible, and cook it as soon as possible. If it is to be stored for a short period, wrap it in heavy wax paper, and place in freezer of refrigerator. Handle with care, as bruised or punctured flesh or skin deteriorates more rapidly. If it is to be frozen, after wrapping in wax paper, wrap in aluminum foil or freezing paper.

Lean fish needs fat when cooking and especially when broiling, but fat fish loses fat during cooking and therefore needs less. When substituting one fish for another in a recipe, it is better to substitute a fat fish for a fat one and a lean fish for a lean one. Fat fish include butterfish, eel, herring, mackerel, *uloa*, *opakapaka*, pompano, sable, salmon, shad, tuna, trout, and whitefish. Among the lean fish are sea bass, bluefish, cod, croaker, flounder, grouper, haddock, hake, halibut, mullet, rockfish, porgy, sea trout, striped bass, swordfish, whiting, *mahi mahi*, carp, pickerel, smelt, perch, pike, and all shellfish.

Japanese-Hawaiian Boiled Bass

SERVES 4

Ready Tray
2   quarts water
1 1/2   tablespoons fresh lemon juice
2   pounds fresh bass, cleaned and cut 3" × 3" × 1/2"
        salt and pepper to taste
2   tablespoons peanut oil
1/4   cup chopped scallions
1/2   cup Kikkoman Hawaiian teriyaki sauce, heated

In deep kettle, bring water to rolling boil. Add lemon juice, and add fish. Return to boil. Turn off heat, cover kettle, and let fish stand in hot water 15–20 minutes, depending on thickness of fish. Drain well, place on platter, and season with salt and pepper. Pour oil over fish, sprinkle with scallions, and pour a little sauce over. Serve remaining sauce with fish.

This fine way to boil fish produces silky flesh, moist and smooth. Fish should be cooked just before serving.

Korean-Hawaiian Carp

SERVES 6

Ready Tray
1   3-pound carp
3   tablespoons Kikkoman soy sauce
2   tablespoons sesame oil
    water
2   medium onions, chopped coarse
2   large tomatoes, chopped coarse
4   large fresh mushrooms, sliced, or 2 large dried mushrooms, soaked in hot water and sliced
    fresh-ground black pepper to taste
1   long white radish, sliced thin
    Chinese parsley leaves

Clean and scale carp, leaving head intact. Rub carp well inside and out with 1 tablespoon soy sauce and 1 tablespoon sesame oil. Place on rack in oval roasting pan with small amount water in bottom. Steam until tender, adding more water if necessary. Before carp is done, heat remaining sesame oil in a skillet. Saute onions until golden brown. Add tomatoes and mushrooms, and cook to thick sauce, stirring to prevent burning. Add remaining soy sauce and pepper, mix well, and pour into deep platter; place steamed carp gently in sauce. Arrange radish slices on fish to resemble scales. Garnish with parsley leaves at intervals along back of fish. Serve with steamed rice and soy sauce. A little prepared mustard is often served in separate saucer to dip fish in.

Fish and Shellfish Entrées

Frog Legs Provençale

SERVES 4

Ready Tray
2	large cloves garlic, crushed gently
1/4	pound butter
4	pairs frog legs, separated and dredged lightly in flour
1	medium tomato, peeled and chopped
1/2	cup white wine
	salt and fresh-ground black pepper to taste
	juice of 1/2 lime
1	teaspoon fine-chopped fresh parsley
2	cups steamed wild rice

In skillet sauté garlic in butter. Add frog legs, and sauté until browned on both sides. Remove garlic. Add tomato and wine, and simmer gently until thoroughly blended. Season with salt and pepper. Sprinkle with lime juice, and garnish with parsley. Serve at once with rice.

This dish was born in Italy. The French received credit for the recipe however. Today it is one of the most popular dishes in Australia and New Zealand.

Stuffed Baked Fish

SERVES 4–6

Ready Tray
2	cups cooked rice
6	anchovy fillets, cut in small pieces
4	hard-cooked eggs, chopped fine
1	teaspoon fine-chopped fresh parsley
2	raw egg yolks
1	whole 4-pound haddock or bass, cleaned
	salt and fresh-ground black pepper to taste
1/2	cup bread crumbs
6	tablespoons melted butter
2	tablespoons water

Combine rice, anchovies, eggs, parsley, and egg yolks. Rub inside of the fish with salt and pepper. Stuff with rice mixture, and skewer closed. Rub outside with bread crumbs. Place in shallow baking pan. Pour butter over fish, and add water. Bake, uncovered, in 350° F. oven 45 minutes, basting with pan juices from time to time.

Grilled Mustard Herrings New Zealand

SERVES 6

Ready Tray
6	whole fresh herrings, filleted and cleaned
	oatmeal
1/4	cup butter
1/4	cup flour
2	cups milk
	salt and fresh-ground black pepper to taste
1	teaspoon dry mustard
1	tablespoon vinegar

Dredge herring fillets thoroughly in oatmeal, pat with palms of hands so that oatmeal adheres to fish on both sides. Grill long enough to cook fish without burning. In saucepan melt butter, and blend in flour until smooth. Gradually add milk, stirring constantly over low heat until sauce is smooth. Season with salt and pepper. Blend in mustard and vinegar. Pour sauce over grilled herrings, and serve with potatoes boiled in their jackets.

Fat must not be used when grilling herring, for they are rich in their own fat.

Salmon in Ti Leaves

SERVES 3

Ready Tray
3	salmon steaks, 1/2 inch thick, halved lengthwise
6	large ti leaves, trimmed
	salt to taste
4	tablespoons salad oil
4	tablespoons fresh lemon juice
1/4	teaspoon rosemary
1/4	teaspoon fresh-ground black pepper
6	thin lemon slices
3	tablespoons fine-chopped fresh parsley or green onion

Place each fish slice on ti leaf, and season with salt. Combine oil lemon juice, rosemary, and pepper. Pour 1 1/3 tablespoons of this mixture over each fish portion. Place lemon slice on each piece, and sprinkle with parsley. Close leaves, as in envelope, and put in baking dish. Brush outside with additional oil. Bake at 375° F. 45–50 minutes. Ti leaves may be removed before serving, or guests may unwrap their own.

Allow 2 packets for each serving. Ten-inch squares of aluminum foil can be substituted for ti leaves; omit brushing with oil, and remove foil before serving on dinner plates.

Grilled or Barbecued Mahi Mahi

SERVES 4

Ready Tray
1/4	pound butter
1 1/2	tablespoons salad oil
1/2	teaspoon garlic powder
1 1/2	tablespoons Kikkoman soy sauce
2	teaspoons lemon juice
2	pounds *mahi mahi* steaks, cut 1 inch thick
	lemon wedges
	fresh watercress

Melt butter, and combine thoroughly with other ingredients, except fish, lemon wedges, and watercress. Pour over fish, and marinate 45 minutes. Barbecue over hot charcoals until "flaky," grill on griddle, or fry in greased hot skillet. Serve with lemon wedges, and garnish with watercress.

Honolulu Trout

SERVES 6

Ready Tray
- 6 whole medium trout, cleaned
- 1 cup Kikkoman Hawaiian teriyaki sauce
- 4 tablespoons brown sugar
- 1/4 cup Kikkoman plum wine
- 1 tablespoon fresh chopped ginger
- 2 cloves garlic, crushed
- 1/2 cup melted butter
- 1/4 pound almonds, ground fine
- 1 cup cornmeal
- 1/2 teaspoon paprika
- lemon wedges

Lay trout in shallow pan or baking dish. Combine teriyaki sauce, sugar, wine, ginger, and garlic. Pour over fish, and marinate 1 hour. Remove fish from sauce, and drain on paper towels. Brush inside and entire outside with melted butter. Add remaining butter to sauce. Combine almonds, cornmeal, and paprika. Roll fish in this mixture. Grill over medium heat 5–7 minutes on each side, brushing with remaining sauce. Serve with lemon wedges.

Tahitian Swordfish Bake

SERVES 4

Ready Tray
- 2 pounds fresh swordfish steaks, quartered
- 1/3 cup fresh lime juice
- fresh-ground black pepper to taste
- 2 large, firm tomatoes, halved horizontally
- 1/2 cup melted butter
- 1/3 cup dry bread crumbs
- 1 teaspoon fine-chopped fresh parsley
- 1/2 teaspoon dried savory
- 4 medium bananas, peeled and scraped lightly

Place fish in large shallow baking dish, and sprinkle with half the lime juice. Season with pepper. Brush tomato halves with melted butter. Combine crumbs, parsley, and savory, and spoon evenly over tomato halves. Arrange tomatoes and bananas around fish. Brush fish and bananas with butter, and sprinkle butter generously over tomatoes. Bake in preheated 375° F. oven 7 minutes. Turn fish and bananas; sprinkle fish lightly with remaining lime juice. Brush fish and bananas with butter, and bake 7 minutes longer, or until fish is flaky and tender. Serve on hot plates, garnished with tomato half and banana for each serving.

Sole Diable New Caledonian

SERVES 4

Ready Tray
- 4 tablespoons flour
- 1 teaspoon salt
- 1/4 teaspoon black pepper
- 4 fillets sole
- 2 tablespoons butter
- 3/4 cup beer
- 1 1/2 teaspoons Worcestershire sauce
- 1/2 teaspoon dry mustard

Season flour with salt and pepper, and dredge fish in mixture. Melt butter in baking dish. Arrange fillets in it. Combine beer, Worcestershire sauce, and mustard; pour over fish. Bake, uncovered, at 375° F. 35 minutes, basting frequently.

Chinese-Hawaiian Ginger Sole

SERVES 4–6

Ready Tray
- 4 thick fillets of sole, halved crosswise
- 3 egg yolks
- 2 tablespoons beer
- 6 tablespoons cornstarch
- 1/2 teaspoon salt
- 3/4 cup dry bread crumbs
- fat
- 1/4 cup water
- 4 tablespoons peanut oil
- 1/3 cup cider vinegar
- 1/2 cup chicken broth
- 1/4 cup sugar
- 2 tablespoons catsup
- 2 tablespoons chopped fresh ginger or 1 teaspoon powdered ginger
- salt and fresh-ground black pepper to taste

Wash and dry fillets with cloth. Beat together egg yolks, beer, 5 tablespoons cornstarch, and 1/2 teaspoon salt. Dredge fish in mixture and then in breadcrumbs, coating thoroughly. Heat fat to 365° F., and fry fillets without crowding, until browned on both sides. Keep fish hot. Mix remaining cornstarch with water, and combine in saucepan with oil, vinegar, broth, sugar, catsup, ginger, salt to taste, and pepper. Cook over low heat, stirring constantly, until thickened. Serve with fish, or pour over fish before serving.

Fish and Shellfish Entrées

Marinated Salmon Steaks

SERVES 6

Ready Tray
2	pounds fresh or frozen salmon steaks
1/4	cup fresh orange juice
1/4	cup Kikkoman soy sauce
2	tablespoons catsup
2	tablespoons fine-chopped parsley
2	tablespoons salad oil
1	tablespoon fresh lemon juice
1/2	teaspoon basil
1	clove garlic, chopped fine

Thaw fish, if frozen. Place salmon steaks in single layer in shallow baking pan. Combine orange juice, soy sauce, catsup, parsley, oil, lemon juice, basil, and garlic. Blend thoroughly, pour over fish, and set aside 30 minutes, turning after 15 minutes. Remove fish from marinade, and reserve sauce for basting. Place fish on well-greased broiler pan. Set 3 inches from heat, and broil 4–6 minutes, or until golden brown; turn, baste with remaining sauce, and broil 4–6 minutes, or until fish flakes easily with fork.

Fresh salmon livers are very good when salted and peppered to taste, rolled lightly in flour, and fried golden brown on both sides in butter.

Whale Steak Chasseur

SERVES 4

Ready Tray
4	eye-of-fillet whale steaks, cut 4" × 3" × 3/4"
1	bay leaf
6	whole peppercorns
1	tablespoon fine-chopped fresh parsley
2	tablespoons olive oil
1	cup dry red wine
	water
1	medium onion, sliced thin
2	medium tomatoes, peeled, seeded, and chopped coarse
	salt and fresh-ground black pepper to taste
1	medium clove garlic, crushed (optional)
1/2	pound small button mushrooms
4	thick slices sourdough French bread, toasted

Place whale steaks in deep pyrex baking dish. Add bay leaf, peppercorns, parsley, 1 tablespoon olive oil, and wine. Marinate in refrigerator overnight, turning occasionally. Drain, reserving marinade, rub with a little of the remaining olive oil, and place in baking dish. Pour 1/4 inch of water in bottom of baking dish. Bake at 400° F. 5 minutes, turn, reduce heat to 325° F., and bake 30–40 minutes, or until tender, basting with pan juices or a little oil if necessary. Meanwhile strain 1 cup marinade.

Sauté onion in remaining oil until golden. Add strained marinade, and bring to boil over medium heat. Add tomatoes, and season with salt and pepper. Add garlic. Simmer sauce 10–15 minutes, or until thick. Sauté mushrooms quickly in butter, add to sauce, and mix lightly. Place whale steaks on toasted French bread, pour sauce over, and serve with buttered rice and fresh tossed salad.

Shellfish

Most types of shellfish are sold alive, fresh, frozen, or canned. The best temperature for storing fresh shellfish is close to 32° F.; higher temperatures cause rapid deterioration in quality.

Fresh shrimp are available headless with shells on or off. The meat should be firm, with little or no odor. Thawed frozen shrimp have a stronger odor. The color of the shells ranges from gray to light pink, sizes from jumbo to very small. There are 15 or fewer larger shrimp to the pound and as many as 60 small ones. Do not keep fresh shrimp more than 24 hours. If necessary to keep longer, cook, and refrigerate for future use.

When purchasing live lobster, be sure legs are moving and the tail curls under body when lobster is picked up. Cook as soon as possible after purchasing. Lobster may be refrigerated at close to 32° F. a short time. Do not attempt to keep it fresh by putting it in salted water, for water will not be cold enough and salt content will differ from what lobster is used to. There is little meat in 1 lobster, so allow 1–1 1/2 pounds whole lobster per serving. When purchasing cooked lobster, be sure that the shell is bright red and that there is no unpleasant odor.

There are two types of crabs: the hard-shell and the soft-shell. The latter is a hard-shell crab that has shed its shell and has not yet had time to harden its new one. The soft-shell crab may be purchased alive or frozen. When buying live crabs, be sure that legs are moving. They may be refrigerated up to 24 hours only. Cooked crab is bright red and should have no disagreeable odor.

Clams may be purchased in shells or shucked. The shells of live clams are closed tight or spring closed when tapped. If shell will not close, clam is dead and should not be used. Shells of good clams open when cooked. Live clams may be kept in refrigerator at 32° F. 2 days. The color of fresh shucked clams ranges from pale to deep orange in color. The liquid is clear and has a fresh odor.

Like clams, live oysters in shells are closed tight or spring closed when tapped. If shell does not close, oyster is dead and should not be used. Live oysters in shells may be kept at 32° F. in refrigerator for no more than 2 days. Shucked oysters are plump, cream-colored, and packed in clear liquid.

Scallops are available fresh or frozen. The meat is the adductor muscle (which opens and closes the shell) of the scallop. There are two varieties. Sea scallops come in marshmallow shapes, ranging in color from white to orange or pink. Smaller bay scallops are more delicate in flavor and are creamy white, light tan, or light pink. Both varieties have a sweet odor before cooking. Fresh scallops may be kept in refrigerator at 32° F. 2 days before using.

Mussels may be purchased alive in shells or canned. Live mussels have dark-purple oval shells and pink-orange flesh. The shells should be closed tight. If they are not, run cold water over them 2 minutes, and if they remain open do not use them, as they are spoiled. The shells open when cooked. They may be kept in refrigerator at 32° F. no more than 2 days.

Portuguese-Hawaiian Abalone

SERVES 4

Ready Tray
- 3 eggs, beaten
- 1 cup tomato sauce
- 2 pounds abalone, sliced and pounded
- 1 cup medium-coarse cracker crumbs
  paprika
- 1/2 cup fine-chopped green bell pepper
- 1/4 pound butter
  salt to taste
- 2 large limes, cut in wedges

Combine eggs and tomato sauce. Marinate abalone in mixture 30 minutes. Lift abalone from marinade, and dip quickly in crumbs, coating each side. Sprinkle both sides with paprika and green pepper. Pat lightly to hold pepper in place. Sauté in butter over medium-high heat no more than 1 minute on each side. Salt to taste. Serve on hot plates with lime wedges.

Abalone Sauté

SERVES 4

Ready Tray
- 2 large abalone steaks, 1/4-inch thick, halved and pounded
  salt and fresh-ground black pepper to taste
- 1 cup flour
- 2 eggs, lightly beaten
- 1/2 cup sweet butter
- 1/4 cup olive oil
  juice of 1 lemon
- 2 tablespoons fine-chopped fresh parsley
  fresh parsley sprigs
  lemon wedges

Season abalone with salt and pepper. Roll in flour, dip in eggs, roll again in flour, and dip finally in egg. Heat 1/4 cup butter and oil thoroughly in shallow skillet, and brown abalone 1 minute on each side. Remove steaks to heated serving platter. Pour off fat in skillet. Add remaining butter, and cook over medium heat until it turns nut brown. Add lemon juice and chopped parsley, stir thoroughly, and pour over abalone. Garnish with parsley sprigs and lemon wedges, and serve immediately.

Never overcook abalone, as it will be tough.

Chinese-Hawaiian Abalone

SERVES 4

Ready Tray
- 4 dried mushrooms
  water
- 1 cup chicken broth
- 1 can abalone (16 oz.), cut in 1-inch pieces, and liquid
- 1 cup green onions 1-inch slices
- 1/2 cup celery 1/2-inch slices
- 5 water chestnuts, sliced thin
- 1 tablespoon Kikkoman soy sauce
- 1 tablespoon white wine
- 2 tablespoons cornstarch dissolved in 2 tablespoons water

Soak mushrooms in water to cover 2 hours. Cut in 1/8-inch strips. Heat broth and abalone liquid; add vegetables, and simmer 5 minutes. Add remaining ingredients, and simmer until sauce is thick and clear. Serve with boiled rice.

Clams

On restaurant menus, large clams on the half shell are called "cherrystones" and smaller clams are called "littlenecks."

Raw clams may be purchased already opened, but it is advisable to wait until shortly before eating. If they remain open several hours, they tend to shrink and lose flavor. Some of their freshness can be restored by sprinkling them with ice-cold bottled clam juice or salt water (1 teaspoon salt to 1 pint water) just before serving. Raw clams should be served as cold as possible.

Fish and Shellfish Entrées

There is a mechanical clam opener, which does a good fast job if you want to open your own clams. They can also be opened neatly with an oyster knife, a short, stubby utensil with blunt blade and round handle.

The clam is a self-assertive creature who refuses to know his place and resists all care and cultivation because he does not stay put very long. He waits patiently until you are right on top of him and then deftly burrows out of sight in the sand faster than you can dig. Care has to be taken when digging for clams by hand because razor clams can cut your hands.

Along the Australian barrier reef one can find Tridacna clams, which sometimes weigh more than 500 pounds apiece; they can fasten onto the anchor chain of a tugboat and keep it from budging.

There is a variety of green clam, the Toheroa, which is undoubtedly the giant of all edible clams and is found along the New Zealand coast. It forms the basis of many fine dishes, but it is hard to find outside New Zealand, and there is no adequate substitute for it.

Soft-shell clams, generally known as "steamers," have a milder but richer flavor than the hard-shell clams have. The best are about 2 inches long, and a dozen generally are sufficient to serve one person. The shells of raw soft-shell clams are normally open, with the necks protruding. Do not try to separate the steaming-hot shells of a cooked soft-shell clam; just pull off brown skin covering neck, lift clam out of shell, dip it in hot clam broth, then in melted butter, and finally drop it in your mouth.

As steamer clam keeps its shell open in its sandy natural habitat, it is frequently full of that habitat. To remove the sand from soft clams, wash well under cold, running water, and scrub thoroughly with brush. Place in large kettle, and cover with cold water. Add 2 tablespoons salt and 2 tablespoons cornmeal or oatmeal for each gallon of water in which clams are steeped. Let clams remain in this water in refrigerator overnight. Before steaming, remove clams from water, and wash with fresh water. Place in steamer kettle or large pot with tight-fitting cover. Add 1 cup water for each quart of clams. Bring water to boil, reduce heat, and let the clams steam 6 minutes, stirring a few times so that those on top may be in closer contact with the boiling water. When clams are wide open, remove from pot, place on platter, and cover with cloth to keep hot. The liquid remaining in pot is clam broth or clam juice. It may be used for clam-juice cocktails or clam soup but generally is served along with the steamers. A little fine-chopped garlic and fine-chopped parsley with a little oil may be added to to the pot of clams before they are steamed to add a delicious flavor. Pour off liquid from steamer, avoiding as much as possible the sediment remaining on bottom of pot, and strain through several thicknesses of cheesecloth. For each guest, provide a small dish of melted sweet butter, to which a little fresh lemon juice has been added, and a cup of strained clam broth. Be sure to have an ample supply of large napkins on hand when serving this delicacy.

Clams Elizabeth

SERVES 2

Ready Tray
24	littleneck or cherrystone clams in shells
	water
	rock salt
1/2	cup white wine
	juice of 1 large lemon
1	cup fine bread crumbs
2	teaspoons fine-chopped chives or green onions
2	teaspoons fine-chopped fresh parsley
1	large clove garlic, chopped fine
1/2	teaspoon oregano
	salt and fresh-ground black pepper to taste
1/4	cup melted butter
1 2	cup grated Parmesan cheese

Wash and scrub clam shells thoroughly. Cover with water, and soak clams in shells 1 hour to wash sand out of clams. Drain and open clams with clam opener, oyster knife, or a short, stubby, blunt-bladed instrument. Drain juice into mixing bowl, and put clams on half shells in flat baking dish or pie plate that has been spread with 1/2-inch thick layer of rock salt. To clam juice add wine and lemon juice, stir, and pour a little sauce over each clam. Combine bread crumbs, chives, parsley, garlic, oregano, salt, pepper, and butter.

Spread mixture over clams, sprinkle on cheese, and bake at 350° F. 10–12 minutes, or until lightly browned on top. Avoid overbaking. Serve in very hot baking dish.

Fresh clams help to wash themselves, by opening and closing shells to flush out sand. Placing rock salt in pan makes it possible to set clam shells so that they do not tilt and lose their juice.

Clam–Pepper Roast

SERVES 4–6

Ready Tray
- 3 dozen fresh clams and liquor
- 2 whole small green onions, chopped fine
- 1 medium green bell pepper, chopped fine
- 1 large clove garlic, chopped fine
- 3 tablespoons butter
- fresh-ground black pepper to taste
- 1 1/2 cups fine bread crumbs
- paprika
- 4–6 slices toast, lightly sautéed in butter

Open clams and reserve liquor, adding water if necessary to make 1 1/2 cups liquid. In electric frying pan or skillet over low heat, sauté onions, green pepper, and garlic in butter until tender but not browned, stirring constantly. Add clam liquor, shelled clams, and black pepper. Bring to slow simmer, reduce heat, and simmer 5 minutes. Add bread crumbs, mix lightly, and pile into clam shells. Bake at 450° F. until golden brown. Sprinkle with paprika before serving with toast.

Clams may also be served on top of toast, but then bread crumbs should be omitted.

How to Prepare Live Crabs

It is easier than you may think to manage a live crab in your kitchen. You need a heavy knife or cleaver, a mallet or hammer, and rubber gloves. Although the gloves are not essential, they are handy, as some broken shell pieces are rather sharp.

Grasp live crab from the rear, getting a good hold on the last one or two legs of either side; place, back down, on cutting board.

Position heavy, sharp knife or cleaver in direct center of crab, between legs. Hit back of knife with mallet or hammer one quick, hard blow to kill crab instantly.

Take firm hold on front claw, and twist off where it joins body; repeat with other claw and legs. Scrub and rinse well, and set aside. Pull off top shell, prying with knife if necessary. Remove gills and spongy parts under shell, saving creamy crab butter; wash well. Hold each leg and claw piece on edge. Crack shell with mallet or hammer to open each section. Lift meat out.

Tap back of knife with mallet to cut body cavity first in half, then each half into several chunks. Rinse away loose shell pieces.

To boil live whole crabs for use in chilled dishes, heat about 8 quarts water, enough for 2 or 3 crabs, to boiling with 2 tablespoons salt in large kettle. Grasp live crabs from rear, getting a good hold on the last one or two legs on either side, and drop into boiling water. Cover kettle, and simmer 15–25 minutes, depending upon size of crabs, after water returns to boil. Lift out with tongs, and cool until easy to handle. Crack, and clean each crab as for live crabs.

Crab Legs Kikko

SERVES 4

Ready Tray
- 2 dozen shelled crab legs
- flour
- 2 eggs, lightly beaten
- 1/4 pound sweet butter
- salt and fresh-ground black pepper to taste
- 1/2 cup Kikkoman Hawaiian teriyaki sauce
- 2 teaspoons dry mustard
- 1/4 cup pale dry sherry
- 2 tablespoons cognac
- 2 cups steamed domestic or wild rice

Dredge crab legs gently in flour; then dip in beaten eggs. In large stainless-steel skillet sauté crab legs in 1/8 pound butter until golden brown, season with salt and pepper, and set aside. In saucepan over medium heat, blend 1/8 pound butter, teriyaki sauce, and mustard until smooth. Season to taste with pepper. Place sautéed crab legs in sauce, and heat gently. Add sherry, and turn onto serving platter. Pour cognac around outer circumference of dish, ignite, and serve over rice.

Lemon halves can be provided if desired, but do not encourage the use of lemon, which tends to destroy the piquant flavor of the sauce.

Crab-and-Shrimp Gumbo

SERVES 8

Ready Tray
- 3 slices bacon
- 2 pounds raw shrimp, shelled and deveined
- 3/4 cup fine-chopped onion
- 3 cloves garlic, crushed
- 2 (10-ounce) packages frozen whole okra
- 1 (8-ounce) can tomato sauce
- 1 (1-pound) can whole tomatoes
- 2 tablespoons seafood crab or shrimp boil
- 1 1/2 teaspoons salt
- 5 cups water
- 1 quart water
- 1 tablespoon salt
- 4 live hard-shell crabs
- 1/2 teaspoon filé powder
- 4–6 cups hot cooked rice

Fish and Shellfish Entrées

Fry bacon until crisp; drain on paper towels, and set aside. Measure 2 tablespoons bacon fat into Dutch oven. Add shrimp, onion, and garlic. Sauté until onion is tender and shrimp are pink. Cut okra in 1-inch pieces, and add to shrimp with tomato sauce, tomatoes, crab boil, 1 1/2 teaspoons salt, and 5 cups water. Bring to boil, reduce heat, and simmer, covered, 1 hour. Meanwhile in large saucepan, bring 1 quart water and 1 tablespoon salt to boil. Place crabs in colander; wash in cold water until clean. Plunge crabs head first into boiling water; bring water to boil again. Reduce heat, and simmer, covered, 10 minutes. Drain, cool, and halve with shells on. Add crabs to okra mixture. Simmer 1/2 hour longer. Add filé powder. Remove from heat; crumble bacon over top. Serve with rice.

Filé consists of pulverized sassafras leaves and is is used as a thickener in gumbos and other soups.

Soft-Shelled Crabs with Fig Fritters Tahiti

SERVES 6–8

Ready Tray
1	cup flat beer
1 1/3	cups sifted flour
2	whole eggs
24	dried figs
24	almonds, shelled and blanched or 1 cup pine nuts
1	cup red wine, heated
1	small stick cinnamon
4	whole cloves
	corn oil
1/2	teaspoon salt
18	very small soft-shelled crabs

Beat beer, flour, eggs, and salt until smooth. Set aside 30 minutes. Place figs in steamer or in strainer over kettle of boiling water. Cover, and steam 30 minutes, or until figs are completely soft. Drain. Stuff center of each fig with 1 almond or a few pine nuts. Place figs in small bowl, and cover with wine. Add cinnamon and cloves, and steep 20 minutes. Dry each fig, dip into beer batter, and fry in oil, heated to 360° F., until golden. Drain, and keep warm. Clean and dry each crab, dip into batter, and fry, a few at a time in oil heated to 375° F. Keep temperature constant until all crabs have been fried golden brown on both sides. Drain on paper towels, and serve with fig fritters.

How to Prepare Live Lobster

Lobsters must be alive and green when you buy them, to yield their most succulent flavor. Do not cook any but the freshest lobsters. The number of lobsters to buy depends upon their size and how they are to be prepared. Most people will eat a whole boiled or broiled lobster of 1 1/2 pounds or less. People who especially relish lobster may eat whole ones weighing as much as 2 pounds, although most people are satisfied with half a lobster this size.

Of course, if you are combining the meat with celery and mayonnaise in salad or in a dish with sauce, 2–3 pound lobsters are more economical. Two of them will yield 5 or 6 servings. Whatever size you select, you must cook the lobsters as soon as possible.

It is customary to discard intestinal vein and little stomach sac from which it starts. The grayish, fringed parts in the upper body are not eaten because they are spongy and tasteless. But the dark greenish-gray liver, or tomalley, which turns a bright green when cooked, is a great delicacy. When making dishes like *Lobster à l'Américaine*, a chef removes the tomalley from the raw lobster and uses it to thicken the sauce. The roe, which has a bright coral color when cooked, also has a delicate flavor.

If you decide to broil lobsters, you can ask the fish dealer to split them. It is best to learn to do it yourself, however. First, practice picking up lobster by top side of body just behind head; it cannot nip you if you hold it this way, nor can the tail grip and cut you because it always curls under the body. You must work with a big, strong, very sharp knife with a good point. A quick, clean cut through the tough shell and body flesh is your aim. The cutting board on which you work must be heavy and strong too.

There are two ways to split lobster. It can be laid on board with either underside or outer shell uppermost. The first way is better for small, young lobsters and the second way for larger, heavier ones. Either way plunge point of the knife into lobster directly at point where body and tail meet, to sever the spinal cord. Many cooks prefer to leave enough of back shells of small lobsters uncut so that halves remain joined when opened up. Spread lobster on the board, shell side down, and, after severing spinal cord, cut through body and tail without quite cutting through back shell at center; then open up lobster.

It is easier to halve large lobster from shell side. Spread lobster on board with shell side up, and, after severing spinal cord, plunge point of the knife in again, and cut up through body; then insert knife again, and cut down through tail. In either case, after turning up halves to keep flesh intact in half-shells, remove intestinal vein and stomach sac. Finally, with dull edge of big knife, crack each side of 2 large claws.

A simple way to extract claw meat in one piece is to cut off claw at first joint and to break off small pincer. Lay large pincer on board, and with sharp cutting edge, hit it about 1 inch from joint. Then turn it over, and do the same on other side. Now pick up pincer with your left hand, and pull off pointed end of shell. Shell will separate at where you cut it, leaving claw meat in one piece. The claw meat below the joint will also come out easily.

Boiled Lobster

SERVES 2–4

Ready Tray
1 1/2 tablespoons salt
8 quarts boiling water
3 live 1 1/4–1 1/2-pound lobsters
  lemon wedges
  melted butter or mayonnaise

Salt water, and plunge lobsters in. If they are to be served hot, cook 20–25 minutes, depending on size. Remove, split lengthwise, and discard intestinal veins and stomach sacs. Crack claws, and place lobsters, cut sides up, on serving platter; garnish with lemon wedges, and serve with melted butter. If lobsters are to be served cold, cook 15 minutes, remove kettle from heat, and cool lobsters in cooking liquid 15 minutes. Remove lobsters from kettle, cool, and chill thoroughly. Split bodies, discard intestinal veins and stomach sacs, and crack claws. Serve with lemon wedges and mayonnaise.

Pressure-Cooked Lobster

Ready Tray
1 pound lobster or lobster tail
  water

Put about 1/4–1/2 inch water in bottom of pressure cooker. Put in lobster and pressure-cook 10 minutes. Take out lobster, and remove meat according to instructions for *Boiled Lobster*. Serve with melted butter, cheese sauce, or mayonnaise. Lobster is delicious hot or cold.

Combine 1/3 ounce dry mustard with 2 ounces mayonnaise, and squeeze 1 tablespoon fresh lime or lemon juice into mixture, to make an excellent dip for cold lobster.

Lobster is very good prepared in the pressure cooker. The meat is tender and free of the stringiness and strong taste that it has when broiled or boiled in water. The Italians invented the first pressure cooker. It consisted of a section of steel pipe with another pipe welded over one end and a threaded cover on the other. Excess steam escaped through the threads, which were not airtight.

Broiled Lobster

SERVES 6

Ready Tray
1 tablespoon salt
  water
3 whole fresh lobsters
5 tablespoons Kikkoman soy sauce
1 tablespoon sherry
1/2 teaspoon ground red pepper
1/2 cup melted butter

Add salt to water, and boil lobsters 20 minutes. Cool, remove legs, and shell. Halve lobsters lengthwise, halfway through. Combine soy sauce and sherry, and add lobster. Broil 4 inches from heat, basting with sauce several times. When lobster is ready to serve, sprinkle with red pepper, and spoon a little melted butter over top. Serve remaining butter in small bowl to be passed at table.

Guy Brault's Lobster à l'Américaine

SERVES 4–6

Ready Tray
2 1 3/4–2-pound lobsters
  salt to taste
1/4 cup hot olive oil
4 tablespoons butter
4 medium size cloves, shallots sliced thin
1 medium carrot, chopped fine
1 small onion, chopped fine
  pinch thyme
1 bay leaf
1 sprig fresh parsley, chopped fine
1/2 cup dry white wine
1/4 cup brandy
1/2 cup tomato puree
1/2 cup fish broth
2 cloves garlic, crushed
3 medium tomatoes, peeled, seeded, and chopped
1 1/2 teaspoons flour
1/2 teaspoon fine-chopped fresh chervil
1/2 teaspoon fine-chopped fresh tarragon
  hot boiled rice

Remove and crack lobster claws. Cut tail sections from bodies, and slice tails crosswise in 3 or 4 pieces. Split body sections lengthwise, and dis-

Fish and Shellfish Entrées

card intestinal veins and stomach sacs. Remove tomalleys, and reserve. Salt lobster meat and shells, and sauté meat in olive oil 6 minutes, or until shells turn red. In 1 tablespoon melted butter, sauté carrot and onion until lightly browned. Season with thyme, bay leaf, and parsley. Add lobster pieces, 1 tablespoon butter, shallots, and wine, and sprinkle with brandy. Ignite, and when flame dies down add tomato puree, broth, 1 clove garlic, and tomatoes. Cover pan tightly, and cook 20 minutes over medium heat. Remove lobster pieces, and take meat from shells. Strain sauce. Cream reserved tomalleys with remaining butter and flour. Add remaining garlic clove, chervil, and tarragon. Add tomalley mixture to sauce, and reheat, but do not boil. Add lobster meat, correct seasoning, and cook 2 minutes longer, or until meat is heated through. Serve with rice.

Of all the recipes for *Lobster à l'Américaine* this one is the finest.

Lobster Thermidor

SERVES 4–6

Ready Tray
3	cups cooked lobster meat, cut in 1/2-inch pieces
1/2	cup sherry
1/4	cup butter
5	tablespoons flour
2	cups milk
1/2	teaspoon dry mustard
1	tablespoon fine-chopped fresh parsley
1	teaspoon Kikkoman soy sauce
1/8	teaspoon white pepper
1/8	teaspoon dried dill
1/8	teaspoon sweet basil
1 1/2	cups fresh mushrooms, sliced through caps and sautéed in butter
2	eggs, slightly beaten
1	cup buttered bread crumbs mixed with 1/2 cup grated Parmesan cheese

Put lobster meat in large bowl, pour sherry over, and set aside. Melt butter in saucepan, and blend in flour, stirring over low heat. Add milk slowly, and continue cooking over low heat, stirring constantly, until smooth and thick. Add mustard, parsley, soy sauce, pepper, dill, and basil. Blend thoroughly. Add lobster and sherry, then mushrooms. Remove from heat, and stir in eggs. Return to low heat, and cook slowly 1 minute. Spoon into lobster half-shells, individual ramekins, or buttered casserole. Top with crumb-cheese mixture, and bake at 450° F. 10 minutes, or until top is nicely browned.

Flaming Lobster Tahiti

SERVES 2

Ready Tray
2	1–1 1/2-pound lobsters or 2 large lobster tails
1/4	cup melted butter
	juice of 1 lemon
2	cloves garlic, chopped fine
1/4	cup safflower oil
	salt and fresh-ground black pepper to taste
3	teaspoons fine-chopped parsley
1	teaspoon marjoram
3	dashes Tabasco
3	teaspoons capers
1	cup whole canned tomatoes, chopped
1/3	cup light rum, warmed

Split lobsters lengthwise. Brush well with butter, and sprinkle with lemon juice. Place, cut side down, in shallow baking dish. Set under preheated broiler until lightly browned. Remove from broiler. Brown garlic lightly in oil, and season with salt and pepper. Mix well, and discard garlic. Add parsley, marjoram, Tabasco, capers, and tomatoes. Simmer over low heat 10 minutes. Turn lobsters cut side up, and mask evenly with sauce. Bake at 375° F. approximately 20 minutes, or until tender, depending upon size of lobster. Sprinkle rum over lobsters, ignite, and serve flaming.

Spit-Roasted Lobster

SERVES 2–4

Ready Tray
2	1 1/2–2-pound lobsters
	boiling salt water
	melted butter

Put lobsters in boiling salt water 2 minutes. Remove, and fasten securely on spit, running latter just under underside of shell. Roast 15–20 minutes, basting with melted butter once or twice during cooking. Arrange on carving board, and split at table. Serve with melted butter.

Oyster Chop Suey

SERVES 6

Ready Tray
5	tablespoons butter
1	cup thin onion wedges
1 1/2	cups thin diagonal celery slices
2	cups bean sprouts
1/3	cup Kikkoman Hawaiian teriyaki sauce
1 1/2	cups canned mushroom buttons, well drained
	dash cayenne
1	pint oysters and liquor
	fresh toast

In large saucepan melt 3 tablespoons butter, and sauté onion until golden brown but limp. Add celery, bean sprouts, and teriyaki sauce, and cook until celery is tender, stirring occasionally. Quickly sauté mushrooms in 2 tablespoons butter; then add to saucepan, and mix thoroughly Cook oysters in their liquid until edges curl; then add to saucepan. Season chop suey with cayenne, and serve hot with toast.

Fried Oysters

SERVES 2

Ready Tray
- 1/3 cup Kikkoman Hawaiian teriyaki sauce
- 1 pint fresh or canned oysters, drained
- 1 egg, slightly beaten
- 1 cup fine bread crumbs
- 1/4 pound butter
- salt and fresh-ground black pepper to taste

Pour teriyaki sauce over oysters, and marinate 30 minutes. Remove oysters from sauce, reserving sauce; dip oysters in egg, roll in bread crumbs and brown both sides in butter. Season, and serve with teriyaki sauce.

Chinese-Hawaiian Oyster Pie

SERVES 6

Ready Tray
- 3 tablespoons butter
- 2 teaspoons fine-chopped shallots
- 3 tablespoons flour
- 3 dozen oysters and liquor
- 1 tablespoon fine-chopped celery
- 2 teaspoons fine-chopped chervil
- 1 teaspoon fine-chopped onion
- 1 1/2 teaspoons Kikkoman Hawaiian teriyaki sauce
- salt and fresh-ground black pepper to taste
- 3 thin slices ham, cut in small pieces
- 1 single pastry crust, or puff paste
- 2 tablespoons milk

Melt butter in saucepan, and sauté shallots quickly, stirring constantly. Blend in flour thoroughly. Strain oyster liquor through double thickness of cheesecloth, and add; stir until smooth. Add celery, chervil, onion, teriyaki sauce, salt, and pepper (use salt springly, because teriyaki sauce is slightly salty). Simmer 5 minutes, stirring occasionally. Place oysters and ham in large buttered baking dish. Place vegetable mixture on top. Cover top with pastry crust, and brush with milk. Bake 5 minutes at 450° F., reduce heat to 400° F. for 5 minutes, then to 350° F. Bake until crust is delicate brown and well risen. Serve at once with side dish of boiled rice.

Oyster Sausages New Zealand

SERVES 4

Ready Tray
- 1/2 pound raw ground lean lamb
- 1/4 pound suet, chopped fine
- 3/4 cup fresh oysters, chopped coarse, and liquor
- 1/4 cup light cream
- 1/4 teaspoon pepper
- 1 teaspoon salt

Thoroughly mix all ingredients. Shape into rolls about the size of link sausages, or into small patties. Fry over low heat in lightly greased skillet, covered, for 15 minutes. Remove cover, drain off all fat, and continue frying until nicely browned on all sides.

Oyster-Wine Stew Australian

SERVES 6–8

Ready Tray
- 3 pints oysters, shells removed, and liquor
- 1 clove garlic, crushed
- 2 small onions, chopped fine
- 4 tablespoons butter
- 2 1/2 cups milk
- 2 1/2 cups cream
- 1/2 cup fine-chopped celery tops
- 1 bay leaf
- salt and white pepper to taste
- dash cayenne
- 1/2 cup dry white wine
- 1 teaspoon fine-chopped parsley
- 1 teaspoon paprika

Chop 1 pint oysters coarse; leave remaining oysters whole. In skillet sauté garlic and onions in 3 tablespoons butter until golden brown. Put milk and cream in top of double boiler, and heat gently. Add butter mixture, celery tops, bay leaf, and chopped oysters. Mix well, and cook over low heat 20 minutes. Do not allow to boil. Strain through sieve, and return strained liquid to top of double boiler. Put remaining oysters in saucepan with their liquor, and season with salt, pepper, and cayenne. When edges of oysters begin to curl, remove from heat, and add to cream sauce in double boiler. Add 1 tablespoon butter and wine. Sprinkle parsley and paprika over top, and serve hot.

How to Prepare Scallops

Bay scallops are best in cold weather, but in summer months shipments do come to market from cold northern waters. Scallops are not only delicious but also practical and economical. No trimming is necessary. A pound of scallops is a

Fish and Shellfish Entrées

pound of food, and they can be prepared in many ways: sautéed, fried in deep fat, or prepared with various sauces. They can be ready for the table in a matter of minutes.

There is one very, very important rule to remember when cooking scallops; it cannot be emphasized too strongly. Do not overcook them, or their fine, tender flesh will shrink and become as tough as leather; abalone too should be cooked only 1 minute on each side over high heat and in a very hot pan. To cook scallops in fat, allow only 3 minutes, 5 minutes at the most. To cook them in their own juices or in liquid like *court bouillon*, which is not as hot as hot fat, 6 minutes are enough. Never boil scallops; reduce heat when liquid reaches boiling point, and simmer until done.

Dry scallops very carefully before sautéeing or frying, and put them into very hot fat so that they brown quickly before any of their moisture can cook out. The brown, crusty surface serves to protect the inner succulence.

Never try to cook scallops ahead of time and keep them hot for later serving. They must be served as soon as they come from the fire on heated plates or in the shells in which they were cooked.

A pound of sautéed or deep-fried scallops will serve 3 or 4 people, but combined with mushrooms and sauce, a pound of scallops will serve 6.

Sautéed Scallops

SERVES 4–6

    Ready Tray
- 2 pounds scallops, cut in 1-inch squares
- 1 cup milk
- 1/2 cup flour
- 4 tablespoons safflower oil
- salt and fresh-ground black pepper to taste
- juice of 1/2 lemon
- 4–6 teaspoons butter
- 1 teaspoon fine-chopped fresh parsley
- lemon wedges

Wash scallops, and dry thoroughly. Dip in milk, then in flour. Shake off surplus flour. Heat oil until very hot, and saute scallops, searing them quickly so that juices will not escape, no more than 5 minutes, until golden brown on all sides. Remove to serving platter, season with salt and pepper, and sprinkle lightly with lemon juice. Pour off oil in pan, add 1 teaspoon butter per serving, and cook over medium heat until nut-brown in color. Pour browned butter over scallops, sprinkle with parsley, and garnish with lemon wedges.

Shrimp Lau Lau

SERVES 4

    Ready Tray
- 1/2 pound cooked shrimp or lobster, chopped fine
- 1 small onion, chopped fine
- 1 small clove garlic, crushed
- 2 tablespoons fresh lemon juice
- 2 tablespoons tomato paste
- 1 1/2 teaspoons fine-chopped fresh parsley
- 1/2 teaspoon monosodium glutamate
- 1/2 teaspoon turmeric
- boiling water
- 8 large iceberg-lettuce or Chinese-cabbage leaves
- 1 pound fillet of sole, quartered
- 1/2 cup butter
- 1/4 teaspoon ground ginger
- 1 teaspoon fine-chopped fresh parsley
- 2 tablespoons fresh lemon juice

In saucepan combine shrimp, onion, garlic, 2 tablespoons lemon juice, tomato paste, 1 1/2 teaspoons parsley, monosodium glutamate, and turmeric. Cook over low heat until all liquid is absorbed. Set aside. Pour boiling water over lettuce to soften and blanch. Drain, and arrange two overlapping leaves on board. On the leaves, place 2 tablespoons shrimp mixture, a piece of sole, and then 2 more tablespoons shrimp mixture. Roll overlapping leaves lengthwise, tucking in ends to form envelope. Repeat until 4 rolls are made. Set 9-inch glass pie plate on bottom of large skillet, and arrange rolls on top. Pour in enough boiling water to cover bottom of skillet but not to reach rim of glass plate; cover tightly and steam 10–12 minutes. While rolls steam, combine remaining ingredients, and bring to boil. Slice rolls about 1 1/2 inches thick, and serve with sauce over top.

Paradise Isle Deviled Shrimp

SERVES 4

    Ready Tray
- 1 egg, slightly beaten
- 1/2 teaspoon celery salt
- 1/8 teaspoon Tabasco
- 1 pound raw shrimp, shelled and deveined
- 1 cup bread crumbs
- 1/4 cup butter, or more
- 1 medium onion, chopped fine
- 1 clove garlic, chopped fine
- 1 1/3 cups beef broth
- 1/2 cup dry gin
- 2 tablespoons Kikkoman soy sauce
- 2 teaspoons dry mustard
- 1/4 teaspoon Tabasco
- juice of 1 fresh lemon
- 2 cups hot steamed rice

Combine egg, celery salt, and 1/8 teaspoon Tabasco. Dip shrimp first into egg mixture, then into bread crumbs, and fry in butter until golden brown on all sides. Keep hot. Add more butter to skillet if necessary, to make 2 tablespoons, and sauté onion and garlic 5 minutes, stirring constantly. Add broth, gin, soy sauce, mustard, and Tabasco. Simmer over low heat 10 minutes. Just before serving, add lemon juice. Arrange shrimp on mound of rice, and pour sauce over before serving.

Coquilles Saint-Jacques Tahitian

SERVES 6

Ready Tray
1 1/2 cups chicken broth or water
1 1/2 cups dry white wine
3 shallots, chopped fine
2 celery branches with leaves, cut in 1-inch pieces
3 sprigs fresh parsley
1 bay leaf
8 whole peppercorns
2 pounds whole bay scallops or sea scallops, sliced 1/2 inch thick
1/4 pound fresh mushrooms, cleaned and sliced thin through stems and caps
4 tablespoons butter
5 tablespoons flour
3/4 cup milk
2 egg yolks
1/4 cup heavy cream
few drops lemon juice
salt and white pepper to taste
1/3 cup grated Swiss or Parmesan cheese

In large, heavy stainless-steel saucepan, bring broth, wine, shallots, celery, parsley, bay leaf, and peppercorns to boil over high heat. Reduce heat, and simmer, uncovered, 20 minutes. Strain liquid through sieve into a 10-to-12-inch enameled or stainless-steel skillet. Add scallops and mushrooms, cover, and simmer 5 minutes. Transfer scallops and mushrooms with slotted spoon to large mixing bowl. Quickly reduce remaining liquid to 1 cup. In large saucepan, melt butter over medium heat. Lift pan from heat, and stir in flour. Return to low heat, and cook, stirring constantly, 2 minutes, or until thoroughly blended, taking care not to let mixture brown. Remove from heat, and slowly whisk in reduced liquid and milk. Return to high heat, and cook, stirring sauce with whisk until thick and coming to boil. Reduce heat, and simmer 1 minute. Combine egg yolks and cream in small bowl. Stir in 2 tablespoons hot sauce; add 2 more tablespoons sauce; then whisk mixture into remaining sauce in pan. Bring sauce to boil over medium heat, stirring constantly, and boil 30 seconds. Remove from heat, and season with lemon juice, salt, and pepper. Sauce should coat a spoon fairly thickly; if too thick, thin with a little more cream.

With bulb baster, draw up and discard any juices that may have accumulated under scallops and mushrooms. Pour in 2/3 of the sauce, and stir gently. Butter 6 scallop shells or shallow 4-inch baking dishes, and set on baking sheet or in broiler pan. Spoon scallop mixture evenly into shells. Spread each portion with remaining sauce, and sprinkle with cheese. Bake in top third of oven 10 minutes, or until sauce begins to bubble; then slide under hot broiler 30 seconds to brown tops lightly. Serve immediately.

Polynesian Shrimp

SERVES 4

Ready Tray
1/2 cup butter
1/3 cup fine-chopped green bell pepper
2/3 cup fine-chopped onions
1/2 cup brown sugar, packed firm
1/4 cup cider vinegar
2 cups canned pineapple chunks with juice
1 teaspoon Kikkoman soy sauce
2 tablespoons cornstarch
1 tablespoon water
1 1/2 dozen breaded shrimp
3 tablespoon (or more) peanut oil
1 1/2 cups rice
3 cups water or broth
2 medium fresh tomatoes, quartered

Melt butter in saucepan. Sauté green pepper and onions until tender. Remove from heat; add sugar, vinegar, pineapple with juice, and soy sauce. Combine cornstarch with 1 tablespoon, water, and add to sauce. Return to low heat, and cook, stirring, until thick and clear. Set aside. Brown shrimp in 1 tablespoon or more peanut oil; keep hot. Combine rice, 3 cups water, and 2 tablespoons peanut oil in 3-quart saucepan. Bring to boil; reduce heat, and stir with fork; cover, and simmer 15 minutes, or until liquid is absorbed. Reheat sauce; add tomatoes, and cook until wilted. Spoon rice around edge of large serving platter; place shrimp in center, and pour hot sauce over all.

Fish and Shellfish Entrées

Snails

SERVES 2

 Ready Tray
 24 snail shells
 1/3 pound soft butter
 1 teaspoon fine-chopped shallots
 1 teaspoon fine-chopped garlic
 1/2 tablespoon fine-chopped fresh parsley
  salt and pepper to taste
 24 snails (1 can)
 3 tablespoons Kikkoman plum wine
  fine bread crumbs (optional)

Cream butter; add shallots, garlic, parsley, salt, and pepper. Blend until smooth. Put a little butter in each shell, put a snail on top, and cover with remaining butter mixture. Arrange shells in baking dish; pour wine around shells. Sprinkle bread crumbs over. Bake at 450° F. 10 minutes, or until butter sizzles and bread crumbs are golden brown. Serve immediately with clamp holders and snail forks.

Canned snails are the easiest fare to prepare, for they have already been thoroughly cooked, and the shells have been cleaned and sterilized. They are available in grocery or gourmet stores. The conventional way to eat snails is to pick up the shell with a clamp holder made for this purpose and to dig out snail with tiny two-tined snail fork. A special pan with rounded indentations to hold snails upright is used for both baking and serving.

Squid

Squid, considered a delicacy by many national groups, is gaining popularity at supermarkets, where it is sold packaged and quick-frozen, as well as fresh. These small, elongated 10-armed cephalopods are plentiful, nourishing, and economical for those who know how to use them. There is little waste in preparing squid. Teeth, eyes, and quill (a pen-shaped structure inside the body) are removed, but the arms are left intact.

The squid is cleaned by cutting the hub containing the arms from the body. Cut across this portion so as to cut out eyes. Squeeze out round sack containing teeth, located in center of cut made across hub. Slit body open, and flatten, unless squid is to be stuffed. Remove quill and scrape inside of body clean with knife. Wash scraped portions, and drain. Squid is now ready for cooking.

Squid may be fried, baked, stuffed, or cooked in sauces and is good served with pasta or rice. Different ethnic groups have special methods of cooking squid. Some marinate it before cooking; others use wine or wine vinegar in cooking. But the basic methods vary little.

Squid Bake

SERVES 6

 Ready Tray
 2 pounds fresh or frozen squid
  salt and pepper to taste
 1 or 2 cloves garlic, sliced thin
 2 tablespoons fine-chopped fresh parsley
 1/4 cup olive oil or salad oil
  juice of 1 lemon

Clean squid, and place squid in pan with olive oil. Bake at 300° F. 15 minutes, turning once. Remove from oven, and drain. Rinse squid again. Season with salt and pepper, and sprinkle with garlic and parsley. Return to oven, and bake 45 minutes. Sprinkle with lemon juice, and serve at once.

Pan-Fried Squid

SERVES 6

 Ready Tray
 2 pounds fresh or frozen squid
 1 egg, lightly beaten
 1/2 cup milk
  salt and pepper to taste
 1 cup flour, bread crumbs, or cornmeal
 1/2 cup oil

Thaw squid, if frozen, and clean. Combine egg, milk, salt, and pepper. Dip squid in mixture; then roll in flour. Heat oil in skillet until very hot. Add squid, and cook quickly 2 minutes on each side. Serve hot or cold.

Stuffed Squid

SERVES 6

 Ready Tray
 2 pounds fresh or frozen squid
 2 cups bread crumbs
 2 teaspoons dried parsley flakes
 2 tablespoons grated Parmesan cheese
 2 tablespoons salad oil
 1 medium onion, chopped fine
  salt and pepper to taste
 1/2 cup oil

Thaw squid, if frozen, and clean. Combine bread crumbs, parsley, cheese, salad oil, onion, salt, and pepper. Stuff squid with crumb mixture. Pour oil into shallow baking dish, and place stuffed squid carefully in pan. Bake, uncovered, at 375° F. 35 minutes, or until tender.

How to Clean a Turtle

The following instructions are for cleaning snapping turtles, the smaller ones. Use reasonable care in handling a live snapping turtle. The safest way to hold it is by the tail. Turn it over on its back. Tease with stick until turtle strikes stick or sticks his head out. Then chop head off with heavy-bladed knife. You can chop off claws now or later; either way will work well. Fill large kettle with water. Add 1 tablespoon salt per gallon of water. Bring to boil. Put in turtle, and boil 30 minutes. Remove from water, and set on its back.

If you have no large kettle or can to boil the turtle in, leave the body in cool place 1–8 hours, depending upon the weather. The hotter the weather the less time turtle should be left before body is cleaned. It takes quite a while after a turtle's head has been chopped off for its heart to stop beating and its reflexes to stop working. It is difficult to clean a turtle if its legs still react as if it were alive, and it is therefore better to wait until the reflexes have stopped. While turtle is on its back, cut belly shell away with sharp knife (a Bull Cook knife, or scimitar butcher's knife, is excellent for this procedure). Find the soft gristle at each joint of top and belly shells. Free under shell of skin, holding it in place, and cut skin from flesh, so that you can remove and throw away the under shell. Skin out four legs, locate joints of legs and body, and cut off legs. Skin neck and meat at base of tail. Cut off and discard outer part from the back. You now have all of edible meat. Leave the entrails intact in the top shell, and throw away. Remove all fat from meat, and wash in mild salt water a few minutes. Use 1 tablespoon salt per quart of water.

Turtle meat is delicious and can be fried, baked, roasted, or used in soup. It does not have a fishy taste. It does, however, have a stringy texture similar to that of frog legs. If you like frog legs, you will like turtle meat. Turtle meat can be substituted for beef or pork in soup recipes. Fry turtle meat in butter as you would beef. All small, medium, and large turtles have very tender meat. To ensure tenderness of old, extra-large turtle, combine 3 parts water to 1 part vinegar in quantities sufficient to cover turtle meat. Add 1 tablespoon salt for every quart of liquid. Marinate turtle meat in liquid overnight. Then rinse well in clean, cold running water, and dry with cloth. Meat is ready to use.

Fried Snapping-Turtle Meat

butter to taste
salt and pepper to taste
turtle meat (size of turtle determines yield)

Heat butter in frying pan. Salt and pepper meat to taste, and fry exactly as you would beef.

Turtle Stew

SERVES 4–6

Ready Tray

2	pounds fresh turtle meat or 2 (1 pound) cans turtle meat, cut in 1-inch pieces
1/4	pound butter
2	cups water
1	medium onion, sliced thin
2	cups celery with leaves, cut 1-inch thick
1	cup dry lima beans, soaked overnight in water to cover, or 1 cup canned lima beans
3	medium potatoes, peeled and cut in 1-inch squares
3	medium carrots, scarped and sliced 1 inch thick
1	small can whole tomatoes
1/4	cup fine-chopped fresh parsley
	salt and pepper to taste

Brown meat on all sides in half the butter; add more butter if needed. Set aside. In large soup kettle, bring water to boil. Add onion, celery, and lima beans; cover, and simmer 30 minutes. Add meat, potatoes, carrots, tomatoes, parsley, salt, and pepper. Cover, and cook 45 minutes longer, or until vegetables are tender. Serve in soup bowls.

If canned lima beans are used, do not add until last 15 minutes of cooking time.

Chinese-Hawaiian Pineapple Duck

Polynesian Steak Broil or Barbecue

Fowl Entrées

5

FOWL ENTREES

Poultry has been prized in China for more than 3,000 years. The eighteenth-century gourmet poet Yuan Mei included chicken and duck among "the four heroes of the table." Legends had grown up about these birds: The rooster, believed to be the incarnation of the masculine cosmic force (yang), symbolized such virtues as "literary spirit" in his crown and "faithfulness" in his crowing at dawn; the duck, because of his affection for his mate, represented marital fidelity. Today the Chinese-Hawaiians have numerous recipes for fowl. Some call for feet, gizzards, even tongues, which may be purchased in Chinese grocery stores.

The most popular and widely available forms of poultry are chicken, turkey, duck, and goose. A fresh bird of high quality is plump, with moist, undamaged skin and good distribution of fat.

Chickens may be purchased as broilers, roasters, or stewing chickens—live, dressed, ready-to-cook, or frozen. The live and dressed birds have not been graded; the latter have been plucked and bled but still have their heads, feet, and internal organs. The ready-to-cook birds are the most commonly available.

Turkeys come either fresh or frozen in a wide range of sizes. The smallest are the young roaster-fryers starting at about 4 pounds. The largest, the young hens or toms, weigh up to 24 pounds and are generally roasted.

Ducks are usually sold as ducklings, fresh or frozen. They range in size from 3 to 5 pounds. Geese are sold fresh or frozen and range in size from 4 to 14 pounds. The most common sizes are from 8 to 12 pounds, however. Both ducks and geese are usually roasted but are equally good braised.

Fresh fowl should be stored no more than 3 days in the coldest section of the refrigerator. Remove neck and giblets before storing. Wrap loosely, as circulation of air helps to reserve quality.

The number of servings you can get from different birds depends on total weight and method of preparation. The lighter the bird for its species, the greater the proportion of its weight is in bone. That is why a large turkey yields more meat per pound.

chickens
    broilers: 1/4–1/2 bird per serving
    fryers: 1/2–3/4 pound per serving
    roasters: 1/2–3/4 pound per serving
    stewing chickens: 1/2 pound per serving

turkeys
  less than 12 pounds: 3/4 pound per serving
  more than 12 pounds: 1/2 pound per serving
ducklings
  3–5 pounds: 1 pound per serving
geese
  8–12 pounds: 2/3 pound per serving

An easy way to test doneness in roasting, baking, or barbecuing whole birds is to grasp leg with thumb and index finger; if it moves forward and backward easily and joints are not stiff, the bird is ready to serve. After roasting a large bird like a turkey, let it sit 30 minutes before carving; it will be much easier to carve, and the bird will still be hot.

Chinese-Hawaiian Chicken Anise

SERVES 4–6

Ready Tray
4	tablespoons melted chicken fat
1	whole 3–4-pound frying chicken, disjointed
4	small green onions, cut in 1-inch lengths
1	tablespoon dark-brown sugar
2	tablespoons Kikkoman soy sauce
1/3	cup anisette or Pernod
1	cup chicken broth

Heat fat in large frying pan. Brown chicken well on all sides, and remove from pan. Add onions to pan, and sprinkle with sugar and soy sauce. Combine liqueur with broth. Return chicken to pan, and pour liqueur mixture over. Cook over low heat, uncovered, 30 minutes. Turn heat high, and cook several pieces of chicken at a time until skin is browned and crisp. Liquid will boil off almost entirely. Serve with plain boiled or fried rice.

Before preparing dry chicken parts, pick off any pieces of fat, and melt in small frying pan. If there is not enough to make 4 tablespoons, add safflower oil to make up the difference. Salt is not necessary because soy sauce is salty.

Chicken Breasts and Mangoes Fiji

SERVES 6

Ready Tray
6	fresh chicken breasts, flattened lightly
3	tablespoons sweet butter
1	teaspoon salt
1	teaspoon curry powder
1/2	teaspoon paprika
1/4	teaspoon white pepper
1/4	teaspoon fresh or dry ground ginger
1	chicken bouillon cube
3/4	cup hot water
2	large fresh mangoes
1	tablespoon cornstarch
1/4	cup water
2	tablespoons white dry wine

Slowly brown chicken on both sides in butter in large skillet; add more butter if needed. Season with salt, curry powder, paprika, pepper, and ginger. Dissolve bouillon cube in hot water, and pour over chicken. Cover, and simmer 30 minutes, or until fork-tender. Meanwhile peel mangoes, remove seeds, and scoop out flesh with ball cutter or teaspoon measure. Remove chicken from skillet, and keep warm. Blend cornstarch and water, stir into chicken drippings, and bring slowly to boil, stirring until thick and clear. Add wine and mango balls, pour over chicken, and serve with steamed rice.

Chicken Momi

SERVES 6

Ready Tray
1 1/2	slices stale sourdough or French bread
1/4	cup light cream
1	small dry onion, chopped fine
6	water chestnuts, chopped coarse
1/4	pound ground veal
1/4	pound ground pork
1/4	pound ground beef
1	egg
2	tablespoons Kikkoman soy sauce
1/4	teaspoon ground ginger
	dash cayenne
	dash monosodium glutamate
6	large chicken breasts, boned and flattened lightly
	salt and pepper to taste
2	tablespoons coconut oil or vegetable oil
2	tablespoons honey
1/4	cup sesame seeds
	fresh pineapple sticks

Soak bread in cream, and mash with fork. Mix softened bread thoroughly with onion, water chestnuts, and remaining ingredients, except chicken, salt, pepper, oil, honey, sesame seeds, and pineapple. Sprinkle chicken breasts with salt and pepper. Put 1/3 cup stuffing on inside or flesh side of each breast. Tuck all four ends of chicken breast over stuffing, and secure with small poultry skewers. Arrange in baking dish, skin side up, and brush with oil. Bake in preheated 325° F. oven 40 minutes, or until tender. Brush with honey and some pan drippings. Sprinkle lavishly with sesame seeds, and bake at 450° F. 10 minutes, or until lightly browned. Serve with pineapple sticks as garnish. (*cont.*)

Fowl Entrées

After breasts have been stuffed and secured with poultry skewers, they may be wrapped in aluminum foil and baked; when breasts are tender, the foil can be removed and the meat brushed with honey, sprinkled with sesame seeds, and browned.

Party Chicken

SERVES 6

Ready Tray
1	cup Kikkoman soy sauce
1	cup water
1/2	cup granulated sugar
1	tablespoon shortening
1	(1 inch) piece fresh ginger
1	large clove garlic, crushed
1	fresh 3–4-pound frying chicken, ready to cook
1/4	cup white wine

Combine soy sauce, water, and sugar. Stir until sugar is dissolved, and set aside. Heat large frying pan, melt shortening, and lightly brown ginger and garlic. Brown whole chicken with ginger and garlic slightly on all sides. Put soy sauce mixture in large kettle, and add wine and chicken. Cover, and simmer 45 minutes, or until tender. Place chicken on large platter, and carve at table.

Pan juices may be served as is or slightly thickened with cornstarch paste. Pour over carved chicken.

Filipino-Hawaiian Holiday Chicken Pochero

SERVES 6

Ready Tray
1/2	cup garbanzos (chick peas)
	water
1	1 1/2-pound chicken, cleaned, boned, and cut into 1/2-inch cubes
1/4	pound beef round, cut in 1/2-inch cubes
1/4	pound lean pork, cut in 1/2-inch cubes
1/4	pound smoked ham, cut in 1/2-inch cubes
2	medium onions, sliced thin
1	medium sweet potato, peeled and cut in 1/2-inch cubes
2	medium Irish potatoes, peeled and cut in 1/2-inch cubes
	salt to taste
1/2	fresh eggplant, peeled, and cut in 1/2-inch cubes
1/4	head cabbage, shredded
2	medium bananas, peeled and quartered
	salt and pepper to taste
1 1/2	teaspoons sugar

Soak garbanzos in water to cover overnight. Drain, cover with water, and cook until tender. Put chicken and meats in large kettle, cover with water, season with salt, cover, and simmer until tender. Add onions and potatoes, and simmer until partially tender. Add garbanzos, eggplant, cabbage, and bananas, and cook slowly until all are tender. Season to taste, and add sugar; stir, and serve in deep soup plates.

Italian-Hawaiian Chicken Marengo

SERVES 8

Ready Tray
2	3-pound broiler-fryers, disjointed
1/4	cup shortening
2	small onions, chopped fine
1	large clove garlic, mashed
1 1/2	cups sliced mushrooms
3	medium, fresh tomatoes, quartered
1/2	cup dry white or red wine
2	tablespoons brandy
	salt and pepper to taste

Brown chicken on all sides in hot shortening over medium heat. Reduce heat, and simmer, covered, 15 minutes. Remove chicken from pan, and keep warm. Add onions, garlic, mushrooms, and tomatoes to pan drippings, and cook 3 minutes, stirring. Add wine, brandy, salt, and pepper. Stir, and raise heat; cook rapidly until liquid is reduced 1/3. Return chicken to pan, partially cover, and simmer 20 minutes, or until fork-tender. Serve chicken with rice.

Slice mushrooms vertically through stems and caps.

Chicken Pot Roast

SERVES 4–6

Ready Tray
3	pounds fresh chicken thighs and drumsticks
1/2	teaspoon salt
1/4	cup Kikkoman soy sauce
2	tablespoons salad oil
1	tablespoon grated fresh ginger root or 1/2 teaspoon ground dried ginger
1	tablespoon Kikkoman plum wine
1	cup sliced fresh or canned mushrooms
1/2	cup fresh or thawed frozen Chinese peas
2	small green onions, cut in 1-inch pieces
1	tablespoon cornstarch
1	cup water
1	tablespoon Kikkoman soy sauce
1	teaspoon monosodium glutamate
1	teaspoon brown sugar

Rub chicken pieces with salt and 1/4 cup soy sauce, and set aside 15 minutes. Heat oil in skillet, and brown chicken well on all sides. Combine ginger and plum wine, pour over chicken, cover, and simmer 30 minutes, or until chicken is tender. Add mushrooms for last 5 minutes of cooking. Transfer chicken to serving dish, and keep warm. To mushrooms in skillet, add remaining ingredients; cook, stirring constantly, until sauce thickens. Pour over chicken, and serve hot.

Tahitian Chicken Prince Hinoi

SERVES 4

Ready Tray
1	3-4 pound frying chicken, disjointed
	salt and pepper to taste
1/3	cup shortening
1	medium onion, chopped fine
1	clove garlic, chopped fine
3	fresh or canned whole tomatoes, drained and chopped coarse
1	teaspoon fine-grated fresh ginger
1	tablespoon grated coconut
1/2	cup Chablis
1	cup chicken broth or consommé
1	cup fresh pineapple, cut in 1-inch cubes

Season chicken with salt and pepper. Brown quickly on all sides in hot shortening. Place in deep casserole. Add onion, garlic, tomatoes, ginger, coconut, wine, and broth. Bake, uncovered, at 350° F. 30 minutes or until chicken is tender. Add pineapple for last 10 minutes of baking time.

The ginger adds a yellowish color to the red of the tomatoes, and the coconut thickens the sauce.

Coconut Chicken Samoan

SERVES 6

Ready Tray
1	cup fresh or dried grated coconut
1	cup milk
2	tablespoons shortening
1	2 1/2-pound chicken, boned and cut in 1-inch cubes
2	teaspoons salt
1/2	cup water
3	tablespoons butter
2	bunches or (8 ounce) packages fresh spinach, stemmed and washed thoroughly

Combine coconut and milk in saucepan. Bring to boil, remove from heat, and soak 30 minutes. Squeeze all liquid from coconut through several thicknesses of cheesecloth, and discard pulp. Heat shortening in large saucepan, and brown chicken well on all sides. Add 1 1/2 teaspoons salt and water. Cover, and simmer 20 minutes, or until tender. Drain well. Melt butter in saucepan, and add spinach and remaining salt. Cover, and simmer 20 minutes; drain well. In large saucepan combine chicken, spinach, and coconut milk; bring to slow boil over low heat, stirring occasionally, and serve.

Coddled Chicken

SERVES 6

Ready Tray
1	4–5 pound roasting chicken, ready to cook
	water
1	small piece ginger root
1	tablespoon salad oil
3	tablespoons Kikkoman soy sauce
1/4	cup fine-chopped fresh green-onion tops

Put chicken in large soup kettle, cover with water, cover, and bring to boil. Add ginger, and bring to boil again. Reduce heat, cover, and simmer 40 minutes, or until chicken is tender. Remove chicken, cool, remove all bones and skin, and cut chicken into 3/4-inch cubes. Combine oil, soy sauce, and onion. Serve over cubed chicken.

This cool dish is good for hot days.

Chinese-Hawaiian Wild Duck

SERVES 4

Ready Tray
2	2-pound wild ducks
2	cloves garlic, minced
1	tablespoon salt
1/2	teaspoon fresh-ground black pepper
1/4	cup melted butter
1	apple, cored and halved
1	tablespoon dry mustard
1/2	cup beer
2	tablespoons Kikkoman Hawaiian teriyaki sauce
1	cup apricot preserves
1	tablespoon lemon juice

Clean, wash, and dry ducks. Make paste of garlic, salt, and pepper; rub into ducks, and brush breasts heavily with butter. Place apple half in each duck. Arrange ducks in shallow roasting pan, breasts up. Roast, uncovered, at 400° F. 15 minutes. Combine mustard, beer, teriyaki sauce, preserves, and lemon juice. Reduce oven heat to 350° F. Pour sauce over ducks, and roast 30–40 minutes longer, basting frequently.

Domestic duck may be prepared in the same way, but roasting time should be 2–2 1/2 hours.

Fowl Entrées

Toad-in-the-Hole Australian

SERVES 6

Ready Tray
1 1/2	cups sifted flour
1/2	teaspoon baking powder
2	teaspoons salt
1	egg, beaten
2	cups milk
3	cups sliced cooked chicken or 6 slices cooked roast beef
3	tablespoons fine-chopped fresh parsley
1/2	teaspoon fresh-ground black pepper

Sift together in large bowl flour, baking powder, and 1 teaspoon salt. Add egg and milk, and beat until smooth. Preheat oven to 350° F. Place chicken in buttered casserole. Sprinkle with parsley, pepper, and remaining salt. Pour batter over chicken. Bake 45–60 minutes, uncovered. Serve in casserole.

Oahu Chicken Wings

SERVES 3–4

Ready Tray
16	chicken wings
	salt to taste
1/2	cup chicken broth
1	clove garlic, peeled and crushed
1/2	cup *okolehao* or sugarcane rum
2	teaspoons sugar
3	tablespoons Kikkoman Hawaiian teriyaki sauce
1/3	cup shortening
1	(8 ounce) can whole mushroom caps
1	tablespoon cornstarch
2	tablespoons water

Rub chicken wings with salt. Combine broth, garlic, liquor, sugar, and teriyaki sauce in large bowl, and marinate chicken wings in mixture 2 hours. Drain, reserving marinade. Heat shortening, and brown wings, adding more shortening as necessary. Drain shortening off, and add marinade to chicken. Cover, and simmer 25 minutes, or until wings are tender. Add mushrooms. Blend cornstarch with water, and thicken pan juices, stirring until sauce is thick and clear. Serve with buttered rice and green salad, or *Victor's Flaming Spinach Salad*.

Fried Duck

SERVES 4

Ready Tray
	salt and pepper to taste
1	5–6-pound duck, cleaned and disjointed
1/4	cup shortening
6	tablespoons Kikkoman Hawaiian teriyaki sauce
1/2	cup water
1	small piece fresh ginger, shredded
1/3	cup Kikkoman plum wine
1/4	cup green-onion sprouts or 1-inch lengths green onions

Salt and pepper duck. Heat shortening in large skillet until very hot, reduce heat, and brown duck slowly on all sides. Combine teriyaki sauce, water, ginger, wine, and onion sprouts. Pour over duck, partially cover, and simmer 25 minutes.

Black-Cherry Chicken Sauté Pago Pago

SERVES 4

Ready Tray
1/2	cup flour
	salt and pepper to taste
2	2-pound broiler-fryers, halved with backbones removed
2	tablespoons sweet butter
2	tablespoons shortening
1	small onion, sliced thin
1/3	cup port wine
1	1-pound can pitted dark sweet cherries and juice
1/4	teaspoon allspice
1	tablespoon lime juice
	fresh lime slices (optional)

Combine flour, salt, and pepper. Dredge chicken lightly in flour mixture. Heat butter in large skillet, add shortening, and melt. Brown chicken on all sides in hot fat, making sure that it is not crowded in skillet. Pour off excess fat, and add onion. Cook until onion is tender but not browned. Remove chicken, set aside. Add wine, and bring to boil, stirring with small wire whisk to loosen brown bits from pan. Return chicken to pan, and add cherry juice, allspice, and lime juice; cover, and simmer 30 minutes, or until chicken is tender, turning once or twice so color is even. Add cherries, and heat through. Correct seasoning. Garnish with lime slices.

Black Duck (Wood Goose) Australian

SERVES 4–6

Ready Tray
18	oysters, shelled and chopped, and liquid
1	cup bread crumbs
2	tablespoons butter
1	teaspoon mixed herbs to taste
	pinch fresh-grated nutmeg
	salt and pepper to taste
1	egg
1	duck, cleaned and dressed (4 1/2–5 pounds)
4	rashers of bacon
1/3	cup melted shortening

Combine oysters, bread crumbs, butter, herbs, nutmeg, salt, pepper, egg, and oyster liquor. Mix lightly. Stuff duck with mixture. Place in baking dish. Cover with bacon. Bake at 325° F., uncovered, 20 minutes per pound plus 1/2 hour, basting well with shortening. Serve with toast and currant jelly.

Sprinkle duck with a little flour, and baste with pan juices during baking period, if desired.

Chinese-Hawaiian Pineapple Duck

SERVES 8

Ready Tray
2	ducklings, cleaned and quartered
3	tablespoons safflower oil
	salt and pepper to taste
1 1/2	cups chicken broth, heated
4	fresh pineapple rings
2	tablespoons cornstarch
3	tablespoons wine vinegar
1/3	cup pineapple juice
1	tablespoon Kikkoman soy sauce
1	teaspoon dry mustard blended with 2 teapsoons water
1	tablespoon minced preserved ginger
1	green bell pepper, cut in 1/2-inch strips
1	large carrot, cut in curls

Brown ducklings in oil. Place in bottom of large pan, and add salt, pepper, and broth. Cover and braise slowly until tender, 1 1/2 hours. Remove duck to hot platter, and keep warm, reserving liquid. Glaze pineapple rings in oiled frying pan until golden. Cut into 1-inch wedges. Blend cornstarch with vinegar and pineapple juice, and add to braising liquid. Cook a few minutes, until thickened. Add soy sauce, mustard, ginger, and green pepper, and simmer 3 minutes. Pour sauce over duck, and place carrot curls on top. The sauce should be the consistency of heavy cream.

Roast Goose New Zealand

SERVES 8–10

Ready Tray
1	12-pound goose, ready to cook
2	teaspoons salt
1/2	teaspoon black pepper
1	tablespoon goose fat or butter
1	cup fine-chopped onions
1/2	cup fine-chopped celery
10	medium potatoes, peeled, cooked, and riced, and cooking water
4	slices white bread, cut in 1/2-inch cubes
1/4	pound ground salt pork
2	eggs, beaten
1	teaspoon poultry seasoning
	salt and pepper to taste

Wipe goose with damp paper towels. Rub cavity and outside well with 2 teaspoons salt and 1/2 teaspoon pepper. Heat goose fat in skillet over medium heat, and partially cook (but do not brown) onions and celery. Add to potatoes with bread, salt pork, eggs, poultry seasoning, salt, and pepper. Stuff goose with dressing, being careful not to pack too tightly, and sew up cavity, or fasten with poultry skewers. Place in large roasting pan, and roast, uncovered, at 375° F. 3 hours, or until tender, basting with potato water.

Chinese-Hawaiian Squab

SERVES 6

Ready Tray
1	cup Kikkoman soy sauce
2	teaspoons fine-chopped fresh ginger
2	teaspoons sugar
2	tablespoons gin
1/2	cup water
6	small squabs, cleaned

In large kettle, combine soy sauce, ginger, sugar, gin, and water, and heat to boiling point. Add squabs, cover, and simmer until tender, approximately 30 minutes. Turn several times during cooking period. Serve hot with pan juices poured over.

Foil-Wrapped Turkey Orientale

SERVES 6

Ready Tray
1	teaspoon sugar
	salt and pepper to taste
1	tablespoon cornstarch
1	tablespoon Kikkoman soy sauce
1	tablespoon salad oil
1	teaspoon *hoisin* sauce (optional)
1	tablespoon dry white wine
1	green onion, chopped fine
1	pound fresh turkey breasts, boned and cut into 1/8" × 1/2" × 1 1/2" pieces
	shortening

Combine sugar, salt, pepper, cornstarch, soy sauce, oil, *hoisin* sauce, wine, and onion. Blend well. Add turkey pieces, and stir thoroughly to coat each piece on all sides. Place each piece of turkey on 6-inch square of aluminum foil, fold in envelope style, and seal. Melt shortening in skillet, to 1-inch depth. Heat thoroughly, carefully drop in packages, and cook 1–1 1/2 minutes on each side. Turkey will be rich, golden brown. Drain, and serve hot in foil.

Hoisin sauce is a Chinese sauce available bottled in Oriental food stores.

Fowl Entrées

New Zealand Turkey Wellington

SERVES 4–6

Ready Tray
1	2-pound frozen boneless turkey roast
1 1/2	cups flour
3/4	teaspoon salt
1/2	cup leaf lard
2 1/2	tablespoons water
1	egg yolk
1	tablespoon water

Cook turkey roast according to package directions, but cut cooking time to 2 hours. Remove from oven and cool. Measure flour without sifting. Sift flour with salt into mixing bowl. Add lard, and blend with pastry blender until mixture is texture of coarse meal. Sprinkle 2 1/2 tablespoons water over flour mixture, and press dough together with table knife. Flour pastry cloth and rolling pin. Place dough on cloth, and shape into ball with hands. Roll dough from center outward to form large circle. Trim to 10″ × 12″ rectangle. Place pastry over top of turkey, and seal bottom and sides with a little cold water. Prick crust to allow steam to escape. Decorate with pastry cutouts from trimmings. Combine egg yolk and 1 tablespoon water, and brush over pastry surface. Place turkey in shallow baking dish, and bake at 425° F. 25–30 minutes, or until crust is golden brown. Slice through crust to serve. Serve with warm *Apricot Sauce*.

South Seas Squab

SERVES 2

Ready Tray
2	squabs, ready to cook
2	teaspoons shortening
	salt and fresh-ground black pepper to taste
1/2	teaspoon grated fresh ginger
1	cup water
1	tablespoon fresh lime juice
1	bay leaf, crushed
1	teaspoon fine-chopped fresh fennel or 1/2 teaspoon dry fennel
1	teaspoon fresh-grated nutmeg
4	1-inch slices fresh pineapple

Rub squabs with shortening, and season with salt and pepper. Place 1/4 teaspoon ginger in cavity of each squab. Place squabs in casserole; add water, lime juice, bay leaf, fennel, and nutmeg. Arrange pineapple around squabs, and bake, uncovered, at 325° F. 1 hour, or until tender, basting frequently with pan juices. Serve with baked yams and tossed green salad.

Portuguese-Hawaiian Roast Turkey

SERVES 8–10

Ready Tray
6	large cloves garlic, chopped fine
3	dried hot chili peppers
3	tablespoons Kikkoman soy sauce
1/2	cup water
1/2	cup wine vinegar
1	10–12-pound turkey, cleaned and ready to cook

Pound garlic and chili peppers in mortar with pestle until very fine. Add soy sauce, water, and vinegar; blend well, and pour over turkey, also rubbing inside with mixture. Set turkey aside 3 hours, turning and basting with sauce every 30 minutes. Place turkey in large roasting pan, cover with aluminum foil, and roast at 225° F. 5–6 hours, or until tender, basting with pan juices. Remove foil for last 30 minutes of roasting so that outer skin will brown evenly. Pass sauce in bowl.

Dried-Fruit Dressing

TO DRESS 5–7-POUND BIRD

Ready Tray
3	tablespoons butter
1	clove garlic, chopped fine
1	medium onion, chopped fine
1	medium green bell pepper, chopped fine
1 1/2	cups rice
3/4	cup mixed dried fruits, chopped coarse
1/3	cup chopped dates and walnuts
1/2	cup white wine
	salt to taste
	dash paprika
	dash cinnamon

In large skillet melt butter, and sauté garlic, onion, and green pepper until just limp. Add rice, and stir until vegetables are well cooked. Add fruits, dates and nuts, wine, and seasonings.

Stuff duck or scooped-out halves of eggplant with rice mixture, being careful not to pack too tightly. Roast according to recipe for fowl or eggplant.

Fruit-and-Rice Dressing for Fowl

Ready Tray
1	cup brown rice
2	cups chicken broth
	grated rind of 1 medium orange
1/2	cup sliced dried apricots
1/3	cup raisins
1/3	cup sherry
1	teaspoon dried tarragon leaves
1	teaspoon dried thyme
1/4	cup heavy cream

Simmer rice in broth in covered saucepan 45 minutes. Drain, and cool. Marinate orange rind and fruits in sherry 2 hours. Combine rice, fruits and marinade, tarragon, thyme, and cream. Toss lightly, and stuff bird.

Stuffing for Roast Duck or Goose

TO STUFF 5-POUND BIRD

Ready Tray
6	dried prunes, pitted, and chopped coarse
1/2	cup white wine
1	medium, tart apple, peeled, cored, and cut in eighths
1	medium banana, peeled and sliced 1-inch thick
	salt and pepper to taste
	dash ground cloves
	dash cinnamon

Soak prunes in wine 2 hours. Combine all ingredients, and stuff bird.

Hawaiian Macadamia Nut–Turkey Dressing

MAKES 10 CUPS

Ready Tray
2	quarts dried bread cubes
1/2	cup butter or margarine
1	cup fine-chopped onions
1	small clove garlic, chopped fine
1/2	cup fine-chopped celery
1/2	cup fine-chopped celery leaves
1/2	teaspoon sage
1/2	teaspoon thyme
1/2	teaspoon crushed bay leaf
1 1/2	teaspoons salt
1/2	teaspoon pepper
1	egg, beaten
2	tablespoons brandy
1	cup macadamia nuts, chopped coarse

Place bread cubes in large bowl. Heat large skillet, add butter, and sauté onions, garlic, celery, and celery leaves. Add to bread cubes, and combine with remaining ingredients. Toss lightly. If dressing seems very dry, add a little milk or broth to moisten slightly. Stuff into ready-to-cook salted turkey.

Old-Fashioned Oyster Dressing

TO DRESS 6–7-POUND BIRD

Ready Tray
2	cups day-old corn-bread crumbs or day-old white bread crumbs
3	cups day-old white bread crumbs
1/2	cup fine-chopped onions
1/2	cup fine-chopped celery
1	tablespoon fine-chopped parsley
	salt and pepper to taste
1/2	teaspoon celery salt
1/2	teaspoon garlic salt
1/4	teaspoon thyme
1/2	teaspoon sage
2	tablespoons melted butter or shortening
1/2–3/4	cup hot water or broth
1	cup minced fresh oysters with liquid

Combine crumbs with onions, celery, parsley, seasonings, and butter. Toss lightly to mix. Add just enough water to moisten. Stuff bird.

Meat Entrées

6

MEAT ENTREES

The Hawaiians are known for luaus with roast pig prepared in the *imu*, or underground oven, along with the *laulaus* wrapped in various leaves. Broiled or fried jerked beef, raw beef strips that have been hung up and "cured" in the sun several days, is very popular.

Pork and beef are daily fare of the Chinese-Hawaiians, and chicken, squab, and duck are festive foods for special occasions. A nine-course dinner will have two chicken courses.

Beef has the upper hand with the Japanese-Hawaiians; sukiyaki is the most popular dish. It is prepared from thin strips of meat and vegetables, each in its special sauce, and cooked at the table. Teriyaki, which runs a close second, is also prepared at the table. Chicken is the favorite fowl.

The Korean-Hawaiians use more beef than pork or chicken. It is generally broiled over hot charcoals or an open fire after marination; this dish is known as *kun koki* and is usually served for special occasions. As a rule beef and pork are used sparingly to add flavor to soups and egg and vegetable dishes.

Pork is the favorite of the Portuguese-Hawaiians; it is roasted and served with wine or vinegar sauce or simmered in diluted spicy vinegar. The fat is removed and spread on bread. After the simmered meat is tender, it is drained and fried.

The Filipino-Hawaiians like pork most. It is generally broiled. The most popular dish is *adobo*, pork chops simmered in water; seasoned with vinegar, garlic, and peppercorns; then fried. Chicken is prepared in the same way and can be combined with the pork *en adobo*. A great feast is barbecued pig *lechon* served with many other meat dishes at the same meal.

All meat is popular among the Australians and New Zealanders, who raise many sheep and cattle on their thousands of acres of grazing lands. Fish and seafood, from the surrounding waters are also great favorites. No meal is complete without tea.

The Tahitians prepare their food in a manner similar to that of the Hawaiians in underground ovens. These feasts are called *tamaaraa* and consist of raw fish, wild bananas, breadfruit, roast pig, and many other delicacies.

The Samoans prefer pork, and no South Pacific feast is complete without it. They are also very fond of barbecued meats flavored with wood smoke from the *imu*. They think that food tastes flat without it.

Pork is also a favorite meat with the natives of the Fiji islands. It is served at a feast whose setting and cuisine are related to those of the Hawaiian luau, with assorted fruits and vegetables and especially curry dishes, for which they are very well known.

Filipino-Hawaiian Bridges Casserole

SERVES 4–6

Ready Tray
1	pound ground round steak
1	tablespoon olive oil
2	medium onions, chopped fine
1/2	cup raisins
	salt and pepper to taste
2	hard-cooked eggs, cut in 6 wedges each
1/2	cup small ripe pitted olives
4	eggs, slightly beaten
2	large cans creamed corn
1/3	cup sugar

Brown meat quickly, in oil, in medium frying pan. Add onions, raisins, salt, and pepper. Sauté until onions are limp. Put mixture into casserole as bottom layer. Arrange egg wedges and olives over meat mixture. Combine beaten eggs and corn thoroughly, pour over meat, and sprinkle with sugar. Bake, uncovered, at 350° F. until top is golden brown.

Pieces of frying chicken may be substituted for ground meat.

Australian Roast Beef and Yorkshire Pudding

SERVES 6–8

Ready Tray
1	4–7-pound standing or rolled beef rib roast
	salt and pepper to taste
1/2	pound flour
	pinch salt
4	eggs
1	quart milk

Heat oven to 325° F. Season meat with salt and pepper. Place, fat side up, in open pan. Do not add water, do not cover, and do not baste. For rare meat roast 18–20 minutes, for medium 22–35 minutes, and for well done 27–30 minutes a pound. (Add 10 minutes a pound for rolled roast.) Put flour and pinch salt in mixing bowl. Break in eggs, add half the milk, stir gradually, and add remaining milk a little at a time until batter is smooth. Beat well 10 minutes, set aside 1 minute, then beat again a few minutes. Place drippings from roasting pan in deep casserole, and heat thoroughly in oven. Pour in batter, and bake 25 minutes. If meat is being spit-roasted, place baked pudding underneath it a few minutes to impregnate it with juices dripping from meat. Cut pudding into squares, and serve with meat or separately.

Filipino-Hawaiian Morcon

SERVES 6

Ready Tray
6	thin slices boiled ham, halved
1	pound round steak, cut in 12 long, thin pieces
2	hard-cooked eggs, sliced thin
1	cup fine-chopped lean pork shoulder
1	small onion, chopped fine
2	medium tomatoes, peeled and chopped
1	celery stalk, chopped fine
	salt and pepper to taste
2 1/3	cups water

Place each strip of ham on strip of steak and slice of egg on ham; roll, and tie securely with string. Combine remaining ingredients. Place meat rolls in large kettle, pour combined ingredients over, cover, and simmer 2 hours, or until meat is tender, turning occasionally. Remove string, and serve whole or sliced in pan with sauce.

This dish is a favorite on special holidays.

Fiji Beef

SERVES 4

Ready Tray
2 1/2	pounds beef sirloin tip, trimmed and cut in 1-inch cubes
1 1/2	teaspoons garlic salt
1	teaspoon paprika
1/4	cup cooking oil or shortening
1	cup canned pineapple chunks with syrup
1	cup beef broth
1/4	cup wine vinegar
1/2	cup sliced celery
1/2	cup sliced green bell pepper
1	cup sliced onions
2	large tomatoes, cut in wedges
2	tablespoons Kikkoman Hawaiian teriyaki sauce
3	tablespoons brown sugar
1	tablespoon cornstarch or arrowroot
1/2	cup water
	salt and pepper to taste

Sprinkle meat with garlic salt and paprika. Brown in hot oil in heavy skillet with cover. Drain off fat. Add syrup from pineapple, broth, and half the vinegar. Cover, and simmer 1 1/2 hours. Add celery, green pepper, and onions; cover, and cook 5 minutes. Stir in tomatoes and pineapple. Blend remaining ingredients and vinegar until smooth, stir into meat, and simmer until thickened.

Meat Entrées

Pot Roast with Apricots

SERVES 6

Ready Tray
1	pound dried apricots
	water
2	tablespoons shortening
4–6	pounds beef chuck roast or brisket
3	cups boiling water
1	medium onion, grated
	salt and fresh-ground black pepper to taste
2	teaspoons lemon juice
1	teaspoon sugar

Soak apricots in water to cover overnight. Drain. Melt shortening in heavy skillet or Dutch oven. Brown meat on both sides over medium heat. Add boiling water, onion, salt, pepper, lemon juice, sugar, and apricots. Cover, and cook over low heat 2 1/2 hours, or until meat is tender, adding a little water if necessary.

Broiled or Barbecued Filet Mignon Béarnaise

SERVES 4

Ready Tray
2	cloves garlic, chopped fine
1/2	cup sweet butter
4	fillets of beef 1 inch thick
4	egg yolks
1	cup butter
2	tablespoons Kikkoman Hawaiian teriyaki sauce
4	tablespoons cognac, heated
1/8	teaspoon tarragon
1/8	teaspoon chervil
	fresh-ground black pepper to taste
1/4	teaspoon fresh parsley, chopped fine
	dash cayenne

Combine garlic with sweet butter, and rub well over steaks. Grill over hot coals or in broiler to desired doneness. In medium heavy-bottomed pan, combine egg yolks, butter, and teriyaki sauce, and cook over low heat, stirring, until thick and smooth. Add cognac, tarragon, chervil, pepper, parsley, and cayenne. Blend until smooth. Pour over steaks.

Bubble and Squeak New Zealand

SERVES 4

Ready Tray
4–8	slices cold cooked roast or corned beef
2	tablespoons drippings or shortening
1	medium head cabbage, boiled, drained, and quartered
1	teaspoon vinegar
	salt and pepper to taste

In large skillet over medium heat, fry meat in drippings; remove to large hot platter. Add cabbage to drippings in skillet, and cook quickly on each side. Add vinegar, season, and arrange around meat on platter.

This dish is one of the most popular conversational breakfast items on the menus of the *S. S. Mariposa* and the *S. S. Monterey* on the South Pacific run. Its special feature is vegetables that have been first boiled (bubble) and then fried (squeak). Cabbage should not be overcooked and should have "bite" to it. A little oil added to the water is very good. Diced boiled potatoes may also be added to the cabbage and cooked until crusty brown.

Chinese-Hawaiian Ginger Beef

SERVES 4–6

Ready Tray
1	fresh papaya
2	cups salted ice water
1	small onion, sliced thin
	shortening
1 1/2	pounds beef tenderloin, sliced paper thin
4	small pieces fresh ginger, sliced thin
2	cups chicken broth
1 1/2	teaspoons cornstarch
1/2	cup water
1 1/2	teaspoons Chinese oyster sauce
2	teaspoons Kikkoman soy sauce
	watercress

Peel papaya, slice, and cut in narrow strips. Soak in ice water 1 hour. Rinse in cold water, and drain. In large skillet sauté onion in a little shortening until soft, and add beef, ginger, and papaya; sauté 2 minutes, stirring carefully so as not to break papaya slices. Add broth, and bring to slow boil. Mix constarch with water. In saucepan combine oyster sauce, soy sauce, and cornstarch mixture. Add to meat, and stir until thickened. Garnish with watercress, and serve with cooked rice.

Hawaiian Jerked Beef

SERVES 6–8

Ready Tray
2	pounds flank steak
1	tablespoon ginger juice
1	tablespoon sugar
2	tablespoons Kikkoman Hawaiian teriyaki sauce
	light oil

Jerked beef was introduced to the islands by ranch cowboys, who broiled it over hot coals. Flank steak is best.

Cut meat into thin strips, and soak in ginger juice, sugar, and teriyaki sauce overnight. Dry, and fry in oil, or broil. It may be sprinkled with salt and set aside 4 hours, then placed in screened box and dried in sun 2 days, turned occasionally so that it dries thoroughly, before frying.

Beef Flambé

SERVES 6–8

Ready Tray
1/2	cup flour
	salt and pepper to taste
1	4–5-pound boneless rump roast
2	medium onions, sliced thin
3	medium carrots, sliced 1-inch thick
3/4	cup Irish whiskey
1	(8 ounce) can tomato sauce
1	cup beef broth
	dash thyme
	dash marjoram

Season flour with salt and pepper, and rub well into meat. Place meat, fat side down, in Dutch oven or heavy skillet with cover, and brown on all sides. Drain off excess fat. Add onions and carrots, and cook until onions are golden brown, stirring to keep from burning. Add 1/2 cup whiskey, tomato sauce, broth, thyme, and marjoram. Cover, and roast at 350° F. 3 1/2 hours, or cook on top of stove at medium or lower heat until tender. Remove meat to serving platter. Strain gravy, forcing vegetables through sieve. Season with salt and pepper, if necessary; heat gravy, and serve with meat. Heat remaining whiskey, set it aflame, and pour over roast. When flames burn out, carve, and serve. Spoon sauce from platter over each serving, adding rest of sauce to gravy.

Sukiyaki

Sukiyaki (from *suki*, "to like," and *yaki*, "to broil") was originally made with fish, as the Japanese people of 1540 did not eat meat or even fowl; as customs changed, they began to use bear grease and bear meat, then water buffalo and India cattle, and finally beef from European bison or buffalo.

Sukiyaki contains quite a few onions, but it has no onion taste. The sauce that sukiyaki is cooked in completely neutralizes the effects of the onions, a real cooking trick in itself.

Celery was not originally used, as it did not grow in Japan. Bamboo sprouts were plentiful and cost nothing and therefore were used in this and many other dishes. Actually, bamboo shoots have little flavor. Celery greatly improves sukiyaki.

Japanese-Hawaiian Sukiyaki

SERVES 8

Ready Tray
1/4	pound sweet butter
4	tablespoons Kikkoman soy sauce
1/2	cup sake or dry white wine
2	teaspoons sugar
3	pounds beef tenderloin, sliced very thin and cut into narrow strips, or boneless raw chicken, sliced very thin
2	cups firmly packed, crisp raw spinach leaves, cut 2 inches long
1	cup green onions, sliced diagonally in 1 1/2 inch lengths
1	cup canned whole broiled mushrooms
	thin stalks asparagus, thin strips zucchini, or slivered green beans
	celery, cut in thin strips
	green bell pepper with seeds removed, cut in rings
1	cup thin-sliced water chestnuts
6	eggs, beaten

Melt butter in chafing dish or skillet at table. Add soy sauce to cover bottom of pan. Add enough sake to cover entire surface of pan. Stir in sugar. Lay meat strips in pan, and cook to individual taste. (The Japanese allow each person to supervise his own portion.) Arrange vegetables in nest around meat. Spoon pan sauce over meat and vegetables constantly. Cook vegetables until just wilted but still crisp. If liquid in pan cooks away, add more soy sauce and sake. (Pan juices may be thickened slightly with flour or cornstarch.) Spoon raw egg into individual side dish for each guest. Serve sukiyaki with hot steamed rice and chilled fruit.

Cooking time for this showy dish is brief, and each vegetable retains its own identity and crispness. All ingredients should be prepared ahead of time so that sukiyaki can be cooked at table in large chafing dish or electric skillet. Guests dip cooked meat strips into raw egg before eating.

Fill large crystal bowl with chopped or shaved ice; spear fresh pineapple tidbits, preserved kumquats, whole fresh strawberries, seedless grapes, and Mandarin orange sections on toothpicks, and stick into ice. Serve with sukiyaki.

Meat Entrées

Steak-and-Kidney Pie New Zealand

SERVES 4

Ready Tray
2/3	cup shredded suet
2	cups flour
1/2	cup water
1	teaspoon salt
1 1/2	tablespoons flour
	salt and pepper to taste
1 1/2	pounds round steak, cut in 1 1/2-inch pieces
2	lamb kidneys, sliced 1/4-inch thick
1	shallot or 1 medium onion, chopped fine
1	tablespoon fine-chopped parsley
3/4	cup red wine or beef consommé

Rub suet into 2 cups flour. Add water and 1 teaspoon salt. Blend until smooth. Roll out. Line deep baking dish or individual ramekins or baking dishes with 2/3 the pastry. Season 1 1/2 tablespoons flour with salt and pepper to taste, and rub into meat. Put meat on pastry liner. Combine remaining ingredients, and spoon over meat. Cover with remaining crust, and cut a few vents to permit steam to escape. Bake at 275° F. or lower 2 hours, or until meat is tender and crust lightly browned. Serve from casserole or in individual baking dishes.

For richer pastry, use more suet and small amount of butter.

Beef Tenderloin Fiji

SERVES 8

Ready Tray
2 1/2	tablespoons fine-chopped scallions
1 1/2	tablespoons fine-chopped onion
1	clove garlic, chopped fine
1/2	cup butter
1 1/2	tablespoons curry powder
1 1/2	teaspoons fresh ginger, chopped fine
2 1/2	tablespoons chili sauce
1 1/2	tablespoons Kikkoman Hawaiian teriyaki sauce
1	fresh medium tomato, peeled and chopped
1 1/3	cups beef gravy
	juice of 1 lemon
16	3 1/2–4-ounce slices beef tenderloin, steamed wild rice
6	sliced water chestnuts
1	cup fresh bean sprouts
1/2	cup canned sliced mushrooms, drained

In large skillet sauté scallions, onion, and garlic in butter 1 minute. Add next 7 ingredients, and cook 2 minutes. Correct seasonings if necessary. Broil beef 1 1/2 minutes on each side. Place on bed of steamed wild rice. Top with sauce, and garnish with water chestnuts, bean sprouts, and mushrooms.

Or place 1/2 cup rice in center of each dinner plate; form ring by rotating bowl of tablespoon to right in rice. Place tenderloin slices in hollow, pour a little sauce over, and garnish with water chestnuts, bean sprouts, and mushrooms.

Japanese-Hawaiian Broiled or Barbecued Teriyaki

SERVES 6–8

Ready Tray
3	pounds filet of beef or round steak, cut 4″ × 3″ × 1/4″
3/4	cup Kikkoman soy sauce
3/4	cup sake or very dry sherry
2	tablespoons sugar
3	teapsoons fine-chopped fresh ginger
1	small onion, chopped fine
2	cloves garlic, chopped fine

Place meat slices between sheets of wax paper, and pound lightly with mallet or flat side of large kitchen knife; score meat by slashing across grain with sharp knife. Place in large flat bowl. Combine remaining ingredients, and pour over meat. Marinate 2 hours, turning occasionally. Broil 1 minute or less on each side over hot charcoals in hibachi at table or in broiler.

To broil on stick, slip 4–6 pieces of meat on bamboo or wooden stick 1/8 inch in diameter and 8–10 inches long. In restaurants meat is partially cooked, sliced thin, and arranged on stick just before serving.

Tahitian Tropical Steak

SERVES 6

Ready Tray
2	pounds beef round steak, cut 2″ × 1″ × 1/2″
1 or 2	tablespoons shortening or oil
2	medium onions, sliced thin
1/2	cup rum
2/3	cup pineapple juice
1/2	cup firm-packed brown sugar
1/2	teaspoon fine-chopped fresh ginger root
2	tablespoons arrowroot
1/3	cup Kikkoman Hawaiian teriyaki sauce
2	tablespoons red wine vinegar
2	medium tomatoes, peeled and quartered
1/2	cup fresh vertical-sliced mushrooms
1	medium avocado, peeled and cut in 1/2-inch strips
1	large ripe papaya, halved, seeded, peeled, and cut into 12 wedges

Brown meat quickly in shortening in large skillet. Add onions and rum, cover, and simmer 30 minutes. Add pineapple juice. Blend sugar, ginger, arrowroot, teriyaki sauce, and vinegar in saucepan until smooth, and cook over medium heat, stirring until thickened. Add to meat, and stir lightly. Place tomatoes, mushrooms, avocado, and papaya around and on top of meat. Heat through. Serve with hot fluffy rice.

Polynesian Steak Broil or Barbecue

SERVES 6

Ready Tray
1	cup Kikkoman Hawaiian teriyaki sauce
1	cup safflower oil
2	cloves garlic, crushed
1	thin slice fresh ginger root
6	thick steaks
2	medium onions, chopped fine
1	tablespoon olive oil
1	(8 ounce) can tomato sauce
1	teaspoon curry powder
	dash ground cinnamon
	dash salt
	dash monosodium glutamate
2	teaspoons cornstarch
1	tablespoon water
1	(9 ounce) can crushed pineapple with syrup

Combine teriyaki sauce, safflower oil, garlic, and ginger. Marinate steaks 2 hours. Broil steaks, reserving 1/2 cup marinade, to desired doneness, or barbecue over charcoal outside or on hibachi indoors. Sauté onions in olive oil until limp. Add reserved marinade and remaining ingredients, except cornstarch, water, and pineapple and syrup, and simmer until mixture comes to boil. Make smooth paste of cornstarch and water, and add to sauce, stirring constantly until thickened. Add pineapple and syrup, and heat thoroughly before serving in separate bowl with steaks.

Tahitian Lamb Chops

SERVES 3–4

Ready Tray
6	baby lamb chops
12	link sausages
6	fresh pineapple slices, 1/2 inch thick
	salt to taste
2	tablespoons melted butter

Sear lamb chops on both sides in hot dry skillet, reduce heat, and cook to desired doneness, pouring off fat as it accumulates. Keep chops warm. Parboil sausages 5 minutes, drain, and sauté over low heat in medium skillet, turning frequently until cooked through. Sprinkle pineapple with salt, and broil 2 inches from moderate flame, basting with butter from time to time until pineapple is nicely browned around edges. Place each chop on pineapple slice, and arrange sausages around chops on serving platter.

One Lamb Meat Ball Fiji

SERVES 4

Ready Tray
1	lamb bone with a little meat on it
1	medium onion, sliced thin
1	clove garlic, crushed
1	medium carrot, sliced thin
	salt and pepper to taste
1/4	teaspoon rosemary leaves
2	quarts water
1	pound lamb shoulder, ground
1	cup cooked rice
1/3	cup fine-chopped fresh parsley
1	egg, slightly beaten
1	large onion, chopped fine
3	tablespoons butter
3	tablespoons currants
3	tablespoons pine nuts or chopped macadamia nuts
1/2	teaspoon allspice
1/2	teaspoon cinnamon
2	egg yolks
	juice of 1 lemon

Place lamb bone, sliced onion, garlic, carrot, salt and pepper, and rosemary in large soup kettle. Add 2 quarts water, cover, and simmer 2 hours, skimming off fat. Strain broth, and bring to boil again.

Meanwhile combine ground lamb with rice, parsley, salt, pepper, and egg. Form large, smooth, round ball, and set aside. In large skillet sauté chopped onion quickly in butter. Remove from heat, and add currants, nuts, and spices, stir lightly, and chill in refrigerator 1 hour for easier handling. Punch hole in meat ball, push currant filling in, and pat hole closed. Tie ball in piece of cheesecloth, and drop into boiling lamb broth. Cover, and simmer until meat is done, 40–50 minutes. Remove ball from broth, remove cheesecloth, and keep ball warm. Beat egg yolks with lemon juice and 1 tablespoon soup. Stir until smooth, and gradually add to soup, stirring until slightly thickened. Carve meat ball at table, and serve slice in center of each soup plate, pouring soup over.

Meat Entrées

Lamb Sate

SERVES 8

Ready Tray
1/4	cup vegetable oil	
1/2	cup vinegar	
1	teaspoon rosemary	
2	tablespoons honey	
1/2	teaspoon black pepper	
2	cloves garlic, crushed	
2	teaspoons Kikkoman soy sauce	
2	pounds lamb, cut in 1-inch cubes	
	preserved kumquats	

Combine first 7 ingredients, and mix well. Add meat, and chill 2 1/2 hours, turning occasionally. Remove meat from marinade, and reserve liquid. Place 4 lamb cubes on each skewer, and broil 5 inches from heat 5–7 minutes, basting with marinade. Turn skewers, and broil 5–7 minutes, basting with marinade. Add kumquats to skewers, and serve over *Wild Rice*.

Flaming Lamb Shanks

SERVES 6

Ready Tray
3/4	cup dry gin
1/2	cup sesame oil
1/2	cup wine vinegar
1	medium onion, chopped fine
1	clove garlic, minced
1	teaspoon tarragon leaves
1	teaspoon basil
2	teaspoons salt
2	teaspoons coarse-ground black pepper
6	lamb shanks
1	tablespoon cornstarch
	water
	mushroom caps

Combine 1/2 cup gin, oil, vinegar, onion, garlic, tarragon, basil, salt, and pepper. Add lamb shanks, and marinate in refrigerator overnight, turning frequently. Arrange shanks on rack in shallow pan, and bake at 350° F. 1 hour, basting often with marinade. Remove lamb to serving platter, skim excess fat from pan juices, and pour juices into 2 cup measure; add remaining marinade and enough water to make 2 cups. Return liquid to pan, and cook and stir to blend in brown bits in pan. Mix cornstarch with small amount of cold water; then add to liquid and cook, stirring, until sauce is thickened. Add more salt, if necessary. Pour sauce into gravy boat. At table heat remaining 1/4 cup gin in ladle, set aflame, and pour into sauce. Pour flaming sauce over lamb shanks, and serve when flames die down. Garnish with mushroom caps.

Colonial Goose New Zealand

SERVES 8–10

Ready Tray
1	8-pound leg mutton
1/2–1	cup lean cooked ham, chopped fine
1	large onion, peeled, parboiled, and chopped fine
1 1/2	cups fine bread crumbs
1/2	cup suet, chopped fine
2	tablespoons melted clarified butter
	salt and pepper to taste
1	tablespoon fresh fine-chopped parsley
1 1/2	teaspoons fine-chopped fresh thyme
1	teaspoon fine-chopped fresh sage
1	tablespoon milk
1	egg, slightly beaten
	salt and pepper to taste
1/2	cup flour
2	tablespoons shortening
1–1 1/2	cups water

Bone mutton, being careful to keep meat intact (or have butcher bone it for you). Combine ham and onion with next seven ingredients, and stir in milk and egg. Fill mutton with mixture, and sew up or skewer opening carefully. Season with salt and pepper, and roll in flour. Melt shortening in roasting pan; place stuffed leg in it, and roast at 450° F. until tender, adding a little water during roasting period and basting from time to time. After first hour of roasting, reduce heat to 350° F. Do not thicken pan juices.

Mutton shoulder may be boned and prepared in the same manner.

Pineapple–Lamb Ragout

SERVES 4

Ready Tray
1/4	cup shortening
1	pound lamb shoulder, cut in 3/4-inch cubes
1/4	cup flour, seasoned with salt, pepper, and marjoram
1	(No. 2) can pineapple chunks and syrup

Melt shortening in heavy kettle. Dredge meat in seasoned flour, and brown thoroughly in kettle. Add pineapple chunks and syrup. Reduce heat to low, cover, and simmer 30 minutes, or until meat is tender. Remove cover, and reduce juices about 5 minutes to thicken.

This dish is good with or served over rice, and a little sour cream on top adds a gourmet touch.

Roast Crown of Lamb Australian

SERVES 6–8

Ready Tray
- 2 teaspoons rosemary
- salt and pepper to taste
- 1 crown roast of lamb
- juice of 1/2 lemon
- 1 cup brown rice
- 2 cups chicken broth
- 1 1/4 cups fresh cranberries
- 3 tablespoons water
- 1/3 cup brown sugar
- 1/2 cup ground lamb
- 1 medium onion, chopped fine
- melted butter
- 3 cups chicken broth
- 1 tablespoon cornstarch
- 1/2 cup water

Combine rosemary, salt, and pepper, and rub into lamb. Sprinkle with lemon juice. Cook rice tightly covered, in 2 cups broth 45 minutes over low heat. Cook cranberries in 3 tablespoons water and brown sugar until they pop but are still whole. Mix cranberries with rice, ground lamb, salt, and pepper; stuff roast. Put onion and 1/2 cup broth in large roasting pan. Roast at 300° F. 1/2 hour, uncovered, basting with remaining broth to moisten filling a little. Roast 45 minutes longer at 300° F. If rice seems dry add melted butter to top. Mix cornstarch with 1/2 cup water. Remove meat to hot platter, and add cornstarch mixture to pan, scraping all onion from pan; add more liquid if too thick. Carve lamb at table, and serve gravy on side.

Have butcher prepare crown of lamb by trimming and tying rib chops. He will also furnish paper frills for top of each chop bone when roast is ready to be served.

Australian Sheep-Station Stew

SERVES 4

Ready Tray
- 3 pounds lamb stew meat or 2 pounds boneless lamb
- 2 tablespoons shortening
- 1 (1 pound) can whole tomatoes
- 1 cup thin-sliced onions
- 2 carrots, sliced 1 inch thick
- 1 tablespoon fine-chopped garlic
- 3 medium potatoes, peeled and cut in eighths
- 1 large bell pepper, seeded and cut in 1/2-inch pieces
- 1 (8 ounce) can tiny peas, drained
- salt and pepper to taste
- 1/4 teaspoon thyme

In large, heavy kettle brown meat in shortening. Add tomatoes, cover, and simmer 30 minutes. Add onions, carrots, garlic, and potatoes. Cover, and simmer 15 minutes. Add remaining ingredients, and simmer 20 minutes, covered.

Roast Pork

The Japanese-Hawaiians are great lovers of pork. The Japanese originally came from China and brought Chinese cooking methods. They were using sugar sauce on hams more than 2,000 years before sugar was known in Europe. Before roasting pork, sprinkle all over with cinnamon, and rub it in well. Poke holes in heavy part of roast with sharp nail or skewer, and work some cinnamon down into meat. Cinnamon has a miraculous effect on pork and removes any strong taste, giving it a delightful fresh taste.

Pork Chops and Fruit Australian

SERVES 6

Ready Tray
- 6 1-inch thick rib pork chops
- 1 medium onion, sliced thin
- 1 (6 ounce) can sliced mushrooms, undrained
- 1/3 cup catsup
- salt and fresh-ground black pepper to taste
- 1/4 teaspoon dried thyme leaves
- 1/4 cup hot water
- 12 dried apricot halves
- 1 medium apple, peeled, cored, and sliced 1/2 inch thick
- 1 medium orange, peeled and sliced 1/2 inch thick

Brown chops well on both sides in large, hot, dry skillet. Remove, and set aside. Sauté onion until golden brown in hot fat in skillet. Stir in mushrooms and liquid, catsup, salt, pepper, and thyme. Add chops to mixture in skillet, overlapping if necessary, cover, and simmer 15 minutes. Meanwhile, pour hot water over apricots in small bowl, and let stand 15 minutes. Add to chops along with apple and orange slices. Cook, basting occasionally with pan juices, 30–40 minutes, or until chops are tender.

Pork Chops Hawaiian

SERVES 4

Ready Tray
- 4 loin pork chops, 3/4 inch thick, trimmed
- salt and pepper to taste
- 1/2 cup white wine
- 1/4 cup honey
- 2 tablespoons wine vinegar
- 2 small green onions, cut in 1-inch lengths
- 1 medium green bell pepper, seeded and cut in 3/4-inch pieces
- 1 cup canned pineapple chunks and syrup

Meat Entrées

1	tablespoon cornstarch
1	tablespoon Kikkoman Hawaiian teriyaki sauce
1	teaspoon fine-chopped fresh mint

Heat large heavy skillet, and rub with a little fat trimmed from chops. Brown chops slowly on both sides. Season with salt and pepper. Blend wine, honey, 1/4 cup pineapple syrup, and vinegar thoroughly, and pour over chops. Cover skillet, and bake at 300° F. 1 hour, or until tender. Remove skillet from oven, and remove chops from skillet. Add onions, bell pepper, and drained pineapple. Simmer on top of stove, uncovered, 5 minutes. Blend cornstarch with teriyaki sauce, add mint and stir into skillet. Cook, stirring, until mixture boils and is thickened. Pour over chops, and serve hot.

Kona Inn Pork Chops

SERVES 6

Ready Tray

6	8-ounce double-rib pork chops
	salt and pepper to taste
2	cups brown sugar
1/2	cup unsweetened pineapple juice
1/2	cup honey
2	teaspoons dry mustard
12	whole coriander seeds, crushed
6	whole cloves
6	orange slices, 1/4 inch thick
6	lemon slices, 1/4 inch thick
6	lime slices, 1/4 inch thick
6	maraschino cherries
	crisp romaine lettuce leaves

Brown chops on both sides in heavy, dry, hot skillet. Season with salt and pepper, and remove to shallow baking dish. Combine sugar, pineapple juice, honey, mustard, coriander, and cloves. Spoon 3 tablespoons mixture over each chop. Bake, uncovered, at 350° F. 1 hour, or until tender, basting with remaining sauce. With toothpick, peg 1 slice each orange, lemon, and lime on each chop; top with maraschino cherry, and baste fruit with sauce. Bake 10 minutes. Arrange on leaf-lined platter with *Honeyed Bananas*.

Puaachi Suckling Pig Tahitian

SERVES 8–10

Ready Tray

1	10–12-pound suckling pig, cleaned and dressed
2	teaspoons salt
2	cloves garlic
1/3	cup lard, butter, or oil
1/2	pound pork liver
1	teaspoon lard
1	medium onion, chopped coarse
4	cloves garlic, chopped fine
4	peppercorns
1 1/4	cups hot water
	salt and white pepper to taste
4	tablespoons bread crumbs, dried
4	teaspoons sugar
4	teaspoons wine vinegar

Rub inside and outside of pig with salt and 2 cloves garlic. Rub outside with 1/3 cup lard. Place in large roaster, and roast, uncovered, at 300° F. for 1 1/2–2 hours, or until tender, basting from time to time with pan juices. This dish may also be prepared on a rotisserie. Rub liver with 1 teaspoon lard, and grill or bake 5–7 minutes, until tender. Cut in pieces, and put through meat grinder, being careful to catch liver and all juice that is extracted. Regrind with onion, 4 cloves garlic, and peppercorns. Add hot water, salt, and white pepper, and stir well. Press through sieve over which clean doubled piece of cheesecloth has been laid. Mash with spoon to extract every bit of essence. Place sauce in saucepan over low heat, carefully add bread crumbs, and stir until mixture thickens, adding more bread crumbs if needed. Do not make sauce too thick. Add sugar and vinegar, and cook, without stirring, 3 minutes. Stir before serving with carved suckling pig.

Chinese-Hawaiian Red Roast Pork Char Sui

SERVES 4

Ready Tray

1	cup Kikkoman soy sauce
1/2	teaspoon red food coloring
1/2	cup sugar
2	pounds lean pork loin
1	1-inch cube fresh ginger root, grated

Combine soy sauce, food coloring, sugar, and ginger in medium saucepan. Simmer until sugar is dissolved, and set aside to cool. Cut pork in four pieces, and soak in sauce 2 hours, turning occasionally. Drain pork, and place on rack over pan of water. Roast at 350° F. 1 hour, or until tender. Turn after 30 minutes, and baste with remaining sauce.

Pork cooked this way is delicious sliced 1/8-inch thick and served hot or cold. It may be shredded and used as topping for dishes like chop suey, chow mein, and fried rice. It very popular in Honolulu and is sold at the food counters of five-and-dime stores there.

Luau-Style Island Pork Roast or Barbecue

SERVES 10

Ready Tray
2	tablespoons salt
1	tablespoon monosodium glutamate
1/2	cup Kikkoman Hawaiian teriyaki sauce
1/2	cup white wine
1	teaspoon fine-chopped fresh ginger
3	cloves garlic, crushed
1/2	cup honey
5	pounds pork loin with skin intact

Blend first seven ingredients thoroughly, and rub into meat. Marinate 2–3 hours, turning every 30 minutes. Roast meat over charcoal until well done, basting frequently with marinade during last hour.

If meat is to be roasted in oven, line large roasting pan with ti leaves, and place pork in pan, skin side up. Roast at 375° F. 1 hour. Pour 1 quart boiling water over skin, and reduce heat to 300° F., and roast 2 1/2 hours. Do not turn pork. Remove meat from oven, detach skin, place skin in dry pan, and return to oven at 250° F. 45 minutes. Skin will be crisp and crumbly and easily digestible. Skim off fat from liquid, and thicken for gravy to serve with pork.

If pork with skin intact is difficult to obtain, bacon rind may be substituted and cooked separately. Ti leaves are available at major florists. Or use large spinach or Swiss-chard leaves in triple thickness.

Filipino-Hawaiian Picadillo

SERVES 2–3

Ready Tray
1	pound ground fresh pork
3	cloves garlic, chopped fine
1	small onion, chopped fine
2 1/2	cups water
2	medium, fresh tomatoes, peeled and chopped
2	medium potatoes, peeled and cut in 1/2-inch cubes
	salt and pepper to taste
	monosodium glutamate to taste

In large heavy saucepan cook pork, stirring constantly, until it renders its fat. Add garlic and onion, and cook until onion is transparent, stirring to prevent sticking. Add water, cover, and simmer 20 minutes. Add tomatoes, potatoes, salt, pepper, and monosodium glutamate. Cover, and simmer until potatoes are tender.

This dish is common among the Filipino-Hawaiians and very good on a cool day.

Paradise Isle Spareribs

SERVES 10–12

Ready Tray
2	matching strips of spareribs
1	medium onion, chopped fine
1/2	cup thin-sliced celery
1	cup fine-chopped macadamia nuts
1/2	cup fine-chopped apple
1	tablespoon peanut oil
1/2	cup canned crushed pineapple, drained
1/4	cup Kikkoman plum wine
1	teaspoon monosodium glutamate
2	teaspoons Kikkoman soy sauce
2	slices fresh bread, crumbled
	salt and fresh-ground black pepper to taste

Sew edges of two strips of spareribs, leaving one edge open. Combine onion, celery, nuts, and apple, and sauté in oil until onion is golden brown. Add pineapple, wine, monosodium glutamate, soy sauce, bread, salt, and pepper (use salt sparingly because soy sauce is salty), and mix thoroughly. Stuff spareribs with this mixture, and sew remaining edge. Place spareribs in roasting pan, and roast uncovered at 350° F. 2 hours, or until meat is tender and browned, basting during cooking period.

Spareribs South Pacific

SERVES 4

Ready Tray
3	tablespoons flour
1	teaspoon salt
4	tablespoons Kikkoman Hawaiian teriyaki sauce
2	pounds lean spareribs, cut in 2-inch pieces
3	tablespoons shortening
1/2	cup sugar
2/3	cup wine vinegar
1/2	cup water
1/2	cup pineapple juice
1	teaspoon grated fresh ginger
1	cup fresh pineapple chunks
1	cup fresh papaya chunks or preserves
1	teaspoon fine-chopped fresh parsley
1	tablespoon sesame seeds

Combine flour, salt, and teriyaki sauce, and coat ribs. Set aside 20 minutes. Heat shortening in large, heavy skillet, and brown ribs on all sides. Drain excess fat from meat, and add sugar, vinegar, water, juice, and ginger. Cover, and simmer until meat is tender, 45–60 minutes. Gently stir in fruit, and simmer 5 minutes longer, uncovered. Sprinkle with parsley and sesame seeds before serving.

When fresh papaya is not available, preserves in jars can be found at all major markets.

Smoked Pork New Zealand

SERVES 6–8

Ready Tray
1	4-pound piece of Canadian bacon or 4-pound picnic ham
1	cup plum preserves
1	cup *Bean Sauce*
2	cloves garlic, gently crushed
1 1/2	teaspoons monosodium glutamate
1/2	cup sugar
	few drops red food coloring
2	tablespoons sesame oil
1	(10 ounce) can beef gravy
1/2	cup honey
1/2	teaspoon ground cinnamon
1	tablespoon chopped preserved kumquats
1/3	cup sherry
4	scallions, chopped fine
4	cups hot steamed rice
1	large avocado, peeled, seeded, and sliced in eighths
1/2	cup preserved kumquats

In large kettle over low heat cook meat in water to cover 1 1/2 hours or until tender. Meanwhile combine plum preserves, bean sauce, garlic, monosodium glutamate, and sugar. Add enough food coloring to make good red color, and stir in oil until smooth. Preheat oven to 325° F. Transfer drained meat to roasting pan, and coat with half the sauce. Roast, uncovered, 30 minutes, basting with remaining sauce. While meat is being roasted combine gravy, honey, cinnamon, 1 tablespoon kumquats, and sherry. Simmer 4 minutes. Remove from heat, and stir in scallions. On large serving platter make ring of rice, and place meat in center. Pour sauce over top. Garnish with avodado and 1/4 cup kumquats.

Bean Sauce

Ready Tray
1	(1 pound) can red kidney beans and liquid
1 1/2	teaspoons Kikkoman soy sauce
1/2	teaspoon sugar
1/2	teaspoon monosodium glutamate

Put beans and liquid through food mill, mash through sieve, or use electric blender to make bean puree. Stir remaining ingredients into puree.

Island Spareribs

SERVES 6–8

Ready Tray
1/2	cup Kikkoman Hawaiian teriyaki sauce
1/4	cup catsup
1/3	cup fresh, unsweetened pineapple juice
2 1/2	tablespoons brown sugar
2	cloves garlic, chopped fine
1/2	teaspoon fine-chopped fresh ginger or 1 teaspoon powdered ginger
4	pounds meaty spareribs, divided at rib sections

Combine teriyaki sauce, catsup, pineapple juice, sugar, garlic, and ginger. Pour over ribs in shallow pan, and marinate 1 hour. Parboil ribs in water to cover 30 minutes. Roast at 350° F. 1 hour, or until tender, turning and basting with marinade sauce, or barbecue over hot coals. Serve with pan juices poured over.

Colony Club Ham Australian

SERVES 10–12

Ready Tray
1	15-pound ham with skin
	water
3	large bottles sauterne wine
2	tablespoons peppercorns
2	pounds brown sugar
1	whole fresh pineapple, peeled, cored, and sliced 1/2 inch thick
6	cooking apples, peeled, cored, and sliced 1/2 inch thick
3	bay leaves, crushed
1/2	cup French mustard
1/2	cup brown sugar
	whole cloves
2	quarts Madeira

Soak ham in extra large kettle with water to cover 7 hours. Drain ham, and wash thoroughly in tepid water. Return ham to large kettle, skin side down, add 2 cups water, sauterne, peppercorns, 2 pounds brown sugar, pineapple, apples, and bay leaves. Cover, and bring slowly to boil; simmer gently 2 1/2 hours, adding hot water to keep ham covered as liquid boils away. (When small bone becomes loose ham is done; do not pierce ham, for juice will escape. Peel off skin while ham is still hot, being careful not to tear fat. Score ham by running sharp knife over fat diagonally in 1-inch widths, first to right over whole ham, then to left.) Cover ham with mustard; then sprinkle with 1/2 cup brown sugar, and spike ham all over with cloves. Place ham in large baking pan, add Madeira, and bake uncovered at 350° F. until thoroughly browned, 30 minutes, basting often with liquid. Remove ham, and allow to set 15–20 minutes before slicing. Served hot or cold.

A sauce may be prepared from the marinade by cutting up fruit in small pieces and thickening liquid with the fruit and a little cornstarch.

Veal in Papaya Lilioukalani

SERVES 4

Ready Tray
2 1/2	tablespoons butter
1	medium onion, chopped fine
2 1/2	pounds veal, trimmed and cut in 3/4-inch cubes
	salt to taste
2	bay leaves, crushed
	pinch thyme
1	large clove garlic, chopped fine
1/4	teaspoon coriander
1/2	teaspoon fine-chopped dried ginger root
2	teaspoons curry powder
1	quart hot stock or broth
1/4	cup tomato sauce
2	tablespoons arrowroot
3/4	cup cream
1	green apple, peeled, cored, and chopped fine
1/4	cup mango chutney
3	tablespoons fresh-grated coconut
4	papayas, with tops cut off and seeds removed
	grated coconut

Heat butter in saucepan, add onion, and simmer until golden brown. Add veal and salt, and cook, stirring, until light brown. Add bay leaves, thyme, garlic, coriander, ginger, and curry powder. Blend well, and add stock and tomato sauce. Bring to boil, cover, and reduce heat to simmer; cook 1 1/2–2 hours, or until veal is tender. Remove meat to separate pan. Blend arrowroot and cream with a little sauce. To sauce add apple, chutney, 3 tablespoons coconut, and arrowroot mixture. Bring to slow boil, and stir constantly 15 minutes. Correct seasoning, and strain through fine sieve over veal. Fill each papaya with meat and sauce. Place in shallow pan. Sprinkle with additional grated coconut, and bake at 350° F. 10 minutes.

This dish was developed by Chef Miyake of the Royal Sheraton Hotel, Honolulu.

Veal Provençale Nouméa

SERVES 2–4

Ready Tray
10	leg scallops of milk-fed baby veal, 2″ × 2″ × 1/4″
	flour
	salt and fresh-ground black pepper to taste
4	teaspoons butter
2	teaspoons olive oil
6	fresh mushrooms, sliced vertically through caps and stems, or canned mushrooms, drained
2	tablespoons diced peeled cucumber
2	tablespoons fine-chopped chives
1	medium tomato, peeled and diced
1	teaspoon garlic butter
2	tablespoons Marsala or sherry

Flatten veal with broad side of butcher knife. Dredge lightly in flour. Season with salt and pepper. Heat frying pan very hot, or heat crepe pan very hot over direct flame. Brown 4 teaspoons butter, and add oil. Sauté meat, browning quickly on both sides. Remove meat from pan to hot plates. Place mushrooms in frying pan, and add cucumber, chives, tomato, and garlic butter, and sauté over hot flame 2 minutes. Add wine, and blend well. Pour sauce over meat, and serve hot.

If fresh mushrooms are used, place in pan first when preparing sauce; if canned mushrooms are used, add to pan after tomatoes. Make garlic butter by adding 2 cloves garlic chopped fine to 1 tablespoon butter and mixing well.

Wild Deer Meat

Wild deer thrive in the forests on the eastern portion of Molokai, Hawaii. They were introduced in 1869 by the Duke of Edinburgh, who had received them as a gift from the Mikado of Japan.

For best results when roasting deer meat, select rump, round, or standing-rib roast. Trim off all skin, fibers, and fat; fat is not tasty and forms tallow when cooled. Work fat out with fingers if necessary, and substitute suet, bacon, or salt pork to combat dryness of meat. Cut added fat in strips 3″ × 1/4″; with sharp point of knife push pieces into meat as far as possible, and lay strips of suet, bacon, or salt pork across top.

Roast deer meat 25–35 minutes a pound 325° F. Be sure to keep 1/4–1/2 inch liquid in bottom of pan while roasting, adding to it during roasting period to keep from drying out. Do not overcook, as meat becomes tough. Also baste frequently during roasting period. Fresh orange juice and ginger ale are excellent basting liquids for game.

Onions, carrots, celery, potatoes, and rutabagas roasted with wild deer meat will keep it from drying out. Always serve meat on hot plates, as it gets tallowy when it cools.

The following marinade is very good for wild deer meat; make enough to cover roast: Combine 1 part vinegar, 1 part water, 1 tablespoon salt, 8 bay leaves, and 8 whole cloves for each quart water. Make slits in meat every 2 inches, so that liquid can

Meat Entrées

penetrate meat. Allow meat to remain in liquid 24 hours in refrigerator. Remove meat from marinade, rinse lightly in cold water, dry with cloth, and set in freezer or other cold place 1–2 hours until chilled and firm. Salt and pepper meat well before roasting.

Wild-Deer Stew Molokai

SERVES 6

Ready Tray

1/2	cup wine vinegar
2	cups Kikkoman plum wine
1	cup fine-chopped Bermuda onions
3	cloves garlic, chopped fine
	salt and fresh-ground black pepper to taste
1	bay leaf
1/4	teaspoon oregano
1/4	teaspoon thyme
3–4	pounds lean venison, trimmed and cut in 1-inch cubes
4	tablespoons shortening
2	cups canned whole tomatoes

Combine vinegar, plum wine, onions, garlic, salt, pepper, bay leaf, oregano, and thyme in large glass or porcelain bowl; do not use metal bowl. Add venison, and marinate overnight in refrigerator, basting frequently. Drain, and reserve marinade. Heat shortening in Dutch oven or casserole, and brown meat well on all sides. Add marinade and tomatoes. Cover, and cook over low heat 1 1/2–2 hours, or until tender. Serve with broad buttered noodles.

Thicken pan juices, if necessary, with 1 tablespoon potato flour mixed with a little water.

Marinated Wild Deer Molokai

SERVES 8

Ready Tray

4–5	pounds round venison roast, trimmed
2	cups wine vinegar
3	cups beer
2	medium Bermuda onions, sliced thin
2	tablespoons mixed pickling spices
3	tablespoons brown sugar
1	tablespoon salt
	flour
5	tablespoons shortening
3	tablespoons flour
1/4	cup beer
1	cup water
2	beef bouillon cubes
1	cup sour cream

Place venison roast in large deep glass or porcelain bowl (do not use metal). Cover with next 6 ingredients. Cover bowl, and refrigerate 3 days, turning meat every day. Remove meat, reserving marinade; dry, and dredge in flour to coat all sides. Brown on all sides in Dutch oven in 5 tablespoons shortening (to 1/4-inch depth). Add 1 cup marinade. Cover, and cook slowly over low heat on top of stove 2 1/2 hours, or until meat is tender. Add more marinade as needed. Remove meat from Dutch oven. Blend 3 tablespoons flour with 1/4 cup beer; slowly add water and 1 cup venison marinade, then bouillon cubes. Cook over medium heat, stirring until thickened. Add sour cream, and stir until just blended; do not allow to boil. Serve gravy with sliced venison roast.

Kangaroo Roast Australian

SERVES 4–6

Ready Tray

1	5-pound boned kangaroo leg roast
1/2	pound sliced bacon
1	cup bread crumbs
1	medium onion, chopped fine
1	level teaspoon marjoram
1	egg
1	tablespoon butter
	salt and pepper to taste
1	cup sherry

Line cavity of roast with most of bacon. Combine bread crumbs, onion, marjoram, egg, butter, salt, and pepper thoroughly. Place this filling over bacon, close cavity, and secure with small metal skewers. Salt and pepper outside of meat to taste. Lard roast with bacon fat, or lay remaining bacon rashers over meat. Place in roasting pan. Pour wine over meat, cover, and roast at 300° F. 2 1/2–3 hours, or until tender. Baste roast with pan juices during roasting period. Remove cover for last 30 minutes, to brown top.

Green onions, cut in 1/2-inch lengths, and peeled and quartered potatoes may be added for last 45 minutes of cooking. Thin-sliced carrots, cooked separately in a little butter and sugar to glaze, complete the entrée. Place roast on large platter, and surround with potatoes, onions, and carrots; serve gravy separately. Carve roast at table.

Kangaroo Steak Australian

SERVES 6

Ready Tray
6	3/4-inch thick boned kangaroo rib steaks
	olive oil
6	rashers bacon
	salt and pepper to taste
2	tablespoons butter
4	small green onions, chopped fine
2	cloves garlic, chopped fine
1/2	cup red table wine

Brush both sides of steaks with olive oil. Wrap rasher of bacon around each steak, and secure with toothpick. Fry in hot, dry frying pan on both sides until well done. Season with salt and pepper. Place meat on hot serving platter. Melt butter in frying pan, and sauté onions and garlic until golden brown. Add wine, a little salt and pepper, and bring to boil quickly. Pour over steaks, and serve at once.

Australian Rabbit

SERVES 4

Ready Tray
1	3–4-pound rabbit, disjointed
1	cup Kikkoman plum wine
1	cup water
	salt and pepper to taste
1/2	bay leaf
1	medium onion, chopped coarse
	flour
2	tablespoons butter
3	slices bacon, diced
1	cup small mushroom caps

Place rabbit pieces in large kettle; add wine, water, salt, pepper, bay leaf, and onion. Simmer gently 1 1/2 hours. Remove rabbit pieces, and flour each lightly. Brown rabbit in butter. Brown bacon, and add to rabbit. Add 1/2 cup or more rabbit stock, cover, and simmer 45 minutes, or until tender. Before serving add mushroom caps. Pan juices may be thickened and served over mashed potatoes or buttered rice.

Pot-Roasted Rabbit Australian

SERVES 4

Ready Tray
1	3–4-pound rabbit, disjointed
1/2	cup flour
1	teaspoon salt
1/4	teaspoon black pepper
1/2	pound bacon, sliced, then halved
1/2	cup broth
1/2	cup rich milk or cream

Wash and dry rabbit. Combine flour, salt, and pepper. Roll rabbit in mixture. Fry bacon slowly in frying pan to extract fat, but do not brown. Remove bacon, and brown rabbit on all sides in bacon drippings. Arrange bacon on bottom of Dutch oven, reserving a few slices. Place rabbit on bacon, and place reserved bacon on top. Cover, and simmer slowly on top of stove 1 hour, turning rabbit from time to time to prevent scorching. No liquid should be needed if Dutch oven is kept covered, but a little broth or milk may be added to keep it from getting too dry. When rabbit is soft but not quite tender, add remaining broth and cream, and keep stirring until quite tender. Serve with boiled or mashed potatoes and pan gravy on side.

Scalloped Brains Australian

SERVES 4

Ready Tray
1 1/2	teaspoons salt
1	quart water
2	sets calves' or sheeps' brains
1/3	cup butter
1/3	cup flour
	salt and pepper to taste
2 1/2	cups milk
1	small onion, peeled and quartered
1/4	teaspoon powdered sage
1/8	teaspoon cayenne
2	tablespoons lemon juice
2	cups cooked macaroni, drained
1/4	cup grated cheese
3	tablespoons bread crumbs
1/4	cup melted butter

Combine 1 1/2 teaspoons salt and water, and soak brains 1 hour. Melt 1/3 cup butter in saucepan over medium heat, and blend in flour until smooth. Season with salt and pepper. Gradually add milk, and simmer, stirring to prevent lumps until thickened. Cool. Remove brains from salt water, rinse, place in saucepan, and cover with fresh cold water. Add onion and sage; cover, and cook slowly 6 minutes. Remove brains, reserving sauce, and pull off membrane gently, for flesh is fragile, and slice 1 inch thick. Mix gently with cooled sauce; add cayenne and lemon juice.

Meat Entrées

Combine macaroni and cheese. Line bottom and sides of buttered baking dish with part of macaroni. Fill with brain mixture, and place remaining macaroni around edge of top. Mix bread crumbs with 1/4 cup butter, and spoon over brains and macaroni. Bake at 375° F., uncovered, until set and golden brown on top. Serve very hot in casserole with green or mixed salad.

Haggis Baggis Australian

SERVES 4–6

Ready Tray
1	sheep's paunch (stomach), cleaned and turned inside out
	water
	sheep's heart, liver, and lights (lungs)
	salt water
	salt and fresh-ground black pepper to taste
1/4	teaspoon fresh-grated nutmeg
1/4	teaspoon cayenne
1	medium onion, chopped fine
1	cup browned oatmeal
1/2	pound beef suet, chopped fine
2	cups brown gravy

Soak paunch in cold water to cover overnight. Drain, place in large kettle, cover with fresh cold water, cover, bring to boil, reduce heat, and simmer 1 1/2 hours. Remove, and sever pipes and gristle. Cook heart, liver, and lights in salted water to cover 30 minutes. Remove from water, and halve liver. Cool thoroughly and grate one half. Chop other half very fine with heart and lungs. Season heavily with salt and pepper. Add nutmeg, cayenne, onion, grated liver, oatmeal, and suet. Mix thoroughly. Fill paunch a little more than half full with mixture, leaving space at top to prevent bursting during cooking. Add 1 cup gravy. Prick haggis here and there with large needle, and sew up opening. To keep haggis from bursting and spilling contents in water during cooking period, wrap in napkin galantine-fashion before putting in water. Place in large pan with water to cover. Cover, and boil gently 3 hours.

To brown oatmeal, fry in the suet until brown.

Haggis Baggis is of Scotch origin and very popular in Australia. When brought in at large banquets, it is accompanied by an escort of pipers. It is usually served wrapped in a well-starched napkin with brown gravy on side, and whiskey is the traditional drink served with it.

Australian Veal Kidneys Flambé

SERVES 4

Ready Tray
3	veal kidneys, trimmed of fat and sliced very thin
1/2	cup fresh mushrooms, sliced vertically through stems and caps
2	teaspoons fine-chopped shallots
1/8	pound butter
1/2	cup brandy
1/2	cup sherry
	salt and fresh-ground black pepper to taste
1/2	teaspoon dry English mustard
1	cup sour cream or thick fresh cream
	trimmed toast triangles sautéed lightly in butter

In frying pan over medium heat, sauté kidneys, mushrooms, and shallots in butter 4 minutes, or until lightly browned. Add brandy and sherry. Ignite; then add salt and pepper. Blend in mustard and sour cream. Heat thoroughly, and serve at once over toast on heated plates.

A pinch of rosemary leaves can be sprinkled in as kidneys are browning for added zest. This dish may also be prepared before guests in blazer pan over Sterno heat.

Ginger Liver

SERVES 4

Ready Tray
2	large onions, sliced thin
3	tablespoons butter or salad oil
4	slices calf's liver, 4" × 4" × 1/2"
4	tablespoons Kikkoman Hawaiian teriyaki sauce
2	tablespoons sherry
1	teaspoon fresh-grated ginger

In large frying pan, sauté onions in 2 tablespoons butter 10–15 minutes, or until golden and limp; lift out with slotted spoon, and place on serving platter to keep warm. Meanwhile trim exterior membrane from liver, and cut meat into 2-inch squares. Add remaining butter to frying pan, and quickly brown liver on one side, 1 minute, over high heat. Turn, and add teriyaki sauce, sherry, and ginger. Cook 2–3 minutes, basting with pan juices. Arrange liver on platter with onions, and pour remaining pan juices over. Serve with sourdough bread and green salad.

Sweetbreads with Apples Australian

SERVES 4

Ready Tray

1	pound fresh sweetbreads
	juice of 1/2 lemon
	boiling salted water
6	tablespoons butter
1/2	pound sliced fresh mushrooms
6	tablespoons apple juice
3	egg yolks, well beaten
3/4	cup heavy cream
	salt and pepper to taste
	buttered toast rounds
1	recipe *Sautéed Apples*

Add sweetbreads and lemon juice to enough boiling salted water to cover meat. Cover, and simmer 10 minutes; drain, and cool, or immerse in cold water. Remove membrane and tubes. Slice 1/4 inch thick. Melt butter in frying pan, add sweetbreads, and cook 10 minutes over low heat, stirring occasionally. Add mushrooms, turning to coat with butter; simmer 5 minutes, covered. With slotted spoon remove mushrooms and sweetbreads; add apple juice to pan, and boil vigorously 1 minute. Reduce heat immediately to below boiling point. Blend egg yolks with cream, and stir slowly into apple juice, stirring constantly until slightly thickened. Return sweetbreads and mushrooms to sauce. Season to taste with salt and pepper. Serve on toast rounds, accompanied by *Sautéed Apples*.

7

SPECIAL BARBECUE RECIPES

All meats to be barbecued should be at room temperature. Tough cuts are excellent when presoaked in papaya juice or the pulp of papaya, skin and all. Do not worry about flavor, as papaya leaves none after cooking. If flavors *are* desired, they can be added with the various marinades. The main flavor is provided by the smoke of an open fire.

Getting the fire going is the same for a simple grill propped on stones as for a fancy store-bought model. Unless slow-burning wood is available, charcoal briquettes purchased in various weights are most satisfactory. They are easily kindled, and burn slowly and intensely. Use more briquettes for food that requires longer cooking than for food that grills quickly. All kinds of starting fuel are good, but be sure to read directions and to follow them carefully. A bucket of sand should be kept near the barbecue to put out the fire when it burns too high.

It takes 30–45 minutes for a small-to-medium charcoal fire to burn to hot coals with gray ash, 1 hour for larger ones, and 1 1/4 hours for a wood fire. Be sure that charcoal and charcoal briquettes are stored in dry place before using, so that they do not absorb moisture that makes them difficult to light. Briquettes of hard wood have low resin contents and a minimum of tar; they smoke less and have little odor, burn longer, and produce even, intense heat without sparks. Soft woods can be used, but they have high resin contents, which give foods an undesirable flavor, produce uneven heat, and give off sparks.

Line firebox with heavy-duty aluminum foil for added fuel economy; it reflects heat and makes cleaning easier. Pour gravel over foil to 3/4–1-inch depth, to permit fire to breathe and even heat distribution while briquettes are burning. After 4–6 barbecues, wash gravel in hot water, and spread out to dry thoroughly before using again, as wet gravel causes pops.

Before cooking wait until flames disappear and all that is visible is bed of glowing reddish color with deposit of fine gray ash on surface of coals. Heat is released through ash in form of infrared rays. The ash also works as in insulator. Tap coals lightly with fire rake or poker to remove ash before starting to barbecue; repeat occasionally during cooking periods. Tapping off excess ashes avoids need for more fuel toward end of the barbecuing.

Put supply of briquettes in firebox and at edge to warm up. Add warm briquettes 15 minutes before needed. Do not dump cold briquettes on live ones, for they reduce temperature of fire and retard barbecuing.

When cooking over grill space briquettes 1/2 inch apart to reduce flare-up; when cooking on spit keep fire well to rear. To keep flare-ups to minimum trim as much fat as possible from meat before placing over hot coals. Heat depends upon how many briquettes are used and how closely they are placed. Learn how to use modest quantity.

Barbecuing time varies, depending upon sizes and shapes of foods to be barbecued, and most meats should be 4–5 inches from heat. As meats are cooked, move them to outer edge of grill to stay hot with minimum additional cooking. When using skewers, space food on them so that heat reaches all sides and cooks food evenly.

A long-handled fork and heavy tongs for turning meats are essential. Sharp knives, cutting board, heavy-bottomed saucepan for sauces, 2-inch paint brush for brushing on sauces, salt and pepper shakers, and good supply of heavy-duty aluminum foil (good for lining firebox and to make disposable pans), pot holders, mitts, wrapping for various foods, and thermometer for testing doneness of turkey and large roasts all help in barbecuing.

The 14-inch heavy-duty aluminum foil just fits most broiler pans and also makes a good wrapping for foods to be cooked on grill and for freezing foods. The 18-inch width is also available. Use foil wraps when banana or ti leaves are unavailable. Breads and buns, wrapped in heavy foil and heated at side of grill while main foods cook, are also an addition to any barbecued feast. Vegetables, potatoes, seafood, and bread are excellent wrapped in foil and barbecued.

To prevent toxic action of foods barbecued over briquette, which give off tar deposits on foods and cause illness to some people, spread sheet of aluminum foil over burning charcoal. Foil allows heat to come through but does not spoil flavor of barbecued foods; in fact, it improves the flavor.

Oahu–Pearl Teriyaki Burgers

MAKES 6 BURGERS OR 3 "STEAKS"

Ready Tray
1 1/2 pounds lean ground beef
1 1/2 cups soft bread crumbs
1/4 cup fine-chopped onions
2 eggs, beaten
2 tablespoons sugar
3 tablespoons Kikkoman Hawaiian teriyaki sauce
1 large clove garlic, chopped fine or put through garlic press
1/2 teaspoon monosodium glutamate
1/8 teaspoon ground ginger

Combine meat and all other ingredients thoroughly. Shape into 6 burger patties or 3 "steaks." Grill 5 inches from coals 10 minutes, or to desired doneness, turning once. Serve on or with toasted buns accompanied by tossed green salad.

Two slices fresh bread should make 1 1/2 cups crumbs.

Japanese-Hawaiian Barbecued Steak

SERVES 4

Ready Tray
1 2-pound sirloin steak, 1 inch thick, quartered
1/2 cup Kikkoman Hawaiian teriyaki sauce
1/3 cup sake or sherry
2 tablespoons sugar
2 tablespoons fine-chopped preserved ginger
1 tablespoon sesame oil

Pound steak 3/4 inch thick, and place in shallow dish. Combine remaining ingredients in small bowl, and pour over meat. Marinate 4 hours at room temperature, or refrigerate overnight, turning occasionally. Lift steaks from marinade, and place on barbecue grill 4 inches above hot coals, and grill 2 minutes on each side, or to desired doneness.

Whole green onions chopped fine make an excellent topping for steak.

Five Islands Flank Steak Teriyaki

SERVES 4–5

Ready Tray
2 pounds flank steak
1 cup beef bouillon, or 2 cubes beef bouillon dissolved in 1 cup hot water
1 teaspoon seasoned salt
1/3 cup fine-chopped small green onions
1/4 teaspoon garlic powder
1/2 teaspoon fresh-ground black pepper
1/2 cup Kikkoman Hawaiian teriyaki sauce
2 tablespoons fresh lemon juice
2 tablespoons honey
12 medium whole fresh mushrooms

Luau-Style Island Pork Roast or Barbecue

Baked Papaya Stuffed with Lobster Curry
and Avocado Fijian

Special Barbecue Recipes

Remove membrane from steak, but do not score or tenderize it. Remove fat and gristle. Cut steak into diagonal strips 1 inch wide. Place in large shallow dish. Combine remaining ingredients except mushrooms, and pour over meat strips; marinate 24 hours in refrigerator. Remove meat strips from marinade, drain, and thread on skewers; cap each with mushrooms. Grill 4–5 minutes 5 inches above hot coals of barbecue or hibachi, turning once.

Korean-Hawaiian Barbecued Beef Kun Koki

SERVES 8

Ready Tray
- 4 pounds beef tenderloin or round steak, trimmed, 5″ × 4″ × 1/3″
- 3 tablespoons sesame oil
- 1 cup Kikkoman Hawaiian teriyaki sauce
- 1 teaspoon monosodium glutamate
- 3 small green onions, chopped fine
- 1 1/2 teaspoons sugar
- 2 cloves garlic, chopped fine
- 2 tablespoons powdered sesame seeds, heated and pounded

Pound meat between sheets of wax paper with mallet or dull edge of large knife. Score with knife lengthwise and crosswise. Combine remaining ingredients in large bowl, add meat, and mix thoroughly. Marinate 1 1/2 hours. Broil in broiler or over charcoal, or pan-broil in hot skillet, turning until meat is cooked to desired degree of doneness. Serve hot.

This dish is usually prepared for special occasions. The meat may be broiled immediately, but it is much better when marinated first.

Chuck Roast New Zealand

SERVES 6–8

Ready Tray
- 1 4-pound chuck roast, 2 inches thick
- 1 teaspoon monosodium glutamate
- 1/3 cup wine vinegar
- 1/4 cup catsup
- 2 tablespoons cooking oil
- 4 tablespoons Kikkoman Hawaiian teriyaki sauce
- 1 tablespoon Worcestershire sauce
- 2 teaspoons prepared mustard
- salt and pepper to taste
- 1/4 teaspoon garlic powder

Sprinkle both sides of roast with monosodium glutamate, and place in shallow baking dish. Thoroughly combine remaining ingredients, pour over meat, and marinate 3 hours, turning several times. Grill 6 inches from hot coals, or broil in stove 6 inches from heat, 35–45 minutes for medium-rare roast, or to desired doneness, basting every 15 minutes.

Chicken Breasts Aloha

SERVES 4

Ready Tray
- 4 fresh chicken breasts, boned
- 1/2 cup Kikkoman Hawaiian teriyaki sauce
- 1/2 cup fresh unsweetened pineapple juice
- 2 tablespoons fresh lemon juice
- 2 large cloves garlic, chopped fine
- 1/2 cup fine-chopped macadamia nuts
- 1 (3-ounce) can deviled ham
- 3 green onions, chopped fine
- 1/4 cup melted butter

Place chicken breasts in shallow dish. Combine teriyaki sauce, pineapple juice, lemon juice, and garlic, and pour over chicken. Set aside 2 hours at room temperature, turning occasionally to ensure even marination. Line firebox of barbecue with 14-inch heavy-duty aluminum foil, and allow coals to burn down until covered with gray ash. Combine nuts, ham, and onions, and spoon onto chicken breasts; roll, and secure with skewers. Brush with butter, and arrange on large sheet of foil. Grill 40 minutes, 5 inches above coals, basting with marinade and turning until delicately browned and tender.

Polynesian Stuffed Chicken

SERVES 4–6

Ready Tray
- 1   5–6 pound roasting chicken, ready to cook
- 1/2   cup wild rice
- 1 1/2   cups water
- 1   pound ground lamb
- 1   egg
- 1   cup chicken stock
- 1   medium onion, chopped fine
- 1/2   cup fine-chopped celery
- 1/3   cup fine-chopped cooked mushrooms
- 1/4   cup olive oil
- 1/4   cup slivered almonds
- 2   teaspoons fine-chopped fresh parsley
- 1   tablespoon fine-chopped pimiento
-     salt and fresh-ground black pepper to taste
- 1/4   teaspoon fresh-grated nutmeg
-     dash thyme
- 1   recipe *Basting Sauce*

Line firebox of barbecue with heavy-duty aluminum foil, and let coals burn down until covered with gray ashes. Wash chicken, and pat dry with paper towels. Parboil rice in water 7 minutes. Drain, and combine with remaining ingredients except sauce. Stuff into chicken, close cavity with metal skewers, and secure chicken carefully on spit, being sure it is balanced. Cook 6 inches from hot coals 1 1/2 hours or until tender, basting with sauce every 15 minutes. When chicken is ready, set aside for 15 minutes before carving.

Basting Sauce

Ready Tray
- 2   tablespoons butter
- 2   tablespoons flour
- 1   cup chicken broth
- 1   (8 ounce) jar orange marmalade

Melt butter in small saucepan, and blend in flour until smooth. Add broth, and stir until thickened. Add marmalade, and blend well. Keep warm on back of grill to baste chicken every 15 minutes.

Paradise Island Chicken

SERVES 4–6

Ready Tray
- 1/2   cup Kikkoman soy sauce
- 2   tablespoons brown sugar
- 2   teaspoons vegetable oil
- 1/3   cup pineapple or orange juice
- 1   large clove garlic, peeled and crushed
- 1/2   teaspoon fresh or ground ginger
- 1   large broiler chicken, disjointed

Combine all ingredients except chicken, and pour over chicken in shallow baking dish; marinate 45 minutes. Drain, reserving marinade, and barbecue 5 inches over hot coals 30–45 minutes, or until tender, basting with marinade and turning occasionally. Serve with hot steamed or baked rice, green vegetable, and tossed salad.

Chicken may also be roasted or broiled in oven.

Polynesian Turkey Barbecue

SERVES 10–12

Ready Tray
- 1   10–12-pound turkey, ready to cook
- 3   teaspoons salt
- 1/2   teaspoon fresh-ground black pepper
- 2   (6 ounce) cans frozen pineapple-juice concentrate, thawed
- 1 1/2   cups water
- 2/3   cup firm-packed brown sugar
- 3/4   cup wine vinegar
- 1/2   cup honey
- 1/2   cup Kikkoman Hawaiian teriyaki sauce

Wash turkey; dry well. Rub inside and out with salt and pepper. Place turkey on spit, according to instructions; set spit in position over hot coals. Combine remaining ingredients in small saucepan, and brush part over turkey. Start rotisserie. Roast, brushing often with sauce, 3–3 1/2 hours, or until turkey is tender and richly glazed. Just before turkey is finished, heat remaining sauce to boiling. Serve sauce with carved turkey.

Sautéed canned pineapple slices and baked yams or sweet potatoes are excellent accompaniments.

Fish Barbecue Bora Bora

SERVES 6

Ready Tray
- 1   (3 1/2 ounce) can flaked coconut
- 1 1/2   cups half-and-half cream
- 6   fillets of sole, ready to cook
-     salt and fresh-ground black pepper to taste
- 1   cup fine-chopped onions
- 2   tablespoons vegetable oil

Combine coconut and cream in small saucepan; heat very slowly to boiling; remove from heat, and set aside 30 minutes. Strain through double thickness of cheesecloth into small bowl, pressing out all liquid. Discard coconut. Sprinkle fish with salt and pepper. In small frying pan, sauté onions in oil until soft and transparent, stirring constantly. Spread onions in center of each of 6 14-inch squares

Special Barbecue Recipes 147

of heavy-duty aluminum foil, and place fish fillet on each. Shape foil around fish, and spoon coconut cream over fish; wrap foil envelope style, and seal tightly. Place packets on barbecue grill 5 inches above hot coals. Grill 25 minutes, turning packets with tongs several times to ensure even cooking. Let each guest unwrap packet.

Skewered Lobster

These combinations may also be served as appetizers, first courses, or entrées, depending upon the amount on each filled skewer. They are excellent cooked on an outdoor grill or indoors on a hibachi.

Thread chunks of cooked lobster meat on skewers, alternating with small mushrooms. Brush with melted butter, and grill over hot coals until lobster is golden and mushrooms are cooked.

Alternate pieces of raw lobster meat with cherry tomatoes and green-pepper squares. Brush with garlic-flavored oil before barbecuing or broiling in oven.

Marinate chunks of raw or cooked lobster in *Tarragon–Butter Sauce* and white wine before cooking.

Heat can (8 oz.) of tomato sauce with 1 tablespoon curry powder, and use as marinade for chunks of lobster. Alternate lobster and pineapple chunks on skewers, and barbecue, or broil in oven.

Tarragon–Butter Sauce

Ready Tray
- 2 tablespoons crushed tarragon leaves
- 2 tablespoons fine-chopped fresh parsley
- 2 tablespoons chopped chives
- 1 tablespoon fresh lemon juice
- 1/2 cup toasted bread crumbs
- 1 cup hot melted butter, clarified

Crush tarragon leaves, parsley, and chives in mortar with pestle; add lemon juice, breadcrumbs, and butter. Or put everything in blender a few seconds.

This marinade is also very good with beef steaks. After meat has been broiled or barbecued, spoon a little over each steak before serving.

Lobster Barbecue

SERVES 6

Ready Tray
- 6 lobster tails with shells intact
- 1/3 cup fresh lime juice
- 1/2 cup coconut oil
- salt and pepper to taste
- 6 banana leaves

Cut membrane of lobster tails down edges and remove. Grasp each tail in both hands, and bend backward toward shell side to crack in 3 places. Combine lime juice, coconut oil, salt, and pepper. Brush liberally onto fleshy side of lobster. Wrap each lobster tail in banana leaf or 12-inch square heavy-duty aluminum foil, place in *imu* or open barbecue over hot coals, and roast 45–60 minutes, or until tender, turning to ensure even cooking.

Barbecued Shrimps Tahitian

SERVES 6–8

Ready Tray
- 24 large raw shrimps in shells
- 1/2 cup Kikkoman soy sauce
- 4 teaspoons sugar
- 1 tablespoon fine-chopped preserved ginger
- 2 cloves garlic, chopped fine
- 1/4 teaspoon fresh-ground black pepper
- 8 fresh chicken livers, halved
- 8 slices lean bacon, halved

Shell shrimps, but leave tails intact; remove sand veins. Place shrimps in large glass bowl. Mix soy sauce, sugar, ginger, garlic, and pepper in small bowl, and pour over shrimps. Chill 45 minutes, turning shrimps in marinade several times. Wrap each liver half in half-slice bacon. Alternate shrimps and bacon-wrapped livers on 6–8 long skewers. Place on grill 5 inches above hot coals. Grill, turning several times, 6 minutes, or until shrimps are tender and bacon is medium crisp.

Barbecued Lamb Chops Australian

SERVES 6

- 6 round-bone lamb chops 1 inch thick, trimmed
- 1 cup light vegetable oil
- 1 cup dry vermouth
- 1 tablespoon fresh lemon juice
- 1/2 cup fine-chopped onions
- 2 large cloves garlic, chopped fine
- 2 teaspoons salt
- 3/4 teaspoon fresh-ground black pepper
- 1/2 teaspoon crumbled basil leaves

Place lamb chops in large shallow dish. Combine all remaining ingredients in small bowl, and pour over lamb chops. Set aside, and marinate at room temperature 4 hours, turning occasionally. Lift chops from marinade, and place on grill of barbecue 5 inches above hot coals. Grill 20 minutes, or to desired doneness, turning and brushing often with marinade.

Shrimps in Foil

SERVES 4–6

Ready Tray
2	pounds large fresh shrimps, shelled and deveined
1/2	cup sliced fresh mushrooms
2/3	cup melted butter
4	tablespoons fine-chopped scallions
3	tablespoons Kikkoman soy sauce
1/4	teaspoon salt
1/4	teaspoon garlic powder
3	dashes Tabasco

Divide cleaned shrimps among 6 12-inch squares heavy-duty aluminum foil. Distribute mushrooms over shrimps. Turn up edges of foil. Combine remaining ingredients in small bowl, and spoon sauce over shrimps and mushrooms. Seal packets tight, and grill close to broiler or over hot coals 5–10 minutes, or until shrimps are pink. Peek into packet after 5 minutes to check.

Fruit in Foil Fijian

SERVES 6

Ready Tray
1	(1 pound 14 ounce) can fruit for salad (3 1/2 cups drained)
2–3	fresh oranges, peeled and sliced 1/2 inch thick to make 1 1/2 cups
1/4	teaspoon curry powder
1/3	cup flaked coconut
1/2	pint sour cream

Mix salad fruit with oranges. Stir curry powder through coconut. Spoon fruit evenly over 6 12-inch squares heavy-duty aluminum foil, sprinkle with curried coconut, and wrap, sealing foil completely with double folds. Grill over hot coals or in 400° F. oven 15–20 minutes. Spoon sour cream over fruit after packets are opened.

These packets may be prepared early in the day and heated on grill while meat, fish, or fowl is being barbecued.

Hawaiian Barbecued Pig

The pièce de résistance of the luau is the whole roasted pig cooked (*kalua puaa*) in an underground *imu*, a pit lined with hot, smooth, round lava stones. Red-hot stones from depths of the *imu* are placed in abdominal cavity of ready-to-cook pig, which is then wrapped in chicken wire and lowered into heated pit. Pig is covered with ti and banana leaves and surrounded by breadfruit, yams, bananas, and *laulaus* of fish and meat, all to be cooked in the *imu*. The entire contents of the oven are then covered with layers of ti and banana leaves. A blanket of burlap is spread over pit, which is then completely covered with earth, and food is left to steam. All this preparation is done 4–5 hours before the feast.

Just before guests are seated the pit is uncovered with great ceremony, and well-done pig and all other delicacies are removed.

Laulaus are ti leaf-wrapped packages of food, especially pork, salmon, or butterfish, with taro tops. If ti leaves are unavailable contents may be wrapped in several layers of large spinach leaves, Swiss chard, cabbage leaves, large grape leaves, or heavy-duty aluminum foil.

Hawaiian Kalua Puaa

SERVES 50

Ready Tray
1	bag ti leaves or corn husks
1	90–100-pound (live weight) pig, dressed
2	cups Kikkoman Hawaiian teriyaki sauce
2	cups ice-cream salt
1/2	pound fresh ginger root, peeled and grated, crushed
6	cups boiling water
2	dozen banana leaves or 5 dozen grape leaves
1	cup salt

Dig hole in ground 3 feet in diameter and 2 feet deep. Place 3 bags dry firewood in bottom, and pile 2 dozen *imu* stones on top. Pour 1 pint kerosene over wood, light it, and allow wood to burn approximately 2 hours or until only live coals remain. Place ti leaves close to *imu*, to make pliable. Clean pig well inside and out, removing all hair and toe nails. Slit pig on belly side from end of ribs to base of tail. Make incisions at the throat and between forelegs and body. Dilute and blend the teriyaki sauce, ginger root, and ice-cream salt; rub pig with this mixture. Rub inside of pig, as well as each incision. Using tongs, remove hot stones from *imu*, and place one in each incision. Fill abdominal cavity with hottest stones. Tie forelegs and hind legs together with ti leaves. Level remaining rocks in *imu*, and place thick layer of banana leaves over them. Lay 4-foot square of chicken wire in center of pit, and lower the pig so that back rests on wire. Pour 2 cups boiling water over rocks in abdominal cavity. Draw wire together over pig, and place any sweet potatoes or *laulaus* around sides. Cover entire pit with thick layer of banana and ti leaves. Spread 12 burlap sacks over leaves, and cover with earth so that no steam escapes. Leave pig to roast 3 1/2 hours.

Special Barbecue Recipes

Scrape earth from bags. Fold bags out from center, being careful not to drop dirt in pit. Remove leaves. Dip hands in bucket of cold water, and remove sweet potatoes and *laulaus* from *imu*. Unfasten wire around pig, and remove stones from abdominal cavity and other incisions. Lift pig and wire out of *imu*, and place in large pan. Sprinkle with 4 cups boiling water and 1 cup salt, and cut meat into individual servings.

Luau Ribs

SERVES 4–6

Ready Tray
1	(13 1/2 ounce) can, crushed pineapple (1 2/3 cups)
1/4	cup molasses
1/4	cup Bahamia-formula mustard
1	teaspoon monosodium glutamate
3	tablespoons fresh lemon juice
4	tablespoons Kikkoman soy sauce
2	tablespoons Worcestershire sauce
	fresh-ground black pepper to taste
	salt to taste
4	pounds spareribs or loin back ribs, in whole strip

Combine all ingredients except salt and ribs in bowl, and set aside. Salt ribs, and place, bone side down, on grill 5 inches from slow hot coals. Watch heat, as ribs tend to dry out and char when cooked too fast. Grill 20 minutes, turn meaty side down, and grill 10 minutes until browned. Turn meaty side up, and brush with pineapple glaze; cook 30–45 minutes until meat is tender (loin back ribs take longer cooking time). Slide piece of foil under thinner end of ribs if they are done before thicker end, and continue cooking.

Chinese-Hawaiian Barbecued Pork

SERVES 8–10

Ready Tray
1	4-pound center-cut pork loin, boned
1	recipe *Soy Marinade* or 1 recipe *Pineapple Marinade*

Place meat in large shallow dish. Pour marinade over pork; let stand 4 hours at room temperature, turning several times, or refrigerate overnight. Lift meat from marinade, and place on spit. Set spit in position over hot coals, and start rotisserie. Roast, brushing often with marinade, 1 1/4 hours, or until meat thermometer registers 185° F. and meat is tender and richly glazed. Slice thin.

Soy Marinade

Ready Tray
1	cup Kikkoman soy sauce
1/2	cup dry sherry
3	tablespoons honey
2	cloves garlic, chopped fine
1/2	teaspoon black pepper

Combine all ingredients in small bowl.

Pineapple Marinade

Ready Tray
1	cup unsweetened pineapple juice
1/2	cup Kikkoman Hawaiian teriyaki sauce
1/2	cup dry sherry
2	cloves garlic, chopped fine
2	tablespoons light or dark brown sugar

Combine all ingredients in small bowl, and pour over meat.

Roast Pork Fijian

SERVES 8–10

Ready Tray
1	8-pound center cut pork loin
1	tablespoon coarse salt
2	tablespoons fine-chopped garlic
2	teaspoons leaf thyme, crumbled
1/2	cup wine vinegar
1/4	cup olive oil
1/2	teaspoon Tabasco

Make cuts near ribs of pork loin; place meat in large shallow dish. Combine salt, garlic, thyme, vinegar, oil, and Tabasco in cup, and brush over pork thoroughly. Chill in refrigerator 24 hours. Place pork on spit. If using meat thermometer, center point in end of roast, and insert without touching bone. Set spit in position over hot coals; start rotisserie. Roast about 4 hours, or until thermometer registers 185° F. and meat is tender. Carve into chops to serve.

Japanese-Hawaiian Sesame Pork

SERVES 6–8

Ready Tray
3	pork tenderloins
1/2	cup Kikkoman soy sauce
3	small green onions, chopped fine
2	large cloves garlic, chopped fine
1	teaspoon ground ginger
1/2	teaspoon fresh-ground black pepper
1/4	cup sesame seeds

Place pork in shallow dish. Combine soy sauce, onions, garlic, ginger, and pepper in cup: pour over pork; sprinkle with sesame seeds. Let stand at room temperature 2 hours, turning occasionally, so that marinade will penetrate meat thoroughly. Lift pork carefully from marinade, and place on grill about 5 inches above hot coals. Grill, turning several times and spooning marinade over top, 30 minutes, or until tender. Slice thin to serve.

If tenderloins are not available, ask butcher to bone 10-inch-long pork loin, then to cut it in three pieces.

Sin-Sul-Lo Barbecue

The *sin-sul-lo* is similar to a chafing dish, and food is cooked in it at the table. It is a metal bowl with a small hollow stem in the center that holds burning charcoal. The *sin-sul-lo* comes in several sizes, and food is prepared to fit particular size used. Small pieces of cooked meat, chicken, egg, vegetables *chen-ya* (vegetables dipped in flour and in egg and fried in fat until golden brown), nuts, and uncooked vegetables are simmered in meat broth in charcoal brazier. The brazier is usually placed on the table, and the individual bowls served from it, as with *Japanese-Hawaiian Sukiyaki*.

Korean-Hawaiian Beef Sin-Sul-Lo

SERVES 6–8

Ready Tray
1/2	pound round steak
3	teaspoons sugar
6	tablespoons Kikkoman soy sauce
2	cloves garlic, chopped fine
	pepper to taste
1 2/3	tablespoons sesame seeds, browned and ground
4	tablespoons sesame oil (part to be used for frying)
2	tablespoons pine nuts
4	tablespoons flour
1	egg, slightly beaten
1/4	pound beef liver
	boiling water
	salt to taste
1/4	pound small tender spinach with roots
3	large fresh mushrooms
2	eggs
3	turnips, peeled
1 1/2	cups salt water
1/3	cup walnuts
1/4	cup pistachio nuts, blanched

Cut 1/8 pound steak in 1 thin 3″ × 5″ slice. Marinate in 1 teaspoon sugar, 1 tablespoon soy sauce, 1/2 clove garlic, pepper to taste; 2 teaspoons sesame seed, and 1 teaspoon oil; set aside 15 minutes. Fry in small amount of oil until tender. Cut into thin strips 1 inch wide. Chop 1/8 pound steak very fine, and add 2 tablespoons soy sauce, 1 tablespoon sesame seeds, 1/2 clove garlic, 1 teaspoon oil, and pepper to taste; mix well. Roll into tiny balls, 1/4-inch in diameter, with pine nut in center of each. Roll in flour, then in beaten egg, and fry in small amount of oil until brown. Cut remaining steak into thin strips 2″ × 1/2″ and mix well with 3 tablespoons soy sauce, remaining sugar, sesame seeds, pepper to taste, 1 clove garlic, and 1/2 tablespoon oil. Place liver in boiling water, and boil 3 minutes. Remove membranes, and cut into thin strips 1/2 inch wide. Season with salt, roll in flour and in beaten egg, and fry in small amount of oil until tender. Remove spinach roots, but be careful not to separate leaves. Put spinach bunches into boiling water, and boil 3 minutes; remove, drain, and press out all water. Run skewer through root ends, placing 6 bunches on each skewer. Press bunches of spinach together, sprinkle lightly with salt, roll in flour and in beaten egg, and fry in small amount of oil. Cut in pieces 2″ × 1/2″. Slice mushrooms through caps and stems, and fry in small amount of oil. Separate 1 egg. Add speck of salt and 1/4 teaspoon flour each to yolk and white, and beat slightly. Fry yolk and white separately in heated oil in skillet until firm on both sides; remove and cut in strip 1/2-inch wide. Cover remaining egg with boiling water, and let stand 40 minutes in warm place. Remove shell, and cut three slices crosswise from center of egg. Boil turnips in salt water until tender; drain, reserving water. Cut turnips 1/4″ inch wide and 1/4″ thick. Place layer of turnips on bottom of *sin-sul-lo*, then layers of uncooked meat, spinach, cooked eggs, mushrooms, liver, and meat slice until *sin-sul-lo* is filled. Place tiny meat balls around center stem of *sin-sul-lo*. Decorate with three slices hard-cooked egg, walnuts, pine nuts, and pistachio nuts. Add reserved turnip water, cover *sin-sul-lo*, and fill center stem with burning charcoal, which may be heated over gas or electric burner until pieces start to burn; then pick up with tongs or chopsticks, and set in center of brazier. Cook 10–15 minutes, and serve from brazier on table.

Special Barbecue Recipes

Hibachi Barbecue

The hibachi, a portable charcoal cooker, is gaining more fans as its special virtues become better known. Besides its portability, which makes it useful indoors or out and for automobile, beach, and boat picnics, the hibachi is easy to use and is a very impressive instrument for cooking hot hors d'oeuvres and other foods. At a large party several should be burning at the same time, and guests can prepare their own specialties; shy people will have lost their reserve by the time that the party is over, for the informality of the small group around each hibachi brings out the hidden culinary abilities of many people.

Hibachi means "fire basin" in Japanese, but this type of cooking was probably first done in China. The hibachi doubled as a room heater and cooking stove. Even today a traditional Japanese trousseau may include a wardrobe of hibachis in a variety of materials, including mulberry, pagoda, and persimmon wood; porcelain; and bronze.

Indoors place hibachi under kitchen range hood, in fireplace, or on back porch or patio to start fire. After initial smoking has subsided, carry hibachi to cooking scene. It is a good idea to keep a window open when using hibachi inside without benefit of hood or fireplace. When party is over any live coals remaining should be dropped, one by one, into a bucket of cold water.

Choose quick-cooking foods for the hibachi. These appetizers are practical and in keeping with the spirit of informal entertaining.

If using bamboo rather than metal skewers, soak them in water several hours beforehand to prevent their charring during cooking period.

Yakitori Hibachi Chicken

SERVES 4–6

Ready Tray
- 1 cup sake or sherry
- 1 cup Kikkoman Hawaiian teriyaki sauce
- 3 tablespoons sugar
- 2 teaspoons fresh-ground black pepper
- 1 1/2 pounds raw chicken, boned, skinned, and cut in 1-inch cubes

Combine all ingredients except chicken in saucepan, and bring to boil. Marinate chicken in sauce 30 minutes, drain, reserving marinade, thread on metal or bamboo skewers, and broil over hot coals in hibachi, basting with marinade and turning until tender and golden brown on all sides.

Hibachi Scallops

MAKES ABOUT 30 PIECES

Ready Tray
- 1 pound fresh or frozen scallops
- 1/3 cup fresh lemon juice
- 3 tablespoons honey
- 3 tablespoons prepared mustard
- 2 tablespoons light oil
- 1 1/2 teaspoons curry powder
-   salt and pepper to taste
- 1/2 cup sesame seeds

Thaw scallops if frozen. Rinse well in cold water, pat dry with clean cloth, and cut into 3/4-inch cubes. Combine remaining ingredients, except sesame seeds, and marinate scallop cubes 1 hour. Drain, reserving marinade, roll scallops in sesame seeds, and thread on metal or bamboo skewers. Broil 4 inches from hot coals 5–6 minutes, basting with marinade sauce; turn, and broil 5–6 minutes longer, basting with marinade. Remove from skewers to hot platter, and serve with picks.

Hawaiian Orange-Blossom Shrimp–Sparerib Hibachi Barbecue

MAKES 16 APPETIZERS

Ready Tray
- 4 pounds lean spareribs, cut into 2" × 1" pieces
-   water
- 1 pound large cooked shrimp, shelled and cleaned
- 1 large green bell pepper, seeded and cut in 1-inch squares
- 8 small white onions, parboiled
- 8 whole, medium, fresh mushrooms
- 1 recipe *Orange-Blossom Sauce*

Cook spareribs in water to cover 30 minutes, drain, and arrange on hibachi grill, leaving space for shrimp skewers. Spear shrimp, green pepper, onions, and mushrooms alternately on 8 skewers. Place on hibachi grill, and brush generously with sauce. Brush ribs with sauce. Grill shrimp over hot coals 5 minutes, turning once. Grill spareribs 10–15 minutes, turning once. Baste shrimps and spareribs with sauce during cooking period.

Hibachi Teriyaki Steak Bits

SERVES 20

Ready Tray
- 3 pounds lean sirloin steak, 1 inch thick
- 2 cups Kikkoman soy sauce
- 3/4 cup sugar
- 1/2 cup sake, sherry, or bourbon
- 1 tablespoon grated ginger root
- 2 cloves garlic, chopped fine
- 1 1/2 teaspoons monosodium glutamate

Slice meat as thin as possible, and cut in 2" × 1" strips. Thread on bamboo skewers. Combine soy sauce, sugar, sake, ginger root, garlic, and monosodium glutamate in saucepan, and cook over very low flame until sugar is dissolved. Cool sauce thoroughly. Dip skewered meat into sauce, and lay skewers neatly on platter. Pour sauce over meat; then broil quickly on hibachi over hot coals, basting with sauce.

Skewers can be prepared well in advance and refrigerated. Leftover sauce may be bottled and refrigerated and used over and over again. Hamburgers marinated in this sauce are exotically different for teen-age parties. Serve on toasted buns with slices of raw Spanish onions.

Beef-Barbecue Sauce

MAKES 3 CUPS

Ready Tray
- 1 cup red dinner wine
- 1 cup beef consommé
- 1/4 cup wine vinegar
- 2 teaspoons mixed thyme, rosemary, and marjoram
- 1 large clove garlic, peeled and crushed
- 1/3 cup grated onion
- 2 teaspoons dry or prepared mustard
- 1/4 cup chili sauce or catsup
- 1 tablespoon brown sugar
- 1 teaspoon salt
- 1/2 teaspoon fresh-ground black pepper
- 2 tablespoons Kikkoman Hawaiian teriyaki sauce
- 1/2 cup light salad oil

Combine all ingredients in medium saucepan, and heat to blend flavors. Cool sauce before using as marinade, and heat again to use as basting sauce.

Seafood Soy Marinade

MAKES 1 CUP

Ready Tray
- 1/3 cup Kikkoman soy sauce
- 1/3 cup salad oil
- 1/3 cup sherry
- 1/2 teaspoon onion powder
- 1/4 teaspoon ground ginger
- 1/4 teaspoon monosodium glutamate
- 1/8 teaspoon garlic powder

Combine all ingredients.

This marinade is very good for scallops, uncooked shrimp, crab, or salmon.

Pork-Barbecue Sauce

MAKES 2 3/4 CUPS

Ready Tray
- 1 cup orange marmalade
- 1/4 cup prepared mustard
- 1/4 cup Worcestershire sauce
- 1 (6 ounce) can frozen pineapple-juice concentrate, thawed
- 1 cup water

Combine marmalade, mustard, Worcestershire sauce, and juice until smooth; stir in water until well blended.

Spicy Barbecue Sauce

MAKES 1 1/2 CUPS

Ready Tray
- 1/4 cup sugar
- 2 tablespoons cornstarch
- 1/2 teaspoon ground allspice
- 1/2 teaspoon ground cloves
- 1 cup Kikkoman soy sauce
- 4 tablespoons white wine
- 4 tablespoons butter

Combine sugar, cornstarch, allspice, and cloves in saucepan. Stir in soy sauce and wine, and cook over medium heat, stirring constantly, until thickened; boil 3 minutes. Add butter, and stir until blended.

This sauce is excellent for all meats, fish, or poultry.

Special Barbecue Recipes

Famous Kikkoman Barbecue Sauce

MAKES 3 CUPS

Ready Tray
- 1 cup Kikkoman Hawaiian teriyaki sauce
- 1 cup white wine
- 2 cloves garlic, chopped fine
- 1/4 cup salad oil
- 1 cup fine-chopped onions
- 1 teaspoon powdered ginger

Combine all ingredients.

Lemon–Soy Steak Sauce

MAKES 1 1/3 CUPS

Ready Tray
- 1 cup Kikkoman soy sauce
- 2 large cloves garlic, chopped fine
- 2 tablespoons prepared mustard
- 1 tablespoon chili powder
- 1/2 cup fresh-squeezed lemon juice, strained
- 1/4 cup salad oil

Blend all ingredients well.

Garnishes, Chutneys, Pickles, Fruits, and Vegetables

8

GARNISHES, CHUTNEYS, PICKLES, FRUITS, AND VEGETABLES

Baked Bananas

SERVES 6

Ready Tray
6   medium cooking or eating bananas, peeled and halved lengthwise
1/2   cup orange sections
1/3   cup brown sugar
2   tablespoons fresh lemon juice
2   tablespoons fresh orange juice

Place bananas in baking dish. Remove membrane from orange sections, and arrange on top of bananas. Sprinkle with sugar. Add lemon and orange juice, and bake, uncovered, at 325° F. 45 minutes. Serve hot or cold.

These bananas are excellent with roast pork.

Honeyed Bananas

Ready Tray
6   medium, firm bananas, peeled
1/3   cup lemon juice
2   tablespoons butter
1/4   cup honey

Dip bananas in lemon juice. Melt butter in skillet, and stir in honey. Add bananas, and cook over low heat, turning gently, until hot and glazed.

Do not overcook bananas. These bananas are very good with any pork dish.

Fried Bananas

SERVES 4

Ready Tray
2   firm medium bananas, peeled and sliced 1 inch thick
1/4   cup light rum
1   egg
1/3   cup bread crumbs
1/4   cup light cooking oil

Sprinkle bananas with rum, and set aside. Beat egg. Dip bananas in egg, roll in bread crumbs, and fry in hot oil until golden on both sides.

Serve hot with chicken, ham, curry, or any island meal for that added something special.

Green-Banana Puree

SERVES 4

Ready Tray
4   firm large green bananas, peeled
1   tablespoon fresh lemon juice
2   cups boiling water

Scrape bananas all over. Rub with lemon juice, and cook in boiling water until tender. Drain, mash, and serve in mound on hot serving platter.

This puree is a good accompaniment for meat dishes.

157

Crystallized Flowers

Ready Tray
1/2 cup rose water
6 teaspoons powdered gum arabic
2 teaspoons castor or fine sugar
    violets, rosebuds, japonica flowers, and geraniums

In top of double boiler put rose water, gum arabic, and sugar; dissolve over medium heat. Remove double boiler from heat, leaving top portion in hot water. Dip the selected fresh blooms in sugar mixture, and allow to drip a little; then dip in dry sugar, shaking off excess. More sugar may be added, if necessary. Dry on grease-proof paper on rack 3 days.

These flowers keep very well in airtight containers and are used as garnish for foods, salads, or beverages.

Kim Chee

Korean-Hawaiians, who like their food very highly spiced, consider pickled raw vegetables indispensable to almost any meal. Their preparation is generally entrusted to the oldest woman of the household, on the assumption that only the judgment that comes with age can produce the fiery blending of ingredients that Koreans prize.

Such vegetables as cucumbers, Chinese cabbage, cauliflower, celery, onions, turnips, and carrots, alone or in any combination, are favorites.

Fresh ginger root, dried fish, shellfish, nuts, and fruits are also added—and always seasoned with the hot red peppers that appears on or with almost all Korean food.

Korean-Hawaiian Pickled Cabbage

MAKES 1 QUART

Ready Tray
2 pounds celery cabbage
1/2 cup coarse salt
1 quart water
1 1/2 tablespoons hot red peppers
1 clove garlic, minced
1 teaspoon fresh ginger, chopped fine
1 tablespoon sugar
2 scallions, chopped fine

Wash cabbage, and cut into 1 1/2-inch pieces. Sprinkle with salt. Add water, and let stand overnight. When cabbage is limp, wilted, but not soft, tear it. Rinse in cold water, and drain. Make paste from remaining ingredients, and rub into cabbage pieces. Pack into 1-quart mason jar, and cover. Place in plastic bag to prevent odors from permeating other foods, and refrigerate 4–5 days.

Celery cabbage is available in major food markets or Oriental stores. Pickled cabbage, or *kim chee*, may also be purchased in jars and is a very popular garnish and condiment.

Marrons and Apricots

SERVES 4–6

Ready Tray
4 fresh apricots, pitted and halved
2 tablespoons honey
8 marrons glacés, bottled in syrup

Brush apricot halves with honey. Butter baking dish. Place apricots in baking dish, cut sides up, and broil 1 minute. Remove from broiler, and top each apricot half with 1 marron; broil 1 more minute.

Serve hot or cold with any kind of game bird.

Orange-Blossom Sauce

MAKES 1 1/2 CUPS

Ready Tray
1 6 ounce can frozen orange-juice concentrate, thawed
1/4 cup prepared mustard
1/3 cup honey
1 tablespoon Kikkoman Hawaiian teriyaki sauce
1 small clove garlic, crushed
1 teaspoon fine-chopped fresh ginger
    root, or ground ginger

Combine thoroughly orange juice, mustard, honey, teriyaki sauce, garlic, and ginger in small bowl, and brush over foods being barbecued on hibachi.

Apricot Sauce

MAKES 2/3 CUP

Ready Tray
1/2 cup apricot preserves
1/2 cup 7-Up or Like
2 tablespoons brown sugar
1 teaspoon vinegar

Combine all ingredients in saucepan, and bring to boil, stirring until sugar is dissolved. Reduce heat, and simmer 10 minutes, or to consistency of syrup.

Sautéed Apples

Ready Tray
4 medium cooking apples, peeled, cored, sliced 1 inch thick
6 tablespoons butter
1 tablespoon sugar

Garnishes, Chutneys, Pickles, Fruits, and Vegetables

Simmer apple rounds in butter in covered frying pan until tender and lightly browned on both sides. Sprinkle with sugar.

Honeyed Peaches

SERVES 8–12

Ready Tray
- 12 canned peach halves, drained
- 1/4 cup honey
- 1 1/2 tablespoons Kikkoman soy sauce
- 1 tablespoon butter

Simmer peaches in saucepan with honey, soy sauce, and butter 5 minutes, or until well coated. Lift from sauce, arrange in dish, and pour remaining sauce over.

These peaches are excellent to dress up turkey platter. Pear and apricot halves and pineapple slices can also be used.

Glazed Pineapple Rings

SERVES 6–8

Ready Tray
- 6–8 fresh pineapple rings
- 1/4 cup butter
- 1/4 cup brown sugar
- juice of 2 limes or 1 lemon

Glaze pineapple rings in butter and sugar in frying pan until both sides are slightly golden brown. Lift onto hot platter; add juice to pan, and cook to syrup. Pour over rings.

Rings are good with meat.

Spiced Pineapple Slices

SERVES 8

Ready Tray
- 1 (1 pound 14 ounce) can pineapple slices with syrup
- 2/3 cup vinegar
- 1 cup sugar
- 1/8 teaspoon salt
- 8 whole cloves
- 1 (3 inch) stick cinnamon

Combine pineapple syrup with vinegar, sugar, salt, cloves, and cinnamon in saucepan, and simmer 10 minutes. Remove from heat, and add pineapple slices. Cover, and chill overnight in refrigerator before using.

This dish is wonderful with meats and in salads.

Pineapple Sticks

SERVES 4–6

Ready Tray
- 1 sugar-ripe pineapple
- 1/4 cup sugar
- 1/2 cup flour
- 1 recipe *Fritter Batter*
- 1 cup fine bread crumbs
- shortening

Peel and core pineapple, and cut in sticks $3'' \times 1/2'' \times 1/2''$. Place in bowl, and sprinkle with sugar, let stand until bowl sweats. Roll pineapple sticks in flour, then in batter, and finally lightly in bread crumbs. Fry in deep hot shortening until crisp.

Serve with chicken or pork or for dessert.

Meat-Stuffed Prunes Australian

SERVES 6

Ready Tray
- 24 large prunes
- water
- 6 tablespoons shortening
- 1 medium onion, chopped fine
- 1/2 pound ground beef
- 1/2 cup canned crushed pineapple, drained
- 4 tablespoons fresh lemon juice
- 3 tablespoons brown sugar
- 3 medium onions, sliced thin
- 1 cup canned tomato sauce
- 4 gingersnaps, crushed
- salt and fresh-ground black pepper to taste

Soak prunes overnight in water to cover. Drain. Remove pits by cutting prunes lengthwise carefully. Melt 2 tablespoons shortening in skillet. Sauté chopped onion 5 minutes, stirring constantly. Add beef, pineapple, 1 tablespoon lemon juice, and 1 tablespoon brown sugar. Cook over low heat 10 minutes, stirring frequently. Stuff prunes with mixture. Melt remaining shortening in saucepan. Sauté sliced onions 10 minutes, stirring frequently. Add tomato sauce, gingersnaps, salt, pepper, remaining lemon juice, and remaining sugar. Add prunes carefully, open sides up. Cover, and cook over low heat 25 minutes. Correct seasoning. Sauce should be both sweet and sour.

Soaking of prunes may be omitted if presoaked variety is used. Serve prunes as accompaniment to meat or poultry dishes or as main course with potatoes.

Grilled Cheese Tomatoes

SERVES 4

Ready Tray
- 2 large tomatoes, halved
- 4 tablespoons butter
- 3 shallots, chopped fine
- 3 tablespoons fine bread crumbs
- 1 tablespoon grated Parmesan cheese
- 1/8 teaspoon garlic powder
- 1/8 teaspoon salt
- 4 tablespoons grated Swiss cheese

Shake seeds from tomatoes. Place tomatoes in greased baking dish. Dot with half the butter. Place under broiler, until they start to brown. Sauté shallots in remaining butter. Add bread crumbs, Parmesan cheese, garlic powder, and salt. Stir until blended. Remove tomatoes from broiler, and spoon shallot mixture evenly over. Top each tomato with 1 tablespoon Swiss cheese; replace under broiler 1 minute, and serve very hot.

Serve with steak or any plain meat dish.

Water Chestnuts

SERVES 4–6

Ready Tray
- 1 1/2 cups sliced fresh water chestnuts
- 1/3 cup sugar
- 1 teaspoon salt
- 1/2 teaspoon dried dill weed
- 1/2 cup white vinegar
- 1/4 cup water

Put water chestnuts in casserole. Combine remaining ingredients in saucepan and bring to boil; remove from heat, pour over chestnuts, cover, and refrigerate 5 hours before serving.

Water chestnuts remain very crisp and crunchy even after cooking, and their delicate flavor enhances salads, vegetables, soups, stews, and casseroles.

Apricot Chutney

MAKES 4 PINTS

Ready Tray
- 1/4 pound dried apricots, chopped coarse
- 1 cup dry red wine
- 1/4 cup pitted dates, chopped coarse
- 1/2 pound fresh cranberries
- 1/4 cup thin-sliced onion
- 1 large clove garlic, chopped fine
- 1/4 cup sliced preserved ginger
- 1/4 teaspoon ground ginger
- 1/2 hot red pepper, chopped fine
- 1/2 teaspoon mustard seed
- 1 teaspoon Kikkoman soy sauce
- 1/4 cup honey
- 1/2 cup dark-brown sugar
- 1/4 cup cider vinegar

Combine all ingredients, and set aside 1 hour. Bring mixture to boil, reduce heat, and simmer 45 minutes, stirring frequently until thick. Pour into hot sterilized jars, and seal.

South Seas Chutney

MAKES 6 PINTS

Ready Tray
- 1 1/2 teaspoons salt
- 3 fresh pineapples, peeled, cored, and shredded
- 1 1/2 pounds fresh plums, peeled, pitted, and chopped
- 3 sweet peppers, freed of pith and seeds and chopped
- 1/4 pound preserved ginger, chopped
- 3 cloves garlic, chopped fine
- 1 chili pepper, chopped fine
- 3 tablespoons sugar
- 1 tablespoon malt vinegar
- 2 cups boiling water

Sprinkle salt over pineapples, and let stand overnight. Combine plums, peppers, and ginger thoroughly. In saucepan combine garlic, chili pepper, sugar, vinegar, and boiling water. Bring mixture to boil, and cook 5 minutes. Add pineapple mixture, and simmer 1 hour, or until thick, stirring frequently. Pour into hot sterilized jars, and seal.

Samoan Chutney

MAKES 4 PINTS

Ready Tray
- 1 cup tarragon vinegar
- 1 cup cider vinegar
- 3 cups sugar
- 1/4 cup fresh ginger root, chopped fine or ground
- 6 cups diced, peeled, firm peaches
- 2 cloves garlic, peeled and chopped fine
- 1 tablespoon salt
- 1/2 pound currants

Cook vinegar and sugar to clear syrup in large kettle. Add ginger root, and cook 20 minutes. Add remaining ingredients, and simmer, covered, 3 hours, stirring occasionally. Pour into hot sterilized jars, and seal.

An asbestos pad placed under kettle helps to prevent scorching; otherwise watch kettle very carefully.

Garnishes, Chutneys, Pickles, Fruits, and Vegetables

Tahitian Mango Chutney

Ready Tray
- 5 pounds green mangoes, peeled and sliced thin
- 2 large onions, chopped fine
- 2 green bell peppers, chopped fine
- 4 cloves garlic, chopped fine
- 1 cup preserved ginger, chopped fine
- 1 cup seedless raisins, chopped fine
- 1 cup ripe papaya, chopped fine
- 1 large fresh lime, seeded and chopped fine
- 1/2 cup pitted dates, chopped fine
- 4 cups vinegar
- 3 cups brown sugar
- 1 tablespoon ground cinnamon
- 2 teaspoons salt
- 1 teaspoon allspice
- 1 teaspoon ground cloves
- 1/2 teaspoon cayenne
- 6 tamarind pods, soaked in water and seeded

Combine all ingredients in large enamel kettle, and stir thoroughly. Bring to boil, reduce heat, and simmer until fruit is tender. Correct seasoning, adding more brown sugar if desired. Pack in hot sterilized jars, and seal.

Tamarind is the fruit of a tropical tree; its soft, acid pulp is used in preserves and chutneys and in a syrup that is used as a flavoring agent in certain drinks. The manager of any gourmet section of large markets can get it for you.

Sweet Guava Pickles

MAKES 3 PINTS

Ready Tray
- 3 pounds large guava shells
- 1 tablespoon whole allspice
- 4 sticks cinnamon
- 30 whole cloves
- 1/3 cup sliced preserved ginger or 3 pieces ginger root, sliced thin
- 4 cups light-brown sugar
- 1 cup wine vinegar

Remove blossom ends from guava shells, halve, and scoop out seeds. Tie spices in cheesecloth bag. Combine all ingredients, and set aside 4 hours. Boil until fruit is tender and syrup has thickened. Seal while hot in hot sterilized jars.

Papaya Pickles

MAKES 1 PINT

Ready Tray
- 1 large, mature, but still green papaya
- 1 tablespoon mixed pickling spices
- 1 cup sugar
- 1/2 cup cider vinegar
- 1/2 cup water
- 1 teaspoon salt
- 1 stick cinnamon
- 1 small, dried, hot chili pepper
- 1 large clove garlic, crushed

Peel papaya, discard seeds, and cut fruit into small pieces. Tie pickling spices in cheesecloth bag. In medium saucepan place sugar, vinegar, water, salt, cinnamon, chili pepper, garlic, and pickling spices. Bring to boil, and boil 5 minutes. Add papaya, and simmer slowly 15 minutes, or until fruit is transparent. Discard pickling spices and garlic, and strain juice into another saucepan. Put fruit with cinnamon and pepper into hot sterilized jar. Simmer syrup until slightly thickened, 5 minutes; pour over fruit, and seal jar.

For sharper pickles, substitute cider vinegar for 1/4 cup water. These pickles are almost like chutney in character; they can be served with curry, broiled chicken, or turkey.

Green-Papaya Pickles

MAKES 2 QUARTS

Ready Tray
- 1 3-pound green papaya
- 1 large carrot
- 1 medium white radish
- 2 1/2 teaspoons salt
- 1 1/2 teaspoons fine-chopped fresh or preserved ginger root
- 3 cloves garlic, chopped fine
- 2 tablespoons brown sugar
- 3/4 cup vinegar

Peel papaya, and shred flesh. Peel carrots and radish, and shred very fine. Add salt, and combine thoroughly. Allow mixture to stand 1 day or overnight. Press out excess liquid, and rinse several times in cold water. Combine ginger, garlic, sugar, and vinegar, and set aside 1 hour. Strain, and add to papaya mixture. Season with more salt or sugar, if necessary. Place in large jar or 2 1-quart jars, cover, and refrigerate 2–3 days before serving.

Fresh-Pineapple Pickles

MAKES 3 PINTS

Ready Tray
- 1 fresh pineapple
- 2 cups sugar
- 2 cups water
-   dash salt
- 1 cup vinegar
- 1 stick cinnamon
- 3 whole cloves

Peel pineapple, and slice crosswise 1 inch thick. Remove core, and cut into sections about 1 inch wide. Combine sugar and water in saucepan; add pineapple pieces, and boil 10 minutes. Remove pineapple. To syrup add vinegar, spices, and salt. Boil until syrup is thick. Add pineapple to syrup, boil 5 minutes, pour into hot sterilized jars, and seal.

Sweet Pickled Radishes

MAKES 2 QUARTS

Ready Tray
- 2 pounds *daikon*
- 1 cup sugar
- 1/4 cup white vinegar
- 1 cup water
- 3 tablespoons salt
- 3 drops yellow food coloring

Wash *daikon*, peel, and slice very thin. Combine remaining ingredients in saucepan, and bring to boil. Place *daikon* slices in 2-quart jar or 2 1-quart jars, and pour hot liquid over. Cool to room temperature, and cover. Refrigerate at least 3 days before serving.

Daikon is the white Japanese radish, available in most supermarkets or Oriental grocery stores.

Avocados

Avocados were introduced into Hawaii in 1825 and have been popular ever since. They have high protein content and in some countries are commonly used as a substitute for meat. They are also rich in unsaturated fatty acids. The basic preparations for avocados are as follows. Halve ripe avocados lengthwise, and twist halves in opposite directions. Strike seed sharply with knife, twist, and remove. To slice or cube, hold avocado half, cut side down, in palm of hand. Begin at top, and peel away skin. Place avocado on cutting board, and slice crosswise or lengthwise, or cube. Or use a melon-ball cutter to remove avocado pulp from cut halves. Avocado balls are especially nice in fresh-fruit compotes, fruit cocktails, and soups.

Avocados will darken rather quickly after cutting unless they are sprinkled with fresh lime or lemon juice before being stored in refrigerator. Wrap in foil or wax paper, and use within a day or so.

Avocado Crème

SERVES 4

Ready Tray
-   juice of 1 medium lemon
- 2 ripe avocados, peeled, seeded, and sliced thin
- 3 tablespoons sugar
- 2 jiggers rum, brandy, or vodka

Put lemon juice in blender. Add avocados and sugar, and blend until smooth. Add liquor, and blend quickly. Pour into sherbet dishes, and chill thoroughly before serving.

Cherimoya

The *cherimoya* is a true aristocrat among fruits and is prized for its delicate flavor and texture. It is sometimes called the "sherbet fruit" because of its natural sherbety texture when chilled. The fruit has a piquant flavor resembling that of a combination of fresh pineapple, strawberries, and bananas, but it also has a unique quality of its own.

This tropical fruit usually comes in a heart-shaped oval with green skin. The skin is rather tough and is indented with what look like very closely set petals. It is a very interesting addition to a fruit bowl, a conversation piece. The *cherimoya* is available from November to May, and the largest fruits are the best. They should be eaten very soon after they become soft, for the fullest flavor.

Halve lengthwise, or quarter, depending on serving size. Serve on pretty plate or on leaf with flower garnish; no accompaniment is needed. The meat may also be scooped out and the seeds removed; meat is then used in blender drinks, sherbet recipes, or with other fruits in cocktails or salads.

Coconuts

Some people say that the coconut originated in the Andes mountains and was carried to the South Seas. The fruit was known as the "Indian nut"; today it is called "coconut," probably because the Spanish and Portuguese likened its inner-shell "face" to a "coco" or bogeyman.

Dried and with the fibrous outer skin removed, the coconut is called "copra" and is used in making industrial oils and soap.

Purified and deodorized coconut oil has a firm consistency at ordinary temperatures and is called "cocoa butter." It is fatty, pure, odorless, taste-

Garnishes, Chutneys, Pickles, Fruits, and Vegetables

less, and very digestible. It is used in diets by people who cannot assimilate butter, and is especially found in vegetarian cooking.

The simplest way to open a coconut is to make an imaginary line around the middle, take a hammer, and tap around line back to where you began. The coconut will split in two when you reach the original point of tapping. Open it over a bowl to catch the milk. Or remove coconut milk by puncturing two of the soft eyes and draining off liquid. Place coconuts in shallow pan, and place in preheated 300° F. oven 45 minutes. If they do not crack, tap lightly with hammer. Remove meat from shell with small spatula or knife, and peel off brown rind. Prepare as desired.

To grate fresh coconut, use hand grater, or cube, and then grate in blender. Coconut keeps well 3–4 days in refrigerator; to keep longer place in airtight containers, and freeze. It will keep indefinitely.

Sauté 1 cup flaked or packaged coconut in 1 tablespoon melted butter or margarine in skillet over medium heat, stirring until golden. To toast coconut, spread thin in shallow pan, and brown in 350° F. oven 8–10 minutes.

To tint coconut, put 1 teaspoon milk or water and a few drops of food coloring or 1 1/2 teaspoons grated orange, lemon, or lime rind into bowl or jar. Add 1 1/3 cups flaked or 1 cup grated coconut, and toss with fork or shake until color is evenly distributed. For rainbow effect, divide coconut in 3 parts, and tint each a different color; then toss together.

To make coconut milk for use in curry recipes, in puddings, or with vegetables, combine in 1-quart saucepan 1 1/3 cups flaked coconut and 1 1/3 cups milk. Simmer, stirring occasionally, until mixture foams up. Strain through very fine strainer or double thickness of cheesecloth until all liquid has been pressed out. Pulp may be mixed with a little sugar and toasted in oven to serve with curry or sprinkle on desserts.

After the coconut meat has been removed from shells, smooth edges, and use shells for individual serving dishes or as cups for tropical drinks. Little bases of florist's clay will keep them from tipping.

Samoan Coconut Milk or Cream

Choose mature coconuts whose flesh is firm but not dry. The more mature the coconut, the smaller the quantity of liquid obtained.

Pierce eyes of coconuts, and drain liquid from inside. Crack coconut, and grate meat, or grind it in meat grinder. Place 1 cup grated coconut in four thicknesses of cheesecloth, or a tea towel with a loose weave. Squeeze out as much liquid as possible. Squeeze remaining coconut 1 cup at a time. The pulp may be discarded or toasted for use in curry dishes or sprinkling over prepared foods before or after cooking.

Coconut milk is used as a sauce in cooking and may have sea water or salted water added if it is to be used with vegetables. Onions and lime juice are added to coconut milk to prepare *miti*, a sauce in which cooked breadfruit and other cooked foods like fish and meat are dipped before being eaten. Coconut milk is seasoned with lime leaves or lime or lemon juice before it is mixed with banana poi or mashed ripe papaya.

A substitute for fresh coconut milk may be prepared by soaking 1 1/2 cups packaged coconut in 1 cup milk or coffee cream 30 minutes, then simmering 10 minutes, cooling, straining through several thicknesses of cheesecloth, and squeezing out as much liquid as possible.

Coconut Pudding Hawaiian

SERVES 4

Ready Tray
- 3 tablespoons sugar
- 1 1/2 tablespoons arrowroot
- 2 cups coconut milk
- 1/4 teaspoon salt

Combine sugar and cornstarch, add 1/2 cup coconut milk, and blend well. Add salt. Heat remaining milk, but do not allow to boil. Add cornstarch mixture, stir until thickened, pour into 8-inch square baking dish, and chill until firm. Cut into squares and serve.

This dish is called *haupia* and is truly a classic of all the islands of the South Pacific and Hawaii; it is served at all luaus and *tamaaras* (Tahitian luaus).

Tropical Figs

SERVES 4

Ready Tray
- 8 fresh figs, peeled and halved
- 1/4 cup light rum
- 3 tablespoons sugar
  juice of 1 lime
  lemon sherbet
  fresh-grated coconut
  sprigs fresh mint

Combine figs, rum, sugar, and lime juice, and chill. Spoon mixture into 4 sherbet dishes, and top each with scoop of sherbet. Sprinkle with coconut, and garnish with mint.

Figs are highly perishable and should be eaten soon after picking or purchase. They are available from May to September in various areas. They should be firm with a little "give"; and the soft and mushy ones are good for stewing or in sauces.

Kiwi Fruit

Kiwi fruit comes from New Zealand and is commonly known as the "Chinese gooseberry." Its unappetizing appearance conceals a unique and delicious fruit. After the fuzzy surface is brushed off and the fruit is peeled, there is meat of a beautiful gooseberry-green color and a flavor both sweet and unusual.

Kiwi fruit is available from June to December. It should be well chilled before peeling, then sliced, quartered, or halved.

Crosswise slices arranged in a pattern are an excellent garnish for cream pies, puddings, and mousses. Alternate slices of kiwi fruit with bananas and strawberries for a colorful fruit appetizer or salad. Or serve sliced as breakfast fruit with a little cream or fresh lime or lemon juice and a sprinkling of sugar.

Litchi Nuts

The litchi nut is a native of China, where the trees are said to bear for 1,000 years. It resembles an oversized peeled grape. When served fresh this fruit does not look like a nut, but when dried and matured it becomes like a nut and therefore is called "litchi nut."

Litchi nuts may be purchased in cans, but fresh ones are best. They are like strawberries in size and shape, but the skin is reddish brown and quite hard, which makes it possible to keep them 2–3 weeks after picking, without loss in flavor. Fresh litchi nuts are available from late May to early August; they are expensive but well worth the price.

Serve as is for eating out of hand—most interesting to peel.

Peel, chill, and serve in small dishes garnished with sprigs of mint. A little crème de menthe or other liqueur poured over the top adds sophistication. Litchi nuts combine well with pineapples, papayas, bananas, and mangoes.

Mangoes

In Hawaii *kamaainas* (old-timers) used to measure time in "mango seasons," rather than in months or years. Mangoes were first cultivated at least 4,000 years ago. They are popular throughout the South Pacific and are used both ripe and green in various ways.

They are available from January through late August and travel very well. Some are oval and flat; others are round. Be sure that you permit mangoes to ripen fully before serving, for under-ripe mangoes may have a very disappointing flavor. Chill before peeling, and always peel from end of fruit. The seed is long and flat, and the meat clings to it, so slice fruit away from seed beginning at top of mango and cutting lengthwise past seed.

Mangoes may be used in all fruit recipes: shortcakes, sherbets, cobblers, and pies.

Mango Mousse

SERVES 8

Ready Tray
- 8 medium, ripe but firm mangoes
- water
- 1 1/2 cups heavy cream, whipped
- 1/4 cup confectioner's sugar
- shaved chocolate

Wash mangoes; cut in small pieces without peeling. Simmer in small amount of water 25 minutes, or until tender. Force through fine sieve, and cool. Fold in whipped cream, and add sugar. Put into sherbet glasses or glass serving dish, and garnish with chocolate. Chill well before serving.

Papayas

Papayas have been a mainstay in the diet of tropical countries for many centuries and are available in most markets the year around. They are also known as "tree melons." Their origin is obscure. The papaya is one of the most healthful of all fruits, high in Vitamins A and C and low in calories. In its green stage it also contains large amounts of papain, the base for all meat tenderizers. It is common practice to wrap tough meats in papaya leaves or to rub meat with papaya juice to tenderize it. Papaya juice is also used in preparation of various remedies and beauty facials. The natives of the South Pacific chew the seeds for health's sake.

Garnishes, Chutneys, Pickles, Fruits, and Vegetables

The papaya resembles the muskmelon, its color fresh deep yellow to salmon; its meat is slightly sweet, and the seeds are the size of peas. If the fruit "gives" to gentle pressure between the palms of the hands, it is ready to eat and may be refrigerated for a week or two.

Papaya is a popular breakfast food in the tropics. The common way to eat it is to halve it, remove seeds (to use in salad dressing), sprinkle fruit with fresh lime or lemon juice, and serve for breakfast or dessert. Papayas can be peeled, sliced, and served with other fruits in salad. Halved papayas filled with shrimp and garnished with lemon are an excellent luncheon salad. *Shrimp Curry Polynesian* in peeled papaya shells, heated and served on beds of rice, is another excellent dish. A little green papaya added to boiling chicken not only tenderizes it but also adds a pleasant sweetness.

Papaya and Crabmeat Supreme

SERVES 2

Ready Tray
1	(6 1/2 ounce) can crabmeat, flaked
2/3	cup thin-sliced celery
2	fresh papayas, chilled
	juice of 1/2 lime
1/2	cup toasted slivered almonds
	lime wedges

Combine crabmeat and celery, and chill. Halve papayas, and remove seeds. Peel, and place on individual shells or salad plates. Sprinkle crabmeat mixture with lime juice, add almonds, and pile into papaya halves; garnish with lime wedges.

Asparagus Australian

SERVES 4

Ready Tray
2	tablespoons butter
1/4	cup water
1/2	teaspoon seasoned salt
1/4	teaspoon monosodium glutamate
1	teaspoon Worcestershire sauce
1 1/2	pounds fresh asparagus, cut in 1-inch lengths
	sour cream

Melt butter in skillet; add water, salt, monosodium glutamate, Worcestershire sauce, and bring to boil. Add asparagus, toss lightly, cover, and cook over medium heat 5 minutes. Serve with sour cream on top.

Green Beans South Pacific

SERVES 4–6

Ready Tray
1	medium onion, chopped fine
1	large clove garlic, chopped fine
2	teaspoons grated lemon rind
1/2	teaspoon fine-chopped green chili pepper
1	medium tomato, peeled and chopped
2	tablespoons light oil
1	(1 pound) can French-style green beans, drained
	salt to taste
1	teaspoon sugar
1	bay leaf
1	cup coconut milk

Pound onion, garlic, lemon rind, chili pepper, and tomato to paste. Sauté mixture in oil 3 minutes, stirring constantly. Add beans, salt, sugar, bay leaf, and coconut milk; cover loosely, bring to boil, reduce heat, and simmer 15 minutes.

Korean-Hawaiian Bean Sprouts

SERVES 6

Ready Tray
4	cups bean sprouts
	boiling water
2	small green onions, sliced 1/2 inch thick
2	tablespoons Kikkoman soy sauce
2	tablespoons roasted sesame seeds
2	tablespoons salad oil
	red pepper and salt to taste

Wash bean sprouts, put in large saucepan, cover with boiling water, and cook 3 minutes; drain. Add onions, soy sauce, sesame seeds, and oil to bean sprouts, and cook 3 minutes until flavors are absorbed. Sprinkle with pepper and salt, toss, and serve.

Breadfruit

The breadfruit has all the qualities of wheat bread and is an important article of food among the islanders of the Pacific. It is sliced and baked or toasted over hot coals; it can be baked whole in an *imu* until outside skin acquires a dark color for a very nutritious food. Its taste recalls that of fresh-baked bread with a slight hint of artichoke or Jerusalem artichoke. To bake, remove core and stem, place 1 tablespoon butter and 1 tablespoon sugar in cavity, replace stem, and bake until tender.

Breadfruit may also be boiled and served with butter, salt, and pepper. Breadfruit chips, made in the same way as potato chips are made, are very good appetizers. To steam: peel, stem, and core. Halve or quarter, and steam, covered, 2 hours. Serve with butter, salt, and pepper. Breadfruit poi is made by the same method as is poi from taro roots.

Breadfruit is extremely important in the Samoan diet. It is picked while still green; the skin is scraped off with a shell. The flesh is baked, with or without wrapping, in the *imu* or in the embers of an open fire.

Japanese-Hawaiian Stuffed Eggplant

SERVES 4

Ready Tray
2	medium eggplants or 4 small Japanese eggplants
1 2/3	cups cooked beef, pork, or shrimp, chopped fine
1/2	cup fine-chopped onion
1	tablespoon Kikkoman soy sauce
	salt and pepper to taste
	deep fat

Peel eggplants, and cut 1 inch from top, reserving tops. Carefully hollow out eggplants for filling. Combine meat with remaining ingredients except fat, mix well, and stuff eggplants; replace tops, and tie with raffia or string, or secure with toothpicks. Heat enough fat in large kettle to cover eggplants. Cook eggplants until they rise to the top and are well browned on all sides. Drain, and serve very hot, sliced.

Japanese eggplant is excellent for tempura. Slice 1/2 inch thick, or cut in narrow strips, unpeeled. Dip in batter, and fry quickly until golden brown.

Japanese eggplant is a miniature version of ordinary eggplant, with the same flavor, texture, and cooking qualities. The best Japanese eggplant is 6–7 inches long, with a firm, dark-purple, glossy skin. It is available most of the year.

Baked Lettuce New Zealand

SERVES 6

Ready Tray
4	heads lettuce
	boiling water
4	tablespoons butter
3	tablespoons flour
1 1/2	cups milk, scalded
1	teaspoon salt
	dash cayenne
1/2	cup bread crumbs
1/2	cup coarse-chopped nuts

Wash lettuce carefully and thoroughly, and remove imperfect leaves. Break each head into quarters with the hands. Pour boiling water over lettuce, and drain well. Cover with fresh water in saucepan, and boil 5 minutes, or until tender. Drain, and press out all excess liquid. Melt 2 tablespoons butter in saucepan, and add flour, stirring until smooth. Gradually stir in milk until boiling point is reached; reduce heat, add salt and cayenne, and simmer 2 minutes. Place lettuce in buttered casserole, and pour cream sauce over; sprinkle with bread crumbs and nuts, dot with remaining butter, and bake uncovered at 425° F. 15 minutes, or until golden brown on top.

Mushrooms Oriental

SERVES 6

Ready Tray
1	cube beef bouillon
2	tablespoons hot water
1/4	medium cauliflower, sliced thin
1	unpeeled zucchini, sliced thin
6	green onions, chopped fine
2	carrots, sliced diagonally
4	stalks celery, sliced diagonally
1	green bell pepper, seeded and sliced thin
1	cup sliced fresh mushrooms
3	tablespoons butter

Soften bouillon in water. Combine vegetables in bowl, and mix lightly. Melt butter in large skillet, and sauté vegetables 5 minutes. Add bouillon, cover, and simmer 2 minutes; toss, and serve hot.

Luau Sweet Potatoes

SERVES 6–8

Ready Tray
1/2	pound sweet butter
6	cups mashed cooked sweet potatoes
3	cups crushed pineapple
2	teaspoons seasoned salt
3/4	cup brown sugar
1/4	teaspoon fresh-grated nutmeg

Melt butter, and combine with all other ingredients except nutmeg. Spread in casserole, sprinkle with nutmeg, and bake, uncovered, at 375° F. until browned on top. Serve in shells or individual vegetable dishes.

Garnishes, Chutneys, Pickles, Fruits, and Vegetables

Chinese-Hawaiian Pea Pods

SERVES 8

Ready Tray
1/2	teaspoon curry powder
1/4	cup butter
1/2	cup green onions, sliced 1-inch thick
2	(8 ounce) packages frozen Chinese pea pods, unthawed
2	tablespoons brown sugar
1/4	cup wine vinegar
1	cup beef broth
3	tablespoons cornstarch
1	(1 pound 4 1/2 ounce) can pineapple chunks and syrup
1	tablespoon Kikkoman soy sauce
2	tomatoes, cut in small wedges
1	(5 ounce) can water chestnuts, sliced thin

In medium saucepan, cook curry powder in butter a few minutes. Add onions and pea pods, and cook only until pods begin to wilt. Stir in sugar, vinegar, and broth. Combine cornstarch with 1/2 cup pineapple syrup, and add to sauce, stirring until thickened. Add drained pineapple, soy sauce, tomatoes, and water chestnuts. Heat through, and serve hot.

Fresh Chinese pea pods are very good boiled 3 minutes and served with butter, soy sauce, salt, and pepper. Do not overcook, as they should be crisp. They may be added to stews and mixed-vegetable dishes just before serving. Sliced water chestnuts, sliced fresh mushrooms, or bean sprouts may be added to pea pods; any combination of the three adds variety to any vegetable dish.

Flaming Sweet Potatoes

SERVES 8

Ready Tray
1/2	pound chestnuts
	water
1	cup milk
	salt and pepper to taste
5	large sweet potatoes
3	tablespoons butter
1/2	cup hot heavy cream
1/3	cup sherry
1/2	teaspoon fresh-grated nutmeg or mace
3	tablespoons brown sugar or chestnut syrup
3	tablespoons dark rum

Slit chestnuts with pointed knife, and boil in water to cover 1 1/2 hours. Drain, shell, and skin while hot. Put chestnuts in saucepan, and add milk, salt, and pepper; cook until tender. Boil sweet potatoes in water to cover until tender. Remove skins, and mash with remaining ingredients, including chestnuts, except rum. Pile into casserole, reheat in oven, add rum, and blaze at table.

This dish is good with the holiday bird. Drained chestnuts in syrup may be used instead of fresh ones.

Potatoes Tahitian

SERVES 6

Ready Tray
4	cups cold water
	salt and white pepper to taste
1 1/2	cups thin-sliced potatoes
6	tablespoons butter
1/2	cup fine-chopped celery
1/2	cup fine-chopped onion
1/2	cup fine-chopped fresh parsley
1	cup toasted coconut flakes

Combine water, salt, pepper, and potatoes in medium saucepan. Cover, and bring to boil; cook 10 minutes, and drain thoroughly. Melt butter in large skillet, and sauté celery, onion, and parsley golden brown. Remove from heat, add coconut, and toss lightly with 2 forks.

This dish is excellent served with roast pork.

Spinach in Coconut Milk Fijian

SERVES 6

Ready Tray
1	cup fresh grated coconut
1	cup milk
2	pounds fresh spinach, washed and drained
1	teaspoon fresh lemon juice
1	teaspoon salt
1/2	teaspoon fresh-ground black pepper
1	large onion, peeled and sliced thin

Combine coconut and milk in saucepan, bring to boil, remove from heat, and set aside 30 minutes. Press all liquid from coconut, and discard pulp. Combine spinach with lemon juice, salt, pepper, onion, and coconut milk in saucepan. Cover, and simmer 15 minutes. Serve hot.

Taro

The taro root is the staple food of the Pacific and South Pacific Islands and the one commonly used for poi, which is made by boiling or steaming roots and mashing or pounding them to paste. Many Hawaiian babies are raised on poi instead of milk and are beautiful examples of the nutritional values of this tuber. The starch grains are the smallest of those in any plant, making them readily digestible. Taro roots can be baked, steamed, boiled, or used in soups as are potatoes; they are available the year around. The entire tuber should be very firm for best results.

The texture and flavor of taro is best when it is boiled or baked with skin on. After boiling until tender, peel, and slice 1/2 inch thick. Brown quickly in a little oil or butter, and season to taste with salt and pepper. Taro may also be served with butter, salt, and pepper as are boiled potatoes.

Wrap taro roots in ti leaves or aluminum foil, and bake in an *imu* or oven; or substitute potato baked in cabbage leaves. Serve with butter, salt, and pepper. Young taro leaves may be baked in ti leaves; spinach or grape leaves may be substituted.

Taro leaves scraped on the outside and soaked in water to cover 30 minutes, drained, then dried and baked can be eaten with salt and butter. These green leaves are known as "luau."

Filipino-Hawaiian Squash Flowers

SERVES 4–6

Ready Tray
2	tablespoons shortening
2	medium cloves garlic, crushed
1	large tomato, sliced
1/4	pound lean fresh pork, sliced fine
1/2	cup water
3	cups (about 20) large squash flowers, with stems and calyxes removed
	salt to taste

Heat shortening in large saucepan, add garlic, and cook until golden brown. Add tomato, and cook until soft. Add pork and cook over medium heat 15 minutes, or until meat is tender. Add water, and bring to boil; add flowers, season, and cook until flowers are wilted, 5–6 minutes. Serve hot.

Curries, Rice, and Eggs

9

CURRIES, RICE, AND EGGS

Curry

A Colonel Cornwell was the first to introduce curry to the Pacific islands. The term "curried" usually implies a dish of almost any cooked food reheated in sauce flavored with curry powder. There are curried eggs and curried sausage, but curried lamb, chicken, or shellfish means a real production. Meat is cooked in the sauce much as in stew.

"Curry" is a British corruption of the Tamil word *kari*. It was so extensively used in the East that it became known as the "salt of the Orient." It need not be scaldingly spicy but can also be light and delicate. The trick lies in restrained use of curry powder and extra seasonings like cayenne, turmeric, paprika, and ginger. As a rule, in areas where the weather is very hot, the natives dress in the sheerest clothes and eat curries to cool off. Gastric juices do not function properly in hot weather, and appetites diminish. They must be stimulated, and, as they respond to highly seasoned foods, curry dishes make excellent warm-weather foods. On some hot summer evening try curry in the chafing dish in the cool of your patio.

The classic way to make curry is to sauté chopped onion, tart apple, and curry powder in butter; then add chicken stock and coconut milk or a combination of stock and evaporated milk cooked together. A little flour is added but not enough to make creamy consistency.

Curry is best when the meat has been chilled in sauce overnight and reheated before serving, with seasonings corrected if necessary. Any meat, except ham, and any kind of poultry or shellfish can be used. Serve all curries with a large bowl of hot fluffy rice, and chutney is a must.

Various condiments are also important. These condiments are numerous, elaborate, and exotic. One hears of "20-boy" and "30-boy" curries, curries accompanied by 20 or 30 different condiments, each served by a different boy. For practical purposes 10–12 condiments make an impressive display; a few selected from each category provide enough choices for individual tastes. But the more the merrier, as long as each adds something definite in flavor or texture. They should be crisp, salty, sweet, or sour. The exception is hard-cooked eggs, with yolks and whites chopped separately. They do nothing exceptional for the curry but are traditional; they count as two more "boys." Chutney is essential; *Tahitian Mango Chutney* heads the list, but peach or apple chutney is an acceptable substitute. Preserved fruits of all kinds—kumquats, chopped guava, mandarin-orange sections, ginger root—and currants, raisins, or dried-apricot strips are good sweet condiments. Chopped nuts, salted almonds, peanuts, chopped preserved ginger, grated orange peel, sliced bananas, chopped sweet onions, shredded coconut, crisp bacon crumbles, shredded dried fish, fresh boiled seaweed, balls of ground salted *kukui* nuts, salted *kukui* or peanuts, native onions, coarse red Hawaiian salt, dried squid, salted liver, and grated coconut are excellent. Many of these condiments are common at luaus. A spoonful of any of them may be sprinkled over an individual serving of curry, according to individual taste.

Curries need no other accompaniment, except perhaps a salad and bread. Tea is better than coffee with curry, and chilled beer is perfect.

Curry powder is one of the oldest and best-known seasoning compounds. It is easy to use and changes commonplace foods into exotic delicacies. It is not a single spice but a blend of 10–32 spices, varying widely in potency and according to individual taste and tolerance. It ranges from fiery hot to mild. In some parts of the world, curry powder is made fresh for each dish and varies from household to household, according to personal idiosyncrasy and seasonal dish. The blend for chicken curry is not the same as that for fish curry, so experiment a little with the commercial brands. The best brands—and the most expensive ones—are stronger and more satisfying.

If, however, you have a good collection of seasonings and are not timid, there is no reason why you cannot mix your own fresh curry powder. Pounding together a pinch of this and a pinch of that in a mortar with a pestle or in a small bowl with a blunt instrument, is satisfactory. After a little practice it is easy to achieve truly individual flavors. The seasoning that gives curry its characteristic rich-amber color is turmeric; use it and any of the following in various combinations, according to taste: pepper, red pepper, coriander, celery seed, ginger, cinnamon, allspice, ground cloves, nutmeg, cumin, fennel, cardamom, and mace. Be sure to omit ginger for seafood curry.

Curry Powder

Ready Tray
2 1/2 teaspoons coriander
1 1/4 teaspoons cardamom
1 teaspoon fenugreek
1 teaspoon cumin
1/2 teaspoon ground cloves
1/2 teaspoon black pepper
1/4 teaspoon fennel
1/4 teaspoon ginger
1/4 teaspoon allspice
1/8 teaspoon red pepper
1–2 teaspoons powdered turmeric

Pound all ingredients together to fine powder; grind in spice mill or pepper mill, or put through blender.

Turmeric is difficult to mill by hand, and it is best to use powdered form. If hotter curry is desired, decrease cloves to 1/4 teaspoon, and increase ginger to 1/2 teaspoon and red pepper to 1/4 teaspoon or more.

Baked Papaya Stuffed with Lobster Curry and Avocado Fijian

SERVES 4

Ready Tray
1/2 Bermuda onion, chopped fine
2 tablespoons olive oil
1 cup rice
3 cups chicken broth
 pinch saffron
 salt and pepper to taste
2 large papayas, halved, seeded, but unpeeled
2 cloves garlic, chopped fine
1/4 cup fine-chopped green onions
1/3 cup fine slices green bell pepper
3 tablespoons butter
1 teaspoon or more *Curry Powder*
1/2 green apple, peeled, cored, and julienned
1/4 cup grated coconut
2 tablespoons cornstarch
1 cup chicken broth or chicken consommé
1 cup cream
2 cups cooked lobster, cut in 1-inch cubes
2 tablespoons Kikkoman Hawaiian teriyaki sauce
1/3 cup Kikkoman plum wine
1 medium avocado, peeled, seeded, and diced
4 tablespoons chutney
4 sprigs fresh watercress

Sauté Bermuda onion and 1 clove garlic in oil in large saucepan until golden brown. Add rice, and brown lightly. Add 3 cups broth, saffron, salt, and pepper. Stir and turn into large casserole. Bake at 350° F. 35–45 minutes, without stirring. Meanwhile bake papayas 10–15 minutes at 350° F. In frying pan sauté green onions, bell pepper, and 1 clove garlic in butter over medium heat 3 minutes. Add curry powder, apple, and grated coconut, and cook over low heat 2 minutes. Blend cornstarch with a little of 1 cup broth until

Curries, Rice, and Eggs

smooth, and add with remaining broth and cream to pan; cook over medium heat, stirring, until thickened. Add lobster, teriyaki sauce, and wine, and heat thoroughly. Add avocado just before serving, and toss very gently. Place 1/2 cup rice in center of each plate, and place papaya half on this bed; then fill papaya half with lobster curry. Sprinkle with toasted coconut; place 1 tablespoon chutney at one side of filled papaya, and garnish other side with watercress.

Be sure to use curry-powder compound without ginger.

Quick, Glamorous Chicken Curry

SERVES 4–6

Ready Tray
1	medium onion, chopped fine
1/2	cup thin-sliced celery
4	tablespoons butter
1 1/2	tablespoons *Curry Powder*
2	cans cream-of-chicken soup
2	cups diced cooked or canned chicken
1/2	cup commercial sour cream
1/2	cup slivered almonds
2	tablespoons chutney
1	(No. 2) can pineapple chunks with syrup
	hot fluffy rice

Sauté onion and celery until golden in 2 tablespoons butter in large skillet. Sprinkle curry powder over, and stir to blend. Stir in soup until smooth; add chicken, and heat thoroughly. Stir in sour cream, heat through, but do not boil. Heat 2 tablespoons butter in saucepan, add almonds, stir, and cook until golden; remove almonds, and set aside. Combine chutney with pineapple chunks and syrup, coating well; add to butter in saucepan, and cook slowly until glazed. Serve chicken curry on bed or ring of rice, and top each serving with pineapple and almonds.

Hawaiian Curry

SERVES 6

Ready Tray
2	tablespoons butter
2	medium onions, chopped fine
2	tart cooking apples, peeled, cored, and diced
2	cloves garlic, chopped fine
2	tablespoons *Curry Powder*
1	cup fresh-grated coconut
2	cups milk
3	tablespoons softened butter
3	tablespoons flour
1	cup diced raw chicken
1	cup raw shrimp, peeled and cleaned
1	cup fresh pineapple chunks

Heat 2 tablespoons butter in skillet, and sauté onions, apples, and garlic until golden. Add curry powder, and blend. Meanwhile soak coconut in milk. After 15 minutes add to sautéed mixture, and simmer slowly. Combine 3 tablespoons butter with flour, and stir into milk mixture until smooth, simmering 15–20 minutes. Add chicken and shrimp and simmer 45 minutes, or until tender, stirring occasionally so that sauce is smooth and free of lumps. Cool at room temperature; then refrigerate overnight. Reheat, and add pineapple just before serving.

If the coconut is fresh, use its milk as part of the liquid.

Australian Chafing-Dish Chicken Curry

SERVES 6

Ready Tray
1	tablespoon *Curry Powder*
1	heaping tablespoon flour
1/2	roasted chicken
4	tablespoons butter
1/2	clove garlic, chopped fine
1	teaspoon fine-chopped onion
1	tablespoon shredded coconut
1/2	teaspoon English mustard
1 1/2	cups chicken broth
	dash powdered ginger
	dash powdered cardamom
3	tablespoons commercial sour cream
1	teaspoon fresh lemon juice
	hot fluffy rice

Combine curry power and flour. Remove and discard skin and bones from chicken. Cut meat in 1/2-inch cubes. Melt butter in blazer pan of chafing dish, and add garlic. When butter is hot sauté onion lightly. Add coconut, mustard, and curry mixture. Mix well, and cook 3 minutes, stirring constantly. Add broth, ginger, and cardamom, stirring until sauce is thickened. Remove from direct heat, and add chicken. Put water jacket full of boiling water over flame of chafing dish; place blazer over water jacket, and simmer 10–15 minutes, or until thoroughly heated. Blend in sour cream and lemon juice. Serve immediately with buttered rice.

This dish is truly glamorous when served in a chafing dish for unexpected company. They will believe that you had a laborious day preparing this masterpiece.

Beef Curry South Pacific

SERVES 4

Ready Tray
1	pound round steak, cut in 1-inch cubes
12	tiny whole onions, peeled
12	slices preserved ginger
1/4	cup butter
1	clove garlic, minced
2	tablespoons *Curry Powder*
1/2	cup red table wine
1/2	cup beer or ale
1/8	teaspoon ground cloves
1/8	teaspoon cinnamon
1/4	teaspoon salt
1	teaspoon fresh lime juice

Alternate meat, onions, and ginger on 7-inch skewers. Place skewers in shallow 8–9-inch baking dish. Melt butter in large skillet, add garlic and curry powder, and cook 2 minutes, stirring constantly. Gradually stir in wine and beer. Add cloves and cinnamon. Pour this sauce over skewered meat, cover, and bake at 300° F. 1 hour, or until meat is tender, turning skewers once during cooking. To serve, place skewered meat on hot platter. Add salt and lime juice to sauce; then spoon over meat. Serve with rice, mixed green salad, and glasses of beer or ale.

Tahitian Curry

SERVES 8–10

Ready Tray
4	medium tomatoes, peeled and chopped
1	medium onion, chopped fine
1	cup diced celery
1	cup melted butter or margarine
2	teaspoons salt
1	tablespoon fresh-ground black pepper
1	teaspoon thyme
1	tablespoon *Curry Powder*
1	quart chicken broth
1	quarts fresh, canned, or frozen coconut milk
1/2	cup flour
1	tablespoon softened butter
	hot rice
	paprika to taste
	fine-chopped parsley

Sauté tomatoes, onion, and celery in a little melted butter until soft and translucent. Add salt, pepper, and thyme, blending well. Add curry powder and broth, and simmer 20 minutes. Add coconut, rest of butter, bring to boil, reduce heat to medium, and cook until mixture has been reduced by one-fourth. Make roux by blending flour and 1 tablespoon butter. Stir into hot sauce, and continue stirring until medium thick. Remove from heat, and strain, pushing as much vegetable pulp through as possible. Serve hot in individual rice rings, and garnish with paprika and parsley.

This dish is excellent with cooked shrimp, crab, or lobster.

Lamb Curry Australian

SERVES 4

Ready Tray
1	cup fine-chopped onions
1	large clove garlic, chopped fine
1	small hot red-pepper pod, chopped fine
3	tablespoons peanut oil
1	tablespoon *Curry Powder*
1 1/2	pound lamb leg or shoulder, cut in 3/4-inch cubes
1	cup water
2	tablespoons tomato paste
	salt to taste
1	teaspoon lemon juice
	hot steamed rice

Fry onions, garlic, and pepper pod in oil 3 minutes. Stir in curry powder, and cook 3 minutes longer. Add meat, and brown lightly, pushing aside onion so that it does not burn. Add water and tomato paste. Cover, and simmer 1 hour, or until meat is tender. Add salt and lemon juice. Gravy should be moderately thick; if not thick enough, add a little cornstarch blended with water. Make ring of rice on serving platter, and put lamb curry in center.

Shrimp Curry Polynesian

SERVES 4

Ready Tray
2	cups milk
1	cup flaked coconut
1	(13 1/2 ounce) can pineapple chunks, drained
1 1/2	cups medium shrimps, cooked, deveined, and shelled
1/2	cup butter or margarine
1 1/2	teaspoons *Curry Powder*
1/3	cup fine-chopped green onions
1/3	cup fine-chopped celery
1/2	cup sifted flour
1	teaspoon garlic salt
1 1/4	cups chicken broth

Curries, Rice, and Eggs

Combine milk and coconut in saucepan, and simmer, stirring, until mixture foams up, 3 minutes. Strain and press out all liquid, and reserve coconut pulp. Sauté pineapple and shrimps in 1/4 cup butter, remove from skillet, and set aside. Add remaining butter and curry powder to skillet. Cook over low heat, stirring, 2 minutes. Add onions and celery, and cook until soft. Blend in flour, garlic salt, broth, and coconut milk. Cook until thickened, stirring, 5 minutes. Stir in pineapple, shrimp, and a little coconut pulp. Serve with steamed rice, chutney, raisins, and coconut chips.

Be sure to use curry-powder compound without ginger.

Old-Fashioned Filipino-Hawaiian Tamales

SERVES 6–8

Ready Tray
3	cups uncooked rice
7	cups coconut milk
	salt to taste
1	teaspoon black pepper
1	cup brown sugar
1	cup ground toasted peanuts
1/4	cup strained *achuete* or few drops red food coloring
18–24	banana leaves or 12–16 corn husks, cleaned and softened
1/2	boiled chicken breast, sliced thin or shredded
1	2-inch square boiled or roasted pork, cut in strips 1/8 inch wide or shredded
1	slice boiled ham, 1/4 inch thick, cut in narrow strips
1	cup small boiled shrimps, shelled
1/2	cup boiled peanuts, halved
4	hard-cooked eggs, sliced thin

Toast rice on griddle until brown. Grind to fine powder in stone or cornmeal grinder, or blend in electric blender. In large kettle put coconut milk, salt, pepper, and sugar; add rice. Cook over low heat, stirring to prevent sticking and scorching, until thick. Add ground peanuts 5 minutes before removing from heat. Divide this paste in half, leaving one half in kettle. Add *achuete* to kettle, and cook 2 minutes to blend color thoroughly. On triple layers of banana leaves or double layers of corn husks, put 3 tablespoons red mixture, then 3 tablespoons white mixture. Pat lightly to flatten; then arrange chicken, pork, ham, shrimps, peanut halves, and egg slices on top. Roll, wrap, and tie securely. Repeat until all ingredients are used. Place wrapped tamales in deep steamer, and cook, covered, over low heat 2 hours. Or stack in deep kettle, half filled with water, cover, and cook over low heat 1 1/2–2 hours. Remove from heat, and cool. Reheat in water to cover, and serve, unwrapped, on heated plates.

Tamales will stay fresh 24 hours if kept in cool place. *Achuete* is red food coloring prepared by soaking 1/4 cup *anatto* seeds in 1/4 cup water. Banana leaves can be softened over direct heat; corn husks should be softened in hot water, then drained.

Authentic Rice Recipe

SERVES 6–8

Ready Tray
3	cups rice
3	cups water
1	teaspoon salt

Wash rice well under running water until water is clear. Drain, and set aside 30–60 minutes. Place rice in large saucepan, and add water and salt. Bring to boil, uncovered, over high heat about 1 minute. Reduce heat to low, cover pan, and cook 20 minutes without stirring or removing cover. Turn off heat, and let stand 10 minutes. Remove cover, and flake rice with fork before serving.

Rice prepared in this manner is extra fluffy and tender.

Fried Rice

SERVES 4

Ready Tray
1	egg, beaten
2	tablespoons butter or oil
2	cups cooked rice
1	cup fine-chopped onion
1/2	cup chopped cooked shrimp or crabmeat, diced bacon, chopped boiled ham, or julienned cooked pork
1/2	cup fresh-cooked green peas, drained
1	tablespoon Kikkoman soy sauce

In large skillet scramble egg in butter. Add remaining ingredients except soy sauce. Stir, and cook over medium heat 5 minutes, stirring lightly. Add soy sauce, stir gently, and cook 2 minutes. Serve with additional soy sauce.

This dish is excellent for lunch or as an accompaniment to a dinner entrée.

Oriental-Hawaiian Fruit Pilaf

SERVES 12

Ready Tray
3/4	cup dried apricots, sliced 1/2 inch thick
6	dried figs, sliced 1/2 inch thick
4	dried peaches, sliced 1/2 inch thick
4	dried prunes, pitted and sliced 1/2 inch thick
2/3	cup sliced pitted dates
2/3	cup seedless raisins
	water
1/2	cup Kikkoman plum wine
1/2	cup Madeira
2	cups brown rice
4	cups water
1	teaspoon salt
1	teaspoon ground cinnamon
1/2	cup butter
1/2	cup chopped browned almonds

Soak all dried fruits until soft in water to cover, drain, and then marinate dates and raisins overnight in plum wine and apricots, figs, peaches, and prunes in Madeira. Wash rice, and place in large kettle; add 4 cups water and bring quickly to boil. Reduce heat, cover, and cook 20 minutes. Stir in salt quickly, cover, and cook 25 minutes over lowest possible heat. When rice is done, toss with cinnamon; put mixture in buttered casserole, and dot with butter. Cover tightly, and bake at 350° F. 10 minutes. Toss fruits through hot rice, and empty into fancy well-buttered mold; let set 5 minutes; then turn out onto platter, and garnish with almonds.

This rice dish is excellent with roast pork or curry. It may be refrigerated and reheated 20 minutes at 350° F.

Tahitian Rice and Fish

SERVES 4

Ready Tray
2	*mahi mahi* fillets
	salt and pepper to taste
4	tablespoons flour
3 1/6	tablespoons butter
3 1/2	tablespoons light salad oil
5	cups water
1	tablespoon *Curry Powder*
2	cups rice
4	bananas, peeled, halved across, and sliced lengthwise
2	lemons, quartered

Season fish with salt and pepper, and set aside 30 minutes; then dry with cloth. Dredge fillets lightly in flour. Heat 1 2/3 tablespoons butter and 2 tablespoons oil in skillet; sauté *mahi mahi* until golden brown on both sides, and set aside. Bring water to boil in large saucepan, stir in curry powder and 1 teaspoon salt, add rice, and boil, uncovered, 12 minutes. Remove from heat and drain. Rice should be half-cooked. Put rice into large buttered casserole, sprinkle with salt and pepper, and bake at 275° F. 15–20 minutes, stirring occasionally to ensure that liquid is absorbed evenly. Heat 1 1/2 tablespoons each butter and oil in skillet, and sauté bananas over medium heat until golden on both sides. Sprinkle with salt and pepper. Mound rice on serving platter, and arrange fish, bananas, and lemon quarters around it.

Be sure to use curry-powder compound without ginger.

Asparagus Rice New Zealand

SERVES 4

Ready Tray
1	pound fresh asparagus, trimmed of hard portions
1 1/2	tablespoons flour
6	cups water
1/4	cup butter
2	cups rice
1/8	pound ham, chopped fine
1	clove garlic, chopped fine
	salt and pepper to taste
3	cups chicken or beef broth

Soak asparagus in water with flour 30 minutes. Remove asparagus, and place in saucepan with water to cover, and cook 12 minutes. Drain, wash thoroughly under running cool water, and cut in 3/4-inch lengths. Heat butter, and brown rice thoroughly. Add ham, garlic, salt, and pepper, and sauté until garlic is golden brown. Add broth, cover, and cook over medium heat until all liquid is absorbed (about 1/2 hour), stirring occasionally. Let stand 5 minutes; then add asparagus, and toss lightly. Turn onto serving platter.

Wild Rice

SERVES 8

Ready Tray
1	teaspoon salt
4	cups boiling water
1	cup wild rice

Add salt to water, and bring to boil. Wash rice in sieve with running water. Add slowly to boiling salted water. Boil gently 25–40 minutes, or until tender. Drain into sieve, and rinse with hot water before serving.

Oriental-Hawaiian Fruit Pilaf

Hawaiian Custard

Curries, Rice, and Eggs

Chinese-Hawaiian Chicken Fried Rice

SERVES 4

Ready Tray

1 1/2	cups rice, washed and drained
1/4	pound chicken, cut in 1/2-inch cubes
1	tablespoon sake or white wine
1	tablespoon Kikkoman soy sauce
3	tablespoons shortening
1/4	pound fresh shrimps, shelled, cleaned, and cut in 1/2-inch pieces
	salt and pepper to taste
1/4	medium onion, chopped fine
1	small carrot, boiled and diced
1/4	cup bamboo shoots, boiled or canned, diced
2	dried mushrooms, soaked in water and cut in 1/4-inch pieces
2	tablespoons green peas, boiled or canned
1	tablespoon fine-chopped leeks
2	eggs, lightly beaten
	monosodium glutamate
1	head romaine lettuce

Cook rice according to basic recipe and cool. Marinate chicken in sake and soy sauce 20 minutes. Heat 1 tablespoon shortening, and sauté chicken over medium heat 1 minute, or until tender. Drain on absorbent paper. Season shrimps with salt and pepper, and sauté quickly in 1 tablespoon shortening. Drain, and set aside. Sauté vegetables except lettuce in 1 tablespoon shortening quickly over high heat, and sprinkle with salt to taste. Combine chicken, shrimps, and vegetables, and toss lightly. Scramble eggs quickly in 1 tablespoon shortening. Add rice, and use spatula to break up and mix well. Add chicken mixture, mix well, and season with salt, pepper, and monosodium glutamate. Cook over medium heat until thoroughly heated, stirring occasionally. Arrange romaine leaves on individual plates or on large serving platter; spoon rice servings on each.

Pork or ham may be substituted for chicken, and vegetables may also be replaced with other favorites.

Japanese-Hawaiian Tempura Combination with Rice

SERVES 4

Ready Tray

3	cups rice, washed and drained
4	tablespoons sake or white wine
2	tablespoons Kikkoman plum wine or Tokay wine
3	tablespoons Kikkoman soy sauce
1	tablespoon sugar
	oil
1/2	cup flour
1	tablespoon cornstarch
1 1/2	tablespoons powdered rice
1	small egg, lightly beaten
1/2	cup water
4	prawns (12 to a pound), shelled with tails intact, cleaned, and butterflied from 1/2 inch from top to tail
4	baby squid (12 to a pound), slightly pounded, peeled, and cleaned, cut in thin strips 1 1/2 inches long
1/8	pound carrots, cut in 1 1/2 inch sticks (julienned)
1/8	pound string beans, Frenched
1/4	pound cleaned and deboned chicken breast or thighs, slightly pounded, cut in narrow strips 2 inches long
1/4	pound celery, cut in 1 1/2-inch sticks

Cook 3 cups rice according to basic recipe; set aside, and keep hot. Combine sake and plum wine in saucepan; heat over low heat 1 minute, and add soy sauce and sugar. Cook until sugar is dissolved, remove from heat, and set aside. Start to heat oil in deep fryer to depth of approximately 2 inches. Meanwhile sift dry ingredients together. Combine egg with water, and add gradually; mix lightly, being careful not to let batter thicken or become sticky. It should splatter slightly when dropped into hot oil. When oil is 320° F. dip prawns in batter, and fry 3 minutes. Remove, and drain on absorbent paper. Mix 1 1/2 tablespoons batter in small bowl with 1 tablespoon each squid, carrots, and string beans. Drop into hot oil, and fry 1 minute on each side, or until batter is golden brown. Repeat until all squid mixture is fried. Mix 1 1/2 tablespoons batter with 1 tablespoon each chicken and celery, and fry as for squid mixture. Place rice in large bowl; dip prawn, squid, and chicken tempura in sake sauce briefly, and arrange attractively on rice. Pour 1 tablespoon sake sauce over top, and serve with additional soy sauce on the side.

This dish is popular for lunch in Hawaii.

Green Rice

SERVES 6

Ready Tray

1	cup uncooked rice
3	tablespoons fine-chopped green onions
1/4	teaspoon *Curry Powder*
3	tablespoons butter
1/3	cup toasted slivered almonds
1	teaspoon salt
1/3	cup fine-chopped parsley
1	pimiento, chopped fine
12–14	medium trimmed ti leaves, spinach leaves, or Swiss-chard leaves
1/4	cup water

Cook rice according to *Authentic Rice Recipe* until just tender; drain. In medium saucepan sauté the onions with curry powder in butter 5 minutes. Combine with rice, almonds, salt, parsley, and pimiento. Spoon rice mixture onto leaves, fold into envelopes, and seal tightly. Stack in baking pan, pour water in bottom of pan, cover, and bake at 400° F. 25 minutes. Serve, and allow each guest to unwrap his own packets.

Heavy-duty aluminum-foil squares can be substituted for leaves.

Korean-Hawaiian Egg Custard

SERVES 6

Ready Tray
4	eggs
1/8	pound cooked lean beef or pork, chopped fine
6	tablespoons fine-chopped green onions with tops
3/4	cup water
1	teaspoon salt
1	tablespoon white sesame seeds, browned and ground
2	tablespoons Kikkoman Hawaiian teriyaki sauce

Beat eggs slightly, add remaining ingredients, and mix thoroughly. Pour into 8-inch square baking dish. Steam over simmering water 20–30 minutes, or until eggs are firm. Cut into squares, and serve.

Meat may be omitted.

Pineapple Rice Australian

SERVES 6–8

Ready Tray
1/2	pound brown sugar
1	cup water
1	medium, fresh pineapple peeled, cored, and cut in 1/2-inch cubes
2	cups unpolished rice
1 1/2	teaspoons salt
6	cups water
1/4	cup coarse-chopped almonds
1/4	cup coarse-chopped cashew nuts
1	teaspoon coriander
1	teaspoon allspice

Simmer sugar and water to syrup in saucepan. Add three-fourths the pineapple, and cook over medium heat 10 minutes. Drain, reserving liquid. Cook rice with salt in water in large saucepan until two-thirds dry. Put cooked pineapple and nuts in top of large double boiler, add rice and spices, stir lightly, and pour pineapple syrup over. Cover, and steam over medium heat until rice is tender but not mushy. Mound on serving platter, and garnish with remaining pineapple.

This dish is excellent with grilled chicken.

Hawaiian Eggs

SERVES 6

Ready Tray
2	tablespoons butter
	salt and pepper to taste
2	teaspoons grated onions
1	tablespoon fine-chopped celery
2	tablespoons flour
1	cup milk
2	cups hot boiled rice, drained
6	hot poached eggs
	paprika to taste
1	teaspoon fine-chopped fresh parsley

Melt butter in saucepan; add salt, pepper, onions, and celery, and cook over medium heat until vegetables are limp. Blend in flour, and gradually stir in milk, until sauce is thickened. Place rice on serving platter, and make indentations with bowl of tablespoon; place eggs in indentations. Pour sauce over all. Sprinkle lightly with paprika and parsley.

Chinese-Hawaiian Eggs Foo Yung

SERVES 8

Ready Tray
8	eggs
1	teaspoon Kikkoman soy sauce
1/2	pound cooked chicken or shellfish, diced
1 1/2	cups fresh or canned bean sprouts, drained
1/4	cup thin-sliced celery
1/4	cup fine-chopped green onions
2	tablespoons peanut oil
2	tablespoons Kikkoman Hawaiian teriyaki sauce
2	tablespoons bourbon
2	teaspoons sugar
2	tablespoons butter
2	tablespoons cornstarch
2	cups chicken bouillon

In large bowl beat eggs with soy sauce. Sauté meat and vegetables in oil 5 minutes; add teriyaki sauce, bourbon, and sugar, and heat through. Pour a little meat mixture into beaten eggs, blend, and continue to add, a little at a time, until both mixtures are well blended. Melt butter in large skillet. Drop egg mixture from large cooking spoon into skillet, and brown pancakes on both sides over moderate heat. If mixture is runny, keep pushing it back into shape with pancake turner as it cooks. It will firm up in a few seconds. Blend cornstarch and bouillon, cook over low heat, stirring, until thick. Serve over pancakes.

For darker sauce, add 1–2 teaspoons soy sauce.

Curries, Rice, and Eggs

Japanese-Hawaiian Lobster Omelet

SERVES 6–8

Ready Tray
6	scallions, chopped fine
6	tablespoons fine-chopped celery
2	tablespoons butter
1/2	cup fish broth
2	tablespoons Kikkoman soy sauce
1/4	teaspoon salt
1/4	teaspoon paprika
	dash sugar
2	cups diced cooked lobster meat
6	egg yolks, beaten until light
	salt and pepper to taste
6	tablespoons fresh cream
6	egg whites, beaten until stiff

Sauté scallions and celery in butter until limp. Add broth, soy sauce, 1/4 teaspoon salt, paprika, sugar, and lobster. Heat over medium heat, and set aside. Season egg yolks, add cream, and fold in egg whites. Pour into large, hot buttered omelet pan. When egg mixture begins to set around edges, spread lobster mixture over top. When omelet has puffed up well, turn over, and brown other side. Cut in wedges to serve, or fold over and slide out of pan onto serving platter.

Any fresh or dried fish may be substituted for lobster.

Egg Rabbit Australian

SERVES 4

Ready Tray
1	medium onion, sliced thin
3	tablespoons butter
3	tablespoons pickled green pepper, chopped fine
	salt and pepper to taste
2	teaspoons sugar
4	teaspoons wine vinegar
1	teaspoon fine-chopped chives
1	teaspoon fine-chopped fresh mint
1	teaspoon fine-chopped fresh parsley
1	fresh tomato, diced 1/4 inch cubes
1/8	teaspoon fresh-grated nutmeg
3	tablespoons grated Parmesan cheese
4	eggs, well beaten
4	slices toast, trimmed and buttered
4	sprigs fresh watercress

Sauté onion quickly in butter in skillet until golden brown. Add pickled pepper, salt, pepper, sugar, vinegar, chives, mint, parsley, and tomatoes. Cook over medium heat until tomatoes are well cooked, stirring occasionally to prevent scorching. Add nutmeg and cheese, and stir until cheese is well blended. Pour in eggs, and mix well. Lower heat, and stir until eggs are cooked but very soft. Mound on toast, and garnish with watercress.

Flaming Omelet South Seas

SERVES 2–3

Ready Tray
4	eggs
2	tablespoons light cream
	salt and pepper to taste
1–1 1/2	cups fresh fruit, cut in small pieces
1	tablespoon honey
1/4	cup liqueur
2	tablespoons butter
1	teaspoon sifted confectioner's sugar
2	tablespoons brandy

Beat eggs with cream, salt, and pepper. Marinate fruits in honey and liqueur for a few hours. Melt butter in omelet pan, coating sides and bottom. Let it get quite hot without burning butter; add eggs, lifting omelet edges several times to let liquid pour into bottom of pan. When eggs are set but still moist, add half the fruit evenly over top, fold omelet, and slide onto hot serving platter. place remaining fruit around omelet, and sprinkle sugar over top. Dribble brandy over fruit, and set ablaze at table.

Five eggs will serve 3–4 people, and 6 eggs will serve 4–5 people, depending on what else is served.

Raspberries or strawberries are good fruits to use, especially when marinated in Curaçao or Cointreau. If sliced peaches are marinated in peach brandy, orange liqueur, or rum, 2 tablespoons rum can be used to flame at table. Fresh pitted cherries marinated in almond extract, kirsch, or rum may also be flamed with rum. Orange juice can replace cream, and orange segments marinated in Curaçao make a nice garnish for edge of platter. Bananas sliced 1/4 inch thick, sautéed in honey and butter, and folded into omelet can also blazed with rum. All these versions are very good for lunch or Sunday brunch.

Breads, Fritters, and Pancakes

10

BREADS, FRITTERS, AND PANCAKES

Hawaiian Banana Bread

MAKES 1 LOAF

Ready Tray
- 1/2 cup butter
- 1 cup sugar
- 2 eggs, beaten light
- 2 1/2 cups sifted enriched flour
- 1 teaspoon baking soda
- 3/4 teaspoon salt
- 3 large very ripe bananas, sieved

Cream butter, and gradually add sugar. Add eggs, and blend. Sift dry ingredients together three times, and add alternately with bananas to butter mixture. Pack into greased loaf pan, and bake at 325° F. 1 hour and 15 minutes, or until done when tested. Turn onto rack, and cool.

Chinese-Hawaiian Bread

SERVES 4–6

Ready Tray
- 5 cups flour
- 5 teaspoons dry yeast
- 1 tablespoon sugar
- 1/2 teaspoon salt
- 2 1/2 cups lukewarm water
- 1 1/2 tablespoons sesame oil
- 1 1/2 tablespoons fine-chopped onion
- 1/2 teaspoon salt
- 1/4 teaspoon pepper

Combine flour, yeast, sugar, salt, and as much of water as necessary to form smooth dough. Place in lightly oiled bowl, and let rise 3 hours over medium-hot water. Do not touch dough while it is rising. After dough has risen, roll out on lightly floured board 1/8 inch thick. Sprinkle sesame oil, onion, salt, and pepper lightly all over. Roll up jelly-roll style, and slice 2 inches thick. Using chopstick or similar implement, press down on center of each piece and pinch upper edges together to form open-ended bun. Steam 15 minutes before serving.

Australian Bubble Bread

SERVES 4–6

Ready Tray
- 2 cups sifted enriched flour
- 1/4 teaspoon baking powder
- 1/2 teaspoon salt
- 1/2 cup grated sharp cheese
- 1/2 cup shortening
- 3 tablespoons boiling water

Sift together flour, baking powder, and salt. Mix in cheese and shortening with pastry blender. Stir in boiling water with fork, until smooth. Cool. Roll on lightly floured board or pastry cloth into oblong shape 1/8 inch thick. Cut in 1 1/2-inch squares. Arrange on lightly greased baking sheet or pan. Prick each piece with fork in 4 places. Bake 10–12 minutes at 400° F.

This bread is very popular in Australia.

Pineapple–Nut Bread Oahu

Ready Tray
1 3/4	cups sifted all-purpose flour
2	teaspoons baking powder
1/2	teaspoon salt
1/4	teaspoon baking soda
1/2	cup raisins
	boiling water
3/4	cup chopped macadamia nuts
3/4	cup sugar
3	tablespoons butter or margarine, softened
2	eggs
1	(8 1/2 ounce) can crushed pineapple and syrup
2	tablespoons sugar
1/2	teaspoon cinnamon

Measure first 4 ingredients into sifter, and set aside. Rinse raisins with boiling water to plump them; drain well, and set aside with macadamia nuts. Gradually beat 3/4 cup sugar into butter. Add eggs, and beat thoroughly. Add raisins and nuts, and mix. Sift in about half flour mixture, and stir until just moist and fairly smooth. Add pineapple with syrup; stir in remaining flour mixture. Quickly but gently spoon batter into greased 9" × 5" × 3" loaf pan. Combine 2 tablespoons sugar and cinnamon, and sprinkle over batter. Bake at 350° F. 60 minutes, or until done when tested. Turn onto rack and cool.

This bread is perfect with coffee and fruit salad.

Filipino-Hawaiian Ensaimada Rolls

MAKES 12 LARGE ROLLS

Ready Tray
1	package dry or compressed yeast
1/4	cup warm water
4 1/2	cups sifted flour
1	tablespoon cream of tartar
1/2	teaspoon salt
3/4	cup sugar
3/4	cup butter or margarine
6	egg yolks
1/2	cup heavy cream
	melted butter
2	cups grated sharp cheese
	sugar

Sprinkle or crumble yeast in warm water in small bowl, and stir until dissolved. Sift flour, cream of tartar, and salt together twice. Stir 1/4 cup sugar and 1/2 cup flour mixture into dissolved yeast. Cover, and let rise in warm place, free from drafts, until doubled in bulk, 30 minutes. Cream 3/4 cup butter, add remaining sugar, and blend thoroughly. Add egg yolks, one at a time, beating well after each addition. Add remaining flour mixture alternately with cream, ending with flour. Stir in yeast mixture, and beat until smooth. Turn onto lightly floured board, and knead lightly until well mixed, 5 minutes. Divide dough into 12 pieces. Roll each piece into 8-inch circle. Brush with melted butter, and spread each with 3 tablespoons cheese. Roll each as for jelly roll; then coil into round bun. Place in ungreased *ensaimada* molds or baking sheets. Cover, and let rise in warm place until doubled in bulk, 1 hour. Bake at 400° F. 15–20 minutes, or until light golden brown. Remove from oven, and brush with melted butter; sprinkle with remaining cheese and sugar. Serve warm.

Cheese–Curry Biscuits Fijian

SERVES 4

Ready Tray
3/4	cup flour
1/2	teaspoon baking powder
2	teaspoons *Curry Powder*
4	tablespoons butter
2/3	cup grated sharp cheese
1	egg yolk
2	tablespoons milk
1/8	teaspoon dry mustard
1/4	teaspoon salt
	dash cayenne

Combine flour, baking powder, and curry powder. Cut in butter with pastry blender or two knives. Add cheese, and continue mixing until smooth. Combine egg yolk, milk, mustard, salt, and cayenne. Add to flour mixture, stirring until dough is formed. Preheat oven to 400° F. Roll dough out 1/8 inch thick on lightly floured board. Cut in any desired shape, place on buttered baking pan, and bake 7–8 minutes, or until golden on top.

Breads, Fritters, and Pancakes

Portuguese-Hawaiian Sweet Bread

MAKES 3-4 LOAVES

Ready Tray
- 2 tablespoons caraway seeds
- 3/4 cup lukewarm water
- 1 compressed yeast cake
- 1 1/4 cups sugar
- 1/2 cup milk
- 1/2 cup butter
- 1 1/4 teaspoons salt
- 7-8 cups flour
- 4 eggs

Wash caraway seeds, drain, and boil in 1/2 cup water 15 minutes. Cool, and strain. Reserve liquid, and discard seeds. Moisten yeast cake in 2 tablespoons lukewarm water; add 1 tablespoon sugar, and stir to smooth paste. Scald milk, add butter and salt, and cool to lukewarm. Add yeast and caraway liquid. Sift flour, place 2 1/2 cups in large bowl, and gradually add liquid ingredients, stirring and pressing out lumps with wooden spoon. Beat dough vigorously; work with hands 15 minutes, or until well mixed, or blend at low speed. Stir in 2 1/2 cups flour, and mix well; cover bowl with clean cloth, and set in warm place to double in bulk. Beat eggs. Reserve 2 tablespoons egg. Add remaining sugar to remaining eggs and stir until sugar is dissolved. Stir into dough, and work in bowl with hands until smooth. Turn onto lightly floured board, and knead 2-3 cups flour into dough until elastic and smooth. When dough is no longer sticky and does not adhere to hands it is ready to be formed into oblong or round loaves. Place loaves in greased loaf pans and round loaves on greased cookie sheets, and allow to double in bulk. Brush surface of each with reserved egg, and bake at 350° F. 50 minutes, or until toothpick comes out clean.

In place of caraway seeds, 1 1/2 teaspoons vanilla extract and 1/2 teaspoon lemon extract or 1/4 teaspoon ground ginger can be used to flavor bread. One cup mashed potatoes may be added with flour if desired; use 1/2 cup lukewarm potato water in place of plain water to soften yeast.

The Portuguese contributed the ukulele and this wonderful sweet bread (*pao doce*) to the Hawaiian islands. The bread is available daily at island bakeries and is a traditional holiday treat. On special occasions coins, charms, thimbles, and even whole eggs at Easter were embedded in the dough. To add whole eggs to dough, when forming the loaves, reserve enough dough to make strips the size of a banana and put two strips over each raw egg and place two eggs in the center of each loaf before the last raising when ready to put loaves in pans.

Drop Scones New Zealand

SERVES 6

Ready Tray
- 1 egg
- 1 cup milk
- 1/2 cup sifted flour
- 1 teaspoon baking powder
- butter

Beat egg and milk together in bowl. Sift flour and baking powder together, and add to egg mixture, mixing until smooth (batter should have consistency of thin cream). Add more flour, if necessary. Lightly butter griddle or large frying pan. Drop batter by tablespoonfuls, and brown lightly on both sides over low heat.

Although drop scones originated in Scotland, New Zealanders consider them a national specialty, owing to the large number of people of Scottish descent living in New Zealand.

Serve this teatime favorite with plenty of butter and jelly.

Fritter Batter

MAKES 1 3/4 CUPS

Ready Tray
- 1 1/2 cups sifted all-purpose flour
- 2 1/4 teaspoons baking powder
- 3/4 teaspoon salt
- 2 egg yolks
- 3/4 cup milk
- 1 1/2 tablespoons salad oil
- 1 teaspoon grated lemon rind
- 1 egg white, beaten stiff

Sift flour with baking powder and salt. Beat egg yolks, milk, and oil until smooth. Gradually add flour mixture, beating until smooth. Fold in egg white and lemon rind.

This batter is for main-dish fritters.

Clam Fritters

MAKES 24

Ready Tray
- 2 (6 ounce) cans whole clams, drained
- 1 recipe *Fritter Batter*
- oil or shortening
- lemon wedges

Dip clams into batter, coating evenly. Deep-fry a few at a time in 2 inches hot oil 3–4 minutes, or until golden brown on both sides, turning once. Drain well on paper towels. Serve hot with *Sour-Cream Tartar Sauce* and lemon wedges.

These fritters are very good as a luncheon dish or as part of a luau or buffet.

Sour-Cream Tartar Sauce

MAKES 1 CUP

Ready Tray
1   cup commercial sour cream
2   tablespoons sweet pickle relish, drained
1/2 teaspoon salt
     dash liquid hot sauce (Tabasco, etc.)
1   teaspoon grated onion

Thoroughly combine all ingredients in small bowl, and refrigerate until well chilled. Serve with shrimp fritters or *Clam Fritters*.

Banana–Ham Fritters

SERVES 4–6

Ready Tray
1   ripe medium banana, peeled and mashed
3/4 cup fine-chopped cooked ham
1   recipe *Fritter Batter*
1/4 teaspoon paprika

Fold banana and ham into fritter batter with paprika. Fry in deep fat at 375° F. until golden brown on both sides. Drop batter into fat with spoon.

Substitute 1/2 cup drained crushed pineapple for banana and 1 can Hawaiian tuna for ham; serve with *Sour-Cream Tartar Sauce* and lemon wedges. Drop from teaspoon for hors d'oeuvres, from tablespoon for main dish.

Sweet Batter

MAKES 1 1/2 CUPS

Ready Tray
1   cup sifted all-purpose flour
1   tablespoon sugar
1   teaspoon baking powder
1   teaspoon salt
2   eggs
1/2 cup milk
1   teaspoon salad oil
1/2 teaspoon vanilla extract
1   teaspoon grated lemon rind

Sift flour with sugar, baking powder, and salt. Beat remaining ingredients in bowl with rotary beater until smooth and light. Gradually add flour mixture, beating until smooth.

This batter is for dessert fritters.

Pineapple Fritters

SERVES 4–6

Ready Tray
     oil or shortening
1   (1 pound 13 ounce) can pineapple slices, drained and halved crosswise
1/2 cup flour
1   recipe *Sweet Batter*
     confectioner's sugar

Heat oil to depth of 2 inches. Roll pineapple in flour, and shake off excess. Then dip in batter, coating evenly. Deep-fry a few at a time 3–4 minutes, or until golden brown, turning once. Drain on paper towels, and sprinkle with sugar.

Serve with *Cardinal Sauce* or *Hawaiian Custard*. Maraschino cherries with stems are very good prepared this way; the stems are used as handles. Or substitute cut-up mangoes, papayas, bananas, oranges, or peaches.

Cardinal Sauce

MAKES 3 1/4 CUPS

Ready Tray
3   tablespoons cornstarch
1 3/4 cups water
1   (10 ounce) package frozen raspberries, thawed
1   (10 ounce) package frozen sliced strawberries, thawed

In saucepan stir cornstarch into water until smooth. Bring to boiling point, and stir until thickened and translucent, 5–8 minutes. Stir in berries, and set aside to cool a little.

Fruit Pancakes

SERVES 2–4

Ready Tray
3   tablespoons butter
3   tablespoons brown sugar
1 1/2 teaspoons cinnamon
1   ripe mango or papaya, peeled, seeded, and julienned
1   tablespoon confectioner's sugar
1/2   cup sifted flour
1/3   teaspoon salt
1/4   teaspoon baking powder
2–3   tablespoons milk
1/3   cup sour cream
2   eggs, well beaten
       confectioner's sugar
       anise or cinnamon

Breads, Fritters, and Pancakes

Melt butter in frying pan, and sprinkle with brown sugar and cinnamon. Add mango, and cook until half tender, 3 minutes; set aside. Combine dry ingredients, except remaining confectioner's sugar and anise. Combine milk and sour cream. Add dry ingredients and liquid alternately to eggs. Pour over fruit, and mix lightly. Pour 2 tablespoons batter on lightly buttered hot griddle or frying pan and brown on both sides. Repeat until all batter has been used. Combine confectioner's sugar and anise, and sprinkle over pancakes.

"Down Under" Pancakes New Zealand

SERVES 6

Ready Tray
- 3/4 pound potatoes, peeled
- 3/4 pound hot potatoes, boiled in jackets
- 3 cups flour
- 3/4 teaspoon baking soda
- 1/2 teaspoon salt
- buttermilk
- piece bacon rind
- butter
- sugar

Grate raw potatoes into cloth placed in sieve over bowl. Drain grated potatoes, reserving juice. Squeeze raw-potato pulp until dry; set juice aside to settle, and reserve pulp. Peel boiled potatoes, and mash. Mix well with raw-potato pulp. Sift flour with baking soda and salt. Carefully pour off potato juice, retaining starch that has settled to bottom. Add starch to flour. Combine thoroughly with potato mixture. Stir in enough buttermilk to soften pancake batter enough to drop from spoon. Beat well, and set aside 5 minutes. Rub hot griddle with bacon rind. Drop spoonfuls of batter on griddle, and fry slowly until brown and risen. Turn, and brown other side. Butter, sprinkle with sugar, and serve hot.

These pancakes are a delicious substitute for potatoes and gravy. Care must be taken not to add too much buttermilk; as quality of potatoes varies an exact amount cannot be given.

Japanese-Hawaiian Pancake Rolls

MAKES 12

Ready Tray
- 2 cups flour
- 1 cup or less boiling water
- 2 tablespoons sesame oil
- 6 tablespoons *miso*
- 1/2 tablespoon Kikkoman soy sauce
- 3 tablespoons cool water
- 3 tablespoons sesame oil
- dash monosodium glutamate

Mix flour with boiling water to form dough. Knead 10 minutes into soft dough, shape into long sausage, and cut into golf-ball-size pieces. Flatten each with palm of hand. Brush half the pieces with sesame oil, and cover each with unoiled piece. Roll sandwiches into pancakes 5 inches around. Fry on both sides in flat, ungreased pan over low heat. Remove from pan, and pull halves apart. Steam; fold into quarters, cover with cloth, and keep warm. Combine remaining ingredients, and spread over pancakes. Roll to form round sandwich, and eat with the fingers.

Miso is Japanese bean paste. These rolls can be used as wrapping for scrambled eggs with shrimp, fried bean sprouts, fried pork, and other foods, which are added on top of *miso* sauce. Chopped onion can be spread over *miso* sauce before other foods are added, to enhance the flavor of pancakes.

South Pacific Pancake

SERVES 2

Ready Tray
- 1 cup pineapple tidbits and syrup
- 2 teaspoons fresh lime juice
- 1 teaspoon grated lime rind
- 2 tablespoons butter
- 1/3 cup sifted flour
- 1/4 teaspoon salt
- 1 teaspoon fresh lemon juice
- 3 eggs, beaten
- 1 cup grated sharp cheddar cheese

Drain pineapple, reserving syrup. Put in saucepan, and stir in 1 tablespoon pineapple syrup, lime juice, and grated rind. Blend, and set aside. Put butter in 12-inch heavy skillet, and heat in 450° F. oven. Remove from oven when butter is melted and skillet is heated through. Sift flour and salt together, and set aside. Combine remaining pineapple syrup and lemon juice. Beat in eggs, and combine with dry ingredients until smooth. Pour batter into skillet. Bake, uncovered, at 450° F. 12 minutes, or until pancake is delicately browned and edges draw away from sides of skillet. While pancake is baking, heat pineapple mixture in saucepan. Sprinkle 1/2 cup cheese evenly over pancake, and roll carefully. Spoon pineapple mixture over pancake, and sprinkle remaining cheese over. Replace in skillet, and broil 3 inches from heat until cheese is melted. Serve from warm serving platter.

Desserts

11

DESSERTS

Trifle Tipsy Cake New Zealand

SERVES 8

Ready Tray
- 1 sponge or plain layer cake 10″ × 8″ × 3″
- 1 (10 oz.) jar currant, raspberry, or apricot jam
- 2/3 cup sherry, port wine, or fruit juice
- 1 1/2 cups milk
- 3 tablespoons flour
- 2 egg yolks
- 1/4 cup sugar
- 1/2 teaspoon salt
- 1/2 teaspoon vanilla extract
- 2/3 cup port wine
- 1 cup heavy cream, whipped
- 24 blanched almonds, halved lengthwise

Halve cake horizontally, make 2 layers, and spread jam between and over top. Place cake in glass serving dish. Pour sherry over and around cake. Bring 1 cup milk to boil in saucepan. Make smooth paste of flour and remaining milk; add to hot milk slowly, stirring until it boils. Remove from heat, and set aside. Beat egg yolks with sugar and salt, and add hot milk slowly; return to heat. Cook over low heat, stirring, until custard forms. Remove from heat, cool slightly, and add vanilla extract. Pour custard over cake, and chill thoroughly. Spread whipped cream over top, insert almonds over top to resemble porcupine, and serve.

A little grated chocolate or caramelized sugar is an attractive addition.

Tropical Compote

SERVES 6–8

Ready Tray
- 1/2 cup cognac
- 1/2 cup Triple Sec
- 1/4 cup toasted macadamia nuts, halved
- 2 cups fresh pineapple, cut in 1/2-inch cubes
- 1 cup sweet apple cubes
- 1 cup papaya cubes
- 1 cup guava cubes
- 1 cup 1/2 inch-thick banana slices
- 1 cup medium whole strawberries, stemmed
- 1 cup pitted cherries
- 1 medium orange, sliced, then halved
- 2 tablespoons sugar
- fresh mint leaves

Combine cognac and Triple Sec, and pour over nuts and fruits in large bowl. Cover, and chill 1–2 hours. Sprinkle with sugar, and serve in individual grapefruit or pineapple shells set in cracked ice; garnish with mint leaves.

Hawaiian Custard

SERVES 4

Ready Tray
5	eggs yolks
5	teaspoons sugar
5	ounces Kikkoman plum wine or Tokay wine

Set small round-bottomed pan into bottom of double boiler, and bring water just to rolling boil. In round-bottomed pan whisk egg yolks, sugar, and wine with small wire whisk until sugar is dissolved; then place over hot-water jacket. Stir gently until eggs thicken, moving custard from sides toward center to allow uncooked liquid to set. Do not stir too fast, or custard will curdle and be spoiled. If water gets too hot, lift pan out of water for a second or two, but continue stirring; then immerse again. When custard is thickened, pour about 2 ounces into each of 4 long-stemmed cocktail glasses.

Always use 1 more egg yolk than there are people to be served, 5 egg yolks for 4 servings and so on. A very nice touch is a sprinkling of fresh-grated nutmeg on surface of custard. Also garnish with large whole strawberries with stems.

Mai Tai Pie

SERVES 6–8

Ready Tray
1	(1 pound 4 ounce) can crushed pineapple
1 1/3	cups sugar
1/4	cup cornstarch
1/4	teaspoon salt
5	eggs
1/3	cup light rum
1	tablespoon butter
1/2	teaspoon grated lime rind
1	teaspoon lime juice
1	baked 9-inch pie shell with fluted rim

Combine undrained pineapple, 2/3 cup sugar, cornstarch, and salt in saucepan. Cook, stirring, over medium heat until boiling and very thick. Separate eggs. Lightly beat egg yolks; stir a little hot pineapple mixture into yolks, and then return to remaining hot mixture. Cook 1–2 minutes longer, stirring briskly, and remove from heat. Blend in butter, rind, and lime juice. Beat egg whites until stiff, and gradually beat in remaining sugar, beating until stiff peaks form. Fold 1 cup egg white into pineapple mixture, and turn into pie shell. Cover filling with remaining egg whites. Bake at 350° F. 10–15 minutes, or until lightly browned.

Kona Coupe Hawaiian

SERVES 3

Ready Tray
6	tablespoons chocolate syrup
1	pint vanilla ice cream
1/2	cup heavy cream, whipped
3	tablespoons Kona coffee liqueur
3	tablespoons Cointreau
3	tablespoons chopped toasted macadamia nuts

Spoon 2 tablespoons chocolate syrup into each of 3 small brandy snifters. Place scoop of ice cream in each. Top with whipped cream. Drizzle tablespoon of each liqueur over cream in each snifter, and sprinkle with nuts.

New Zealand Strawberries Romanoff

SERVES 6

3	ounces kirsch
1	pint fresh or frozen strawberries
3	ounces rum
2	pints vanilla ice cream
3	ounces Cointreau
1	pint whipped cream

Add kirsch to strawberries, and mash lightly with fork. Add rum to ice cream, and mash with fork. Add Cointreau to whipped cream, and whisk. Place large serving spoonful ice cream mixture in glass serving dish. Top with large serving spoonful strawberry sauce; add one large serving spoonful whipped cream.

Fruit Ice

SERVES 6–8

Ready Tray
3–4	cups fresh ripe mango or papaya, pureed
	juice of 1 lemon or lime
1/3	cup honey
1/2	teaspoon gelatin
1/4	cup cold water
	sprigs of fresh mint
	orange liqueur

Combine pureed fruit with lemon juice and honey. Soak gelatin in cold water 3 minutes; then melt over hot water. Combine fruit mixture with gelatin, and freeze in ice tray at normal temperature. Ice should be on mushy side. Serve in parfait glasses garnished with mint and drizzled with liqueur.

Desserts

Flaming Foods and Beverages

To the epicure there are few dishes more exciting, visually and gastronomically, than those that can be set ablaze. Flames are a simple but magical ingredient that makes good food better, in a dramatic way. The function of flaming is to burn off the alcohol and retain the flavor of liquor and liqueurs, so use good ones.

Any liquor can be flamed. Chartreuse is exciting, for its base includes 130 different herbs. Fruity cordials and wines, themselves too low in alcoholic content to burn, can be combined with high-proof liquor. In experimenting with combinations, caution is advisable. Brandy is the traditional flaming liquor and probably the most popular.

Whatever your choice of liquor and whatever the dish, flame it correctly. First warm thoroughly in small pan or ladle over low flame. Ignite either before or after pouring over food, but do not touch match to liquor until match head has burned away. Sulphur is one flavor that you can do without.

Important dinners should end with a flourish, and guests are certain to be impressed with a flaming dessert.

Flaming Baked Alaska

SERVES 20

Ready Tray
1	1-pound pound cake
2	1-quart bricks Neapolitan ice cream
8	egg whites
12	whole maraschino cherries, halved
1 1/2	cups confectioner's sugar
1/2	empty egg shell
4	ounces rum, warmed
	confectioner's sugar

Halve cake lengthwise, and place halves end to end in center of 12–14" × 6–8" oblong platter. Place ice cream bricks as evenly as possible end to end on cake; freeze. Beat egg whites, adding 1 1/2 cups sugar a little at a time until meringue is stiff enough to form peaks. Remove platter from freezer, and spread meringue evenly over entire surface of cake and ice cream. Clean spatula, and pat meringue slowly and gently to form several peaks. Gently place cherry halves, round sides up, alternately between meringue peaks. Place egg shell, rounded side down, in center of top surface. Place Alaska in freezer at least 5 hours. Place wet serving plates and forks in freezer 1 hour before serving time. Five minutes before serving time remove Alaska from freezer and lightly dust surface with confectioner's sugar. Place under hot broiler close to flame until top surface turns golden brown. Remove from broiler, and pour rum into empty egg shell, allowing it to dribble over entire surface of Alaska. By candle light or with lights turned low, ignite rum, and watch amazed and approving expressions of your guests. With heated carving knife (place blade in hot water) halve lengthwise; then slice through center crosswise. Slice individual servings according to the number of guests to be served. Serve on chilled plates with chilled forks.

Serve *Flaming Baked Alaska* at your child's next birthday party. The children's delight will astound you, and their shrieks of joy will reward you for the extra work in preparation.

Baked Plum-Wine Dessert

SERVES 6

Ready Tray
6	eggs
3	tablespoons cold water
1	teaspoon salt
4	tablespoons shortening
3/4	cup sugar
3	teaspoons cinnamon
2 1/2	cups Kikkoman plum wine

Beat eggs, water, and salt together. Melt 1 tablespoon shortening in 9-inch skillet. Pour in 1/4 cup egg mixture, turning pan quickly to coat bottom; cook over low heat until lightly browned on both sides. Repeat process for remaining egg mixture, stacking omelets as they are finished. Add additional shortening as necessary. Combine sugar and cinnamon, sprinkle over each omelet, and roll. Preheat oven to 350° F. Arrange omelets in greased casserole. Pour wine over. Bake 45 minutes, or until wine is almost absorbed. Serve hot with additional sugar and cinnamon as desired.

Cherries Jubilee

SERVES 4–6

Ready Tray
2	tablespoons butter
1	1-inch piece vanilla bean
1	(No. 2) can black or bing cherries, well drained
1	tablespoon sugar
3	jiggers Cointreau or Grand Marnier
3	jiggers brandy
	vanilla ice cream

Heat blazer pan over direct flame until hot. Add butter, spear vanilla bean on fork, and rub center of pan vigorously. Add cherries, and heat. Sprinkle with sugar. Add Cointreau and brandy. Ignite by tilting blazer pan into flame. Serve flaming over 1 scoop of vanilla ice cream per person.

This dessert can be varied with different liquors or liqueurs. The original recipe calls for kirsch and thickening with arrowroot or cornstarch. But this recipe has the epicurean virtues of sweetness and liqueur flavor without thickening.

Crepes

Preparation of crepes separates the men from the boys and the women from the girls. It results either in a telephone call to the fire department to put out the flaming drapes or in an overwhelming impression on guests. Now is the time to grasp your crepe or frying pan firmly in one hand.

Crepes New Caledonian

SERVES 6–8

Ready Tray
- 1 cup unsifted all-purpose flour
- 1/4 cup butter, melted and cooled
- 2 eggs
- 2 egg yolks
- 1 1/2 cups milk
- 3/4 cup sweet butter
- 1/2 cup fine sugar
- 1/3 cup sugarcane rum
- 1/4 cup grated orange rind
- 1/2 cup sweet butter
- 3/4 cup sugar
- 2 tablespoons shredded orange rind
- 2/3 cup orange juice
- 2 oranges, peeled and sectioned
- 1/2 cup sugarcane rum
- 3 tablespoons sugarcane rum
- sifted confectioner's sugar

Combine flour, melted butter, eggs, egg yolks, and 1/2 cup milk; beat with rotary beater until smooth. Beat in remaining milk until mixture is blended. Cover, and refrigerate 45 minutes. Meanwhile cream 3/4 cup sweet butter with 1/2 cup fine sugar until fluffy. Add 1/3 cup rum and 1/4 cup orange rind; beat well, and set aside. Melt 1/2 cup sweet butter in large skillet, and stir in 3/4 cup sugar, 2 tablespoons orange rind, and juice. Cook over low heat 20 minutes, or until rind is translucent, stirring occasionally. Add orange sections and 1/2 cup rum. Keep warm. Slowly heat 8-inch skillet until drop of water sizzles and rolls off. Before cooking each crepe brush skillet lightly with butter. Pour in 2 tablespoons batter, rotating pan quickly to spread batter completely over bottom of skillet. Cook until lightly browned, turn and brown other side, and turn onto wire rack. Spread each crepe with orange butter; fold in half, then in half again, or roll jelly-roll style. When all crepes are ready, place in sauce in chafing dish or skillet, and heat through over very low heat, spooning sauce over crepes. To serve gently heat 3 tablespoons rum in small saucepan just until vapor rises; ignite, and pour over crepes. Serve flaming.

Peach Melba Flambé Australian

SERVES 4

Ready Tray
- 4 vanilla ice-cream balls
- 4 thin silver-dollar-size slices sponge cake
- 4 fresh or canned peaches, halved
- 1 tablespoon brown sugar
- 2 teaspoons butter
- 1 tablespoon sliced toasted almonds
- 2 1/2 tablespoons Cointreau
- 1/3 cup dark rum

Mount ice-cream balls on sponge-cake slices. In crepe pan over direct heat or in frying pan on stove, sauté peaches in sugar and butter. Add almonds, Cointreau, and rum, and flame. While peaches are flaming, ladle over ice-cream balls.

It is most romantic to turn lights very low and to have soft background music while performing this feat.

It was 1888, the year that Dame Nellie Melba, a virtually unknown singer from Australia, was to make her debut at Covent Garden Opera House in London. A dinner party in her honor had been arranged by the maître d'hôtel where she was staying. He escorted her to the kitchen to show her the masterpiece of ice-cream cake that the chef was making, a replica of Covent Garden. In her excitement Miss Melba leaned against some cartons and knocked them over just as a waiter was passing with a large bowl of peaches. He tripped over Nellie's foot, and the bowl of peaches fell on the cake, demolishing it completely. The chef became slightly exercised, as it had taken many hours of preparation and a duplicate could not be made on such short notice. The maître d'hôtel assured him that everything would be all right. "Serve it just as it is," he said, "and we'll call it Peach Melba."

Desserts

Princess Papulie's Hawaiian Delight

SERVES 4

Ready Tray
1	cup grated coconut, toasted dark brown
1	cup grated coconut, toasted light brown
1	cup grated raw coconut
4	pineapple rings, browned on both sides on hot grill
4	Queen Anne cherries
4	vanilla ice-cream balls
1	tablespoon sweet butter
1	heaping tablespoon brown sugar
2	jiggers Cointreau
3	jiggers dark rum
4	silver-dollar-size slices pound cake

Arrange dark-brown coconut in center of large platter, with raw coconut around it and light-brown coconut around that. Place grilled pineapple around outer coconut ring. Place cherry in center of each pineapple ring. Place ice-cream balls on coconut. Present platter to guests; heat butter in crepe pan over direct heat or in frying pan on stove; add sugar, and blend. Sauté pineapple rings on one side; add Cointreau and rum, and flame. While fruit is flaming, quickly roll ice cream balls in coconut, and place on pound cake in glass dessert dishes. Place pineapple ring on top of each ice cream–coconut ball, and ladle flaming syrup evenly over each.

Flaming Strawberries Polynesian

SERVES 6

Ready Tray
3/4	cup rice, washed and drained
1	quart milk
1/2	teaspoon salt
3/4	cup sugar
1	teaspoon vanilla extract
2	envelopes plain gelatin
1/4	cup cold water
1	cup whipping cream
	strawberry leaves
8	large whole strawberries
1/2	cup small strawberries
1/4	cup Cointreau
2	tablespoons brandy

Cook rice in milk with salt and sugar in saucepan until very soft and creamy. Force through fine sieve, and add vanilla extract. Soften gelatin in water, and dissolve in hot rice. Cool rice to lukewarm. Whip cream until stiff, and fold into rice. Turn mixture into ring mold, and chill 2 hours, or until firm. Unmold on cold platter, and garnish outer circumference with strawberry leaves. Place large berries in center of mold. In blazer pan over direct flame or in frying pan on stove crush small berries gently with Cointreau and brandy. Flame crushed nectar, and ladle, flaming, over central portion of mold. Serve individually.

Hawaiian Pineapple Flambé

SERVES 4–6

Ready Tray
1	fresh pineapple
1 1/2	cups light brown sugar
1/4	cup Jamaica rum
1	teaspoon cinnamon
1	cup chopped preserved kumquats
1/2	cup brandy, warmed
	coffee ice cream

Cut off top of pineapple about 2 inches down, and reserve. Remove pineapple meat, but do not pierce outer shell. Dice fruit, discarding hard core, and sprinkle with brown sugar. Return fruit to pineapple shell. Pour rum and sprinkle cinnamon over it. Cover with aluminum foil. Place in baking dish, and bake at 350° F. 30 minutes. Remove foil, replace leafy head, and bring to table. At serving time remove head, add kumquats, pour in brandy, and ignite. Ladle flaming fruit over individual servings of ice cream.

Flaming South Seas Bananas

SERVES 4–6

Ready Tray
	salt to taste
6	medium bananas, peeled, halved crosswise, and sliced lengthwise
2	tablespoons fresh lime juice
3	tablespoons butter
1	cup brown sugar
1	cup Kikkoman plum wine
1/2	teaspoon fresh-ground nutmeg
1/2	teaspoon cinnamon
1/2	teaspoon grated orange rind
1/4	teaspoon ground cloves
1	cup fine-crushed macaroons
3	tablespoons heavy dark rum

Salt bananas lightly, and brush with lime juice. Brown quickly in butter, and arrange in baking dish. Blend sugar, wine, nutmeg, cinnamon, orange rind, and cloves; pour over bananas. Turn bananas in syrup until well coated, sprinkle with macaroons, and bake at 350° F. 10–15 minutes. Flame bananas with rum.

Flaming Date Cake Queen Elizabeth

SERVES 8

Ready Tray
- 1 cup boiling water
- 1 cup chopped dates
- 1 teaspoon baking soda
- 1 cup sugar
- 1/4 cup butter
- 1 beaten egg
- 1 teaspoon vanilla extract
- 1 1/2 cups flour
- 1 teaspoon baking powder
- 1/2 teaspoon salt
- 1/2 cup chopped nuts
- 1 recipe *Icing*
- 1/4 cup chopped nuts
- 3 ounces rum, warmed

Pour boiling water over dates; add baking soda, and let stand. Combine sugar, butter, egg, vanilla extract, flour, baking powder, salt, and 1/2 cup nuts. Add date mixture, and continue mixing until all ingredients are well blended. Bake in round or square cake pan at 350° F. oven 35 minutes. Spread *Icing* on cake, and sprinkle 1/4 cup nuts over top. At table ladle rum over cake, and light with match.

This cake is good with a serving of *Hawaiian Custard*. It has been said that Queen Elizabeth bakes this cake for Prince Philip.

Icing

Ready Tray
- 5 tablespoons brown sugar
- 5 tablespoons cream
- 2 tablespoons butter

Mix sugar, cream, and butter together, and boil 3 minutes.

Flaming Coffees and Tropical Drinks

12

FLAMING COFFEES AND TROPICAL DRINKS

Flaming Coffee

Flaming coffee is not only a spectacular way to bring a dinner to a memorable conclusion; it is also a subtle way to save on electricity. It calls, as it should, for a darkened room; the only light is the flickering burner beneath the chafing dish or over the coffee cups. Touch a match to spiced liquor in shallow pan or ladle, and a blue flame spreads over the mixture, lighting the contented faces of the guests. Pour hot coffee over flaming liquor.

Blazing Tahitian Coffee

SERVES 4

Ready Tray
1   slice lemon peel
1   slice orange peel
4   cubes sugar
2   whole cloves
1   cinnamon stick
1/4 vanilla bean
1 1/2 cups cognac or brandy
2   cups very strong black Kona coffee

In blazer pan of chafing dish over direct flame place fruit peels, sugar, cloves, cinnamon, and vanilla; add cognac, and heat. Warm ladle, and dip up bit of spiced brandy with sugar lump; ignite. When brandy is blazing brightly, lower ladle into pan. Pour coffee over, and blend by dipping up liquid and pouring it back again. When blaze has burned itself out, serve in demitasse cups.

Flaming Hawaiian Coffee

SERVES 8

Ready Tray
1   lemon with thin skin
1   1-inch cinnamon stick
8   whole cloves
3   sugar cubes
3   jiggers (4 1/2 ounces) sugarcane rum
2   jiggers Tia Maria
3   cups hot, strong, black Kona coffee

With sharp knife carefully remove peel from lemon in single long spiral. Place lemon peel, cinnamon, cloves, and sugar in chafing dish over direct heat. In heated ladle ignite rum, and pour over ingredients in chafing dish. Keep ladling flaming rum over ingredients until sugar is dissolved. While rum is flaming, add Tia Maria, gradually add coffee, and continue ladling until flame fades. Serve immediately in demitasse cups.

Volcano Coffee Brew

SERVES 4

Ready Tray
1	orange
1	grapefruit
1	lemon
1	teaspoon whole cloves
1	bay leaf, torn in small pieces
1	cinnamon stick
1	tablespoon sugar
16	whole roasted coffee beans
1/2	cup Triple Sec
2	cups strong black hot Kona coffee
1/2	cup *okolehao*
1/3	cup sugarcane rum
	box whole cloves

Make three chains of citrus rinds at least 8–10 inches long by peeling the three fruits spirally. Punctuate each chain at 2-inch intervals with 1 teaspoon whole cloves. In blazer pan over direct flame, heat bay leaf, cinnamon, sugar, and coffee beans. Puncture citrus pulp with forks, and with napkin squeeze and strain pulp into heated spices and sugar. Hold all three chains together over end of carving fork, and dribble Triple Sec over from height of 12 inches. Ignite, and allow to burn down into liquid. Add coffee, *okolehao*, and rum, and heat through. Flame again. Strain with diable spoon, and serve in demitasse cups immediately.

Okolehao (pronounced *o-ko-lay-how*) is a liqueur distilled from the root of the ti plant. It became the favored drink of Hawaii during the reign of Kamehameha I (1795–1819). It was named after the iron pots used in distilling it. These pots came from whaling ships and were used in pairs. Each pot had a flat side; when they were fitted together they resembled the rump of a plump matron. Hence *okole* for "rump" and *hao* for "iron." Literally *okolehao* means "iron bottom."

South Seas Coffee

SERVES 4–6

Ready Tray
3 1/2	cups coconut milk
1	cup strong, hot, black Kona coffee
1/4	cup brown sugar
	dash salt
4–6	cinnamon sticks

In saucepan bring coconut milk just to boil. Blend in coffee, sugar, and salt. Stir until sugar is dissolved. Serve in hot mugs, and stir with cinnamon sticks.

Coffee Hawaiian

SERVES 4

2	cups strong cold Kona coffee
1	cup cold pineapple juice
1	pint soft vanilla ice cream

Combine all ingredients in mixing bowl, and beat with a rotary mixer at low speed until smooth and frothy. Serve in tall, frosted glasses.

Tropical Coffee

SERVES 4

Ready Tray
4	cups strong, black, cold Kona coffee
4	tablespoons rum
1	cup light cream
	soda water
	simple syrup

Combine coffee, rum, and cream. Chill thoroughly in refrigerator. Pour into tall frosted glasses over cracked ice, and fill with soda water. Stir gently, and sweeten to taste with syrup.

Syrup is made by boiling 1 cup sugar and 1/2 cup water; when mixture thickens, let cool.

Australian Coffee À Go Go

SERVES 4

Ready Tray
	shaved ice
2	ounces Jamaican rum
1	ounce Tia Maria
1	ounce Cointreau
4	egg yolks
1	cup strong, cold, black Kona Coffee

Fill cocktail shaker 1/3 full of shaved ice. Add all ingredients, and blend thoroughly at high speed. Pour into chilled cocktail glasses.

Papaya Nectar

SERVES 2–4

Ready Tray
2	cups diced fresh papaya
1	cup orange juice
1	cup pineapple juice
1/4	cup lime juice
1/4	cup honey
1/4	cup passion-fruit juice
	cracked ice

Flaming Coffees and Tropical Drinks

Mash papaya through sieve, or puree in electric blender, and mix with remaining ingredients thoroughly. Serve in pineapple shells with long straws, and be sure to use plenty of cracked ice.

Australian Ice Tea

SERVES 2

Ready Tray
- 1/2 cup orange juice
- 2 cups cold tea
- crushed ice
- sugar to taste
- lemon wedges

Combine orange juice and tea, and pour over crushed ice in tall glasses. Add sugar, and garnish with lemon wedge.

For tea punch, add ginger ale, soda water, sherry, and lemon juice to tea and orange juice. Amounts vary according to individual taste.

Rum Tea

SERVES 4

Ready Tray
- 4 cups hot tea
- 4 teaspoons sugar
- 4 tablespoons rum
- 4 slices lemon

Combine tea, sugar, and rum. Serve in heated mugs with lemon slices.

Rose-Petal Tea

- 1 cup boiling water
- 1 teaspoon dried rose petals

Pour water over leaves. Serve in tiny cups.

Gather rose buds, unfold separate petals, put in small cardboard box, and dry in sun. A sunny window is good. When dry, store in jar. Tea will be clear.

Hawaiian Ice Tea

SERVES 4

Ready Tray
- 1/4 cup crushed fresh mint leaves
- 4 cups hot tea
- juice of 2 lemons
- 4 tablespoons pineapple juice
- sugar to taste
- cracked ice
- 4 spears fresh pineapple

Soak mint leaves in tea 3 minutes. Remove from tea. Add lemon and pineapple juice to tea. Stir in sugar, and pour over cracked ice in tall glasses, and garnish with pineapple.

Rose Petal–Pineapple Crush

SERVES 6–8

Ready Tray
- 4–5 large roses
- 2 quarts water
- 1 1/3 cups sugar
- 1/4 cup lemon juice
- 3 cups fresh or canned crushed pineapple
- 2 cups cracked ice
- rose petals

Wash roses thoroughly in cold water. Pluck off petals, and place in a large jar, covered pyrex dish, or granite casserole. Pour water over, cover, and set in cool, dark place 4 hours. Do not put near sunshine. Strain water from petals, reserving water. Dissolve sugar in lemon juice, and stir into rose water. Add pineapple and cracked ice. Pour into tall chilled glasses, and place fresh rose petals on top of each glass.

This drink is very refreshing in hot weather. For an exciting tropical beverage, add 2 cups light rum to it.

Hawaiian Tea Punch

SERVES 6–8

Ready Tray
- 1 cup sugar
- 2 cups water
- 1 piece ginger root, 1/2-inch square
- 3 cups strong cold tea
- 1 cup orange juice
- cracked ice
- fresh mint sprigs

In saucepan boil sugar in 1 cup water to clear syrup. Cool thoroughly. Cook ginger in 1 cup water 15 minutes, and set aside to cool. Combine all ingredients except ice and mint, using ginger water and syrup to taste. Chill, and serve over cracked ice in tall frosted glasses garnished with mint.

Mai Tai Punch

MAKES 2 1/2 QUARTS

Ready Tray
- 1 cup light rum
- 1 cup dark rum
- 1/2 cup Cointreau
- 1/3 cup lime juice
- 2 quarts fresh pineapple juice

Combine all ingredients, and serve frosty cold; or pour over large piece of ice in punch bowl, and serve in punch glasses.

Trade Winds Punch

SERVES 4

Ready Tray
- 1/2 cup lemon juice
- 1/4 cup pineapple juice
- 4 teaspoons sugar
- 4 cups hot strong tea
- 1 cup sugarcane rum
- 1/4 cup brandy
- lemon slices

Combine first six ingredients, and serve in heated mugs garnished with lemon slices.

"Down Under" Brandy Shrub

MAKES 6 QUARTS

Ready Tray
- 3 pounds cocktail sugar cubes
- 2 quarts old brandy
- 3 quarts sherry
- peelings from 4 lemons, sliced
- juice of 6 lemons

Combine all ingredients, and let set 5 days; then bottle for future use. Serve as highballs over ice with plain or soda water.

Chi-Chi Cocktail

SERVES 2

Ready Tray
- 1/2 cup pineapple juice
- 1/2 cup vodka
- 2 teaspoons coconut syrup
- crushed ice
- 2 fresh mint sprigs
- 2 pineapple wedges
- 2 orchids

Put liquids in blender, add crushed ice, and blend at high speed a few seconds. Serve in tall, chilled glasses with mint, pineapple, and an orchid in each.

Coco Cocktail

SERVES 20

Ready Tray
- 1/2 bottle 135-proof rum
- 6 ounces crème de cacao
- milk from 2 dry coconuts
- 4 ounces simple syrup
- 2 teaspoons fresh-grated nutmeg
- 1 ounce vanilla extract
- crushed ice

Blend ingredients in small batches in blender. Serve frozen in 3-ounce cocktail glasses.

Simple syrup is made by boiling 1 cup sugar and 1/2 cup water; when mixture thickens, let cool.

Buccaneer's Ghost

SERVES 4

Ready Tray
- 4 jiggers light rum
- 2 jiggers orange Curaçao
- 1 1/2 jiggers red Burgundy wine
- 2 jiggers lemon juice
- 2 jiggers simple syrup
- shaved ice

Combine all ingredients except ice in shaker, and shake thoroughly. Serve in tall glasses over ice.

Buccaneer's Wench

SERVES 4

Ready Tray
- 4 jiggers light rum
- 2 jiggers Cointreau
- 2 jiggers blue Curaçao
- 2 jiggers lemon juice
- club soda
- shaved ice

Combine first 4 ingredients in shaker, top with soda, add shaved ice, shake, and serve in tall glasses over ice.

Tahiti Punch Bowl

SERVES 6

Ready Tray
- 4 ounces yellow Chartreuse
- 1 ounce gin
- 1/2 ounce lemon juice
- 1 block ice
- 1 (13 ounce) bottle champagne

Pour Chartreuse, gin, and lemon juice into punch bowl. Place ice in bowl, and add champagne. Stir slowly, and serve in punch cups.

Ginger Meggs

Ready Tray
- 1 bottle sake, chilled
- 1 bottle Crabbies Green Ginger, chilled
- cracked ice
- crystallized ginger

Combine sake and Green Ginger, pour over cracked ice, and garnish with crystallized ginger.

Vary proportions according to taste. Sake, which is somewhat bland, mixed very well with other liquors. This cocktail has won a gold medal in open competition and is very simple and delicious.

Flaming Coffees and Tropical Drinks

Australian Punch

SERVES 12

Ready Tray
- 1/2 gallon lemon granita or sherbet
- 2 large cans tomato juice
- 2 large cans orange juice
- 3 fifths vodka
- 2 large cans mango juice
- 2 large cans papaya juice

Combine all ingredients in large container, and chill thoroughly before serving.

This drink is excellent for Sunday brunch.

Chinese-Hawaiian Pineapple Shrub

Ready Tray
- 1 large Hawaiian pineapple with rind
- 1 jigger Demarara rum
- 1 jigger amber rum
- 1/2 jigger 150-proof dark rum
- 1/2 jigger Jamaica rum
- 2 jiggers fresh pineapple juice
- 1 jigger fresh lime juice
- 1 jigger honey
- 1 jigger soda water
- few chunks fresh pineapple

Cut pineapple top at slant. Hollow center, leaving about 1 inch of fruit lining shell. Blend remaining ingredients well. Pour into pineapple, chill, and serve with straws, replacing pineapple top before serving.

Akiko Cocktail

- 1 ounce green-tea liqueur
- 2 ounces dry sherry
- ice

Combine liqueur and sherry, stir well with ice, strain, and serve in cocktail glass.

Serve as an after-dinner drink.

Diamond Head Cocktail

- 1 ounce green-tea liqueur
- 1 ounce gin
- 1 ounce heavy cream
- ice

Combine liqueur, gin, and cream; stir well with ice, strain, and serve in cocktail glasses.

Serve as an after-dinner drink.

Purchasing Guide

Game and Gourmet Specialties:

Iron Gate Products Company, Inc.
424 West 54th Street
New York, New York

Most of the products like kangaroo, caviar, pheasant, wild deer, seafoods of all kinds, and beverages are available. Advance notice is necessary to obtain some items.

Gourmet foods:
Farmer's Market
3rd & Fairfax
Los Angeles, California
   General specialties.

May Company (all stores)
Los Angeles, California
   General specialties.

Goldberg Bowen
314 Sutter Street
San Francisco, California

Hosada Bros.
1596 Post Street
San Francisco, California
   Japanese foods.

Kwong Hang
918 Grant Avenue
San Francisco, California
   Chinese foods.

Mow Fung
733 Washington Street
San Francisco, California
   Vegetables.

Normandy Lane
City of Paris
Geary at Stockton Streets
San Francisco, California

House of Hanna
15th and T Streets, N. W.
Washington, D. C.
   Oriental foods.

Shiroma
1058 West Argyle Street
Chicago, Illinois
   Oriental foods.

Oriental Shop
130 East Greene Street
Ithaca, New York
   Oriental foods.

Kyoto Art Co.
2124 Northern Boulevard
Manhasset, New York
   Japanese foods.

Japan Mart Inc.
239 West 105th Street
New York, New York
   Japanese foods.

Wing Fat Company
35 Mott Street
New York, New York
   Chinese foods.

Trinacria Importing Co.
40 East 29th Strest
New York, New York
   Curry.

Index

Abalone
  bites, 56
  Chinese-Hawaiian, 96
  Portuguese-Hawaiian, 96
  sauté, 96
Anchovy spread, Portuguese-Hawaiian, 55
Apples
  sautéed, 158
  sweetbreads with, Australian, 140
Apricot
  chutney, 160
  and marrons, 158
  pot-roast with, 123
  sauce, 158
Asparagus
  Australian, 165
  and rice, New Zealand, 178
Avocado
  general information on, 162
  cocktail, 57
  crème, 162
  dip, 52
  stuffed with seafood, 56
  as stuffing for baked papaya, 172

Bacon
  Hawaiian banana-bacon Pupus, 49
Banana
  -bacon Pupus, Hawaiian, 49
  baked, 157
  bread, Hawaiian, 187
  flaming South Seas, 201
  fried, 157
  green-banana purée, 157
  -ham fritters, 190
  honeyed, 157
Barbecuing
  general information on, 143-44, 150, 151
  special recipes, 143-53

Bass
  boiled, Japanese-Hawaiian, 90
  stuffed baked, 91
Batter
  fritter, 189
  sweet, 190
Bean sprouts
  Korean-Hawaiian, 165
  salad, 76
Beef
  barbecued
    burgers teriyaki, Oahu-Pearl, 144
    chuck roast, New Zealand, 145
    flank steak teriyaki, Five Islands, 144
    Kun Koki, Korean-Hawaiian, 145
    sin-sul-lo, Korean-Hawaiian, 150
    steak, Japanese-Hawaiian, 144
    steak bits hibachi teriyaki, 152
  barbecued or broiled
    filet mignon Béarnaise, 123
    Polynesian steak, 126
    teriyaki, Japanese-Hawaiian, 125
  broiled tenderloin Fiji, 125
  bubble and squeak, New Zealand, 123
  casserole, Filipino-Hawaiian Bridges, 122
  curried, South Pacific, 176
  Fiji, 122
  flambé, 124
  ginger, Chinese-Hawaiian, 123
  jerked, Hawaiian, 123
  jerky Pipikalua, Hawaiian, 49
  Morcon, Filipino-Hawaiian, 122
  pot-roast with apricots, 123
  roast, and Yorkshire pudding, Australian, 122
  steak-and-kidney pie, New Zealand, 125
  sukiyaki
    general information on, 124
    Japanese-Hawaiian, 124
  Tahitian tropical, 125

Beverages, 205-09
Biscuits, Fijian cheese-curry, 188
Blue runner, *see* Fish, raw, Hawaiian
Brains
  lamb's, Australian piquant, 49
  scalloped, Australian, 138
Bread, 187-89
  banana, Hawaiian, 187
  bubble, Australian, 187
  Chinese-Hawaiian, 187
  ensaimada rolls, Filipino-Hawaiian, 188
  pineapple-nut, Oahu, 188
  sweet, Portuguese-Hawaiian, 189
Breadfruit, 166
  chowder Tahitian, 64
Bubble and squeak, New Zealand, 123

Cabbage
  pickles, Korean-Hawaiian, 158
  salad, Chinese-Hawaiian, 76
Cake
  trifle tipsy, New Zealand, 195
  flaming date, Queen Elizabeth, 202
Carp, Korean-Hawaiian, 90
Caviar, poor man's, Australian, 57
Cheese
  grilled, with tomatoes, 160
  -curry biscuits Fijian, 188
Cherimoya, 162
Cherries
  black, *see* Chicken, sauté with black cherries Pago Pago
  Jubilee, 199
Cherry-blossom salad, 75
Chicken
  baked
    Momi, 110
    Prince Hinoi, Tahitian, 112
  barbecued
    breasts Aloha, 145

Chicken—(cont.)
   Paradise Island, 146
   stuffed, Polynesian, 146
   Yakitori hibachi, 151
  breasts and mangoes Fiji, 110
  coconut, Samoan, 112
  coddled, 112
  curried
   chafing-dish, Australian, 175
    Hawaiian, 175
    quick, glamorous, 175
  fried, anise, Chinese-Hawaiian, 110
  with fried rice, Chinese-Hawaiian, 181
  Holiday Pochero, Filipino-Hawaiian, 111
  Marengo, Italian-Hawaiian, 111
  Party, 111
  pot-roast, 111
  sauté with black cherries Pago Pago, 113
  wings Oahu, 113
Chowder
  breadfruit, Tahitian, 64
  green-papaya, Tahitian, 64
Chutney
  apricot, 160
  mango, Tahitian, 161
  Samoan, 160
  South Seas, 160
Clam
  general information on, 96–97
  Elizabeth, 97
  flaming volcano sesame, 50
  fritters, 190
  -pepper roast, 98
Cocktails, 208–09
  Akiko, 209
  Buccaneer's Ghost, 208
  Buccaneer's Wench, 208
  Chi-Chi, 208
  Coco, 208
  Diamond Head, 209
  Ginger Meggs, 208
Coconuts
  general information on, 162–63
  chicken Samoan, 112
  Coco cocktail, 208
  milk or cream, Samoan, 163
  Princess Papulie's Hawaiian Delight, 201
  pudding, Hawaiian, 163
Coeur de Cocotier à la Tahitienne, 76
Coffee, 205–06
  blazing Tahitian, 205
  flaming Hawaiian, 205
  A Go Go, Australian, 206
  Hawaiian, 206
  South Seas, 206
  tropical, 206
  Volcano Brew, 206
Compote, tropical, 195
Coquilles Saint-Jacques Tahitian, 104
Crab
  general information on, 98
  -legs Kikko, 98
  -meat and papayas Supreme, 165

Crab—(cont.)
  and shrimp gumbo, 98
  soft-shelled with fig fritters Tahiti, 99
Crepes, 200
  New Caledonian, 200
Curry, 171–77
  general information on, 171
  beef, South Pacific, 176
  cheese-curry biscuits Fijian, 188
  chicken
   chafing-dish, Australian, 175
   Hawaiian, 175
   quick, glamorous, 175
  dip Suva, 50
  lamb, Australian, 176
  lobster, as stuffing for baked papaya, 172
  powder, 172
  puffs Suva, 52
  shrimp, Polynesian, 176
  Tahitian, 176
Custard, Hawaiian, 196

Date cake, flaming Queen Elizabeth, 202
Deer, *see* Wild deer
Desserts, 195–202
  baked plum-wine, 199
Duck
  black (wood goose) Australian, 113
  fried, 113
  pineapple, Chinese-Hawaiian, 114
  wild, Chinese-Hawaiian, 113

Eggplant
  dried-fruit stuffing for, 117
  stuffed, Japanese-Hawaiian, 166
Eggs, 182–83
  foo yung, Chinese-Hawaiian, 183
  Hawaiian, 182
  pickles, Filipino-Hawaiian, 58
  rabbit, Australian, 183
  see also Custard; Omelet
Escargots, New Caledonia style, 50

Figs
  fritters, and soft-shelled crab, 99
  tropical, 163
Fish, 89–95
  general information on, 89–90
  barbecued, Bora Bora, 146
  raw, Hawaiian, 58
  raw, Nouméa, 58
  and rice, Tahitian, 178
  stuffed baked, 91
  Tahitian, 58
   salad, 75
  See *also* Bass; Carp; Herring; *Mahi mahi*; Salmon; Sole; Swordfish; Trout
Flaming foods and beverages, 77, 80, 129, 167, 199–200, 205–06
Flowers, crystallized, 158
Fowl, 109–18
  general information on, 109–10
Fritters, 189–90
  banana-ham, 190
  batter, 189

Fritters—(cont.)
  clam, 189
  fig, with soft-shelled crab, 99
  pineapple, 190
Frog legs Provençale, 91
Fruit
  cocktail
   litchi, 57
   papayas, 57
   South Pacific, 57
  in foil, Fijian, 148
  ice, 196
  salad
   Australian, 77
   bowl, Hawaiian, 77
   flaming orange Bora Bora, 77
   pineapple-rum, 79

Ginger liver, 139
Goose roast, New Zealand, 114
Green beans, South Pacific, 165
Guava, sweet pickles, 161

Haddock, stuffed baked, 91
Haggis baggis, Australian, 139
Halibut, *see* Fish, Tahitian
Ham
  banana-ham fritters, 190
  Colony club, Australian, 135
  Morcon, Filipino-Hawaiian, 122
  tidbits, flaming sweet-and-sour, 50
Herring, grilled mustard, New Zealand, 91
Hors d'oeuvres, 49–59

I'a Ota, 75
Ice Cream
  Flaming Baked Alaska, 199
  Kona Coupe Hawaiian, 196
  New Zealand Strawberries Romanoff, 196
  Peach Melba Flambé Australian, 200
Icing, 202

Kalua puaa, Hawaiian, 148
Kangaroo
  roast, Australian, 137
  steak, Australian, 138
Kidneys
  steak-and-kidney pie, New Zealand, 125
  veal, flambé, Australian, 139
Kim chee, 158
Kiwi fruit, 164

Lobster
  general information on, 99–100
  barbecued, 147
   skewered, 147
  boiled, 100
  broiled, 100
  curried, 172
  Guy Brault's, à l'Américaine, 100
  omelet, Japanese-Hawaiian, 183
  pressure-cooked, 100
  Rumaki, 55

Index

Lobster—(cont.)
  salad
    South Pacific, 77
    Spanish-Hawaiian, 78
  spit-roasted, 101
Lamb
  barbecued chops, Australian, 147
  brains, Australian piquant, 49
  broiled Sate, 129
  chops, Tahitian, 126
  crown roast, Australian, 130
  curried, Australian, 176
  One Meat Ball Fiji, 126
  and pineapple ragout, 129
  shanks, flaming, 129
  stew, Australian sheep-station, 130
  See also Mutton
Laulaus, 148
  Hawaiian, 51
Lettuce, baked, New Zealand, 166
Litchi nuts, 164
  fruit cocktail, 57
Liver, ginger, 139

Mahi mahi
  grilled or barbecued, 91
  see also fish, and rice, Tahitian
Mackerel, *see* Fish, raw Hawaiian
Mai Tai Pie, 196
Mangoes
  general information on, 164
  chicken breasts and, Fiji, 110
  chutney, Tahitian, 161
  mousse, 164
  salad, 79
Marinade
  pineapple, 149
  seafood soy, 151
  soy, 149
Marrons and apricots, 158
Meat, 121–40
  general information on, 121–22
Meatballs, teriyaki Hawaiian, 51
Mushrooms Oriental, 166
Mustard, Chinese, 56
Mussel-and-potato salad, Japanese-Hawaiian, 83
Mutton
  Colonial Goose, New Zealand, 129

Nectarines on a stick, 51

Omelet
  Baked Plum-wine Dessert, 199
  flaming South Seas, 183
  lobster, Japanese-Hawaiian, 183
Orange salad
  flaming Bora Bora, 77
  and onion, Australian, 79
Orange-blossom sauce, 151, 158
Oyster
  chop suey, 101
  fried, 102
  pie, Chinese-Hawaiian, 102
  salad, Tin Can Isle, Niuafo'ou, 78
  sausages, New Zealand, 102
  -wine stew, Australian, 102

Pancake, 190–91
  "Down Under," New Zealand, 191
  fruit, 190
  -rolls, Japanese-Hawaiian, 191
  South Pacific, 191
Papaya
  general information on, 164
  baked, stuffed with lobster curry and avocado Fijian, 172
  and crabmeat Supreme, 165
  fruit cocktail, 57
  green
    chowder Tahitian, 64
    pickles, 161
  nectar, 206
  salad, Filipino-Hawaiian, 78
Peach
  honeyed, 159
  Melba, flambé Australian, 200
Pea-pods, Chinese-Hawaiian, 167
Pickles
  cabbage, Korean-Hawaiian, 158
  eggs, Filipino-Hawaiian, 58
  fresh-pineapple, 161
  green-papaya, 161
  kim chee, 158
  papaya, 161
  sweet guava, 161
  sweet radishes, 161
Pig, Hawaiian barbecued (*kalua puaa*), 148
Pilaf, fruit, Oriental-Hawaiian, 178
Pineapple
  with duck, Chinese-Hawaiian, 114
  flambé, Hawaiian, 201
  fritters, 190
  glazed rings, 159
  -lamb ragout, 129
  Mai Tai Pie, 196
  -nut bread, Oahu, 188
  -pickles, 161
  -rice Australian, 182
  -rum salad, 79
  spiced slices, 159
  sticks, 159
    Pearl Harbor, 58
Poi, 59
Pork
  barbecued
    Chinese-Hawaiian, 149
    kalua puaa (Hawaiian whole pig), 148
    Luau-style Island, 132
    ribs, Luau, 149
    roast Fijian, 149
    sesame, Japanese-Hawaiian, 149
    shrimp-spareribs (hors d'oeuvres), 55
  chops
    and fruit, Australian, 130
    Hawaiian, 130
    Kona Inn, 131
  picadillo, Filipino-Hawaiian, 132

Pork—(cont.)
  roast
    general information on, 130
    Luau-style Island, 132
    red, Char Sui, Chinese-Hawaiian, 131
    suckling pig Puaachi, Tahitian, 131
  smoked, New Zealand, 135
  spareribs
    barbecued (hors d'oeuvres), 55
    Island, 135
    Paradise Isle, 132
    shrimp and, Hibachi-barbecued, 151
    South Pacific, 132
Potatoes
  -mussel, Japanese-Hawaiian, 83
  Tahitian, 167
Prawns, flaming Tahitian, 52
Prunes, meat-stuffed, Australian, 159
Pudding, coconut, Hawaiian, 163
Punch
  Australian, 209
  Hawaiian tea, 207
  Mai Tai, 207
  Tahiti Punch Bowl, 208
  Trade Winds, 208

Rabbit, pot-roasted, Australian, 138
Rabbit (rarebit), egg, Australian, 138
Radishes, sweet pickles, 161
Red snapper, *see* Fish, raw, Nouméa
Rice, 177–82
  asparagus, New Zealand, 178
  authentic recipe, 177
  and fish, Tahitian, 178
  fried, 177
    with chicken, Chinese-Hawaiian, 181
  fruit pilaf, Oriental-Hawaiian, 178
  green, 181
  pineapple-, Australian, 182
  tamales, Filipino-Hawaiian, 177
  Tempura, Japanese-Hawaiian, 181
  wild, 178
Rumaki
  lobster, 55
  Polynesian, 55

Salads, 75–80
  bean-sprout, Korean-Hawaiian, 76
  cabbage, Chinese-Hawaiian, 76
  cherry-blossom, 75
  coeur de cocotier à la Tahitienne, 76
  fish, Tahitian, 75
  flaming orange, Bora Bora, 77
  fruit, Australian, 77
  fruit bowl, Hawaiian, 77
  Hawaiian Japanesque, 76
  lobster
    South Pacific, 77
    Spanish-Hawaiian, 78
Salads
  macadamia Island, 77
  mango, 79
  orange-and-onion, Australian, 79
  oyster, Tin Can Isle, Niuafo'ou, 78

Salads— (cont.)
    papaya, Filipino-Hawaiian, 78
    Papeete, 83
    pineapple-rum, 79
    potato-mussel, Japanese-Hawaiian, 79
    sesame-seed, Korean-Hawaiian, 79
    spinach, Victor's flaming, 80
    Sunomono, Japanese-Hawaiian, 83
    water-chestnut, 78
Salad dressings, 80–85
    ale 'n oil, Canberra, 83
    banana-cream, 83
    beer-boiled, 80
    boiled, 80
    chutney-cream, 84
    curry, 84
    fruit salad, 84
    ginger, 84
    Green Goddess, 80
    Imperial, 84
    lemon-cream, 84
    orange, 85
    plum-wine fruit, 85
    roquefort, 84
    sweet-sour sesame seed, 85
Salmon
    Papeete Lomi, 58
    steaks, marinated, 95
    in ti leaves, 91
Sashimi, Japanese-Hawaiian, 59
Sauces
    apricot, 158
    barbecue
        beef, 152
        Famous Kikkoman, 153
        lemon-soy steak, 153
        orange-blossom, 151, 158
    pork, 152
        spicy, 152
        tarragon-butter, 147
    bean, 135
        Hawaiian, 55
    Cardinal, 190
    plum, 55
    sour-cream tartar, 190
    soy
        cold, 56
        hot, 56
        lemon-, 153
    See also Marinade
Scallops
    general information on, 102–03
    hibachi-barbecued, 151
    sautéed, 103
Scones, New Zealand drop, 189
Sesame-Seed salad, Korean-Hawaiian, 79
Shellfish, 95–106
    general information on, 89, 95–96
    See also Abalone; Clam; coquilles Saint-Jacques; Crab; Lobster; Oyster; Scallops; Shrimp
Shrimp
    barbecued, Tahitian, 147
    boiled, 51
    broiled or barbecued in foil, 148
    crab and gumbo, 98

Shrimp— (cont.)
    curried, Polynesian, 176
    deviled, Paradise Isle, 103
    hibachi-barbecued with spareribs, 151
    Lau Lau, 103
    Polynesian, 104
    tempura, 56
Shrub
    brandy, "Down Under," 208
    pineapple, Chinese-Hawaiian, 209
Snails, 105
    Escargots New Caledonia Style, 50
Sole
    Diable New Caledonian, 92
    ginger, Chinese-Hawaiian, 92
    See also Fish, barbecued, Bora Bora
Soups, 63–72
    general information on, 63
    abalone
        Chinese-Hawaiian, 63
        clear, 63
    almond, Chinese-Hawaiian, 64
    beef and sweet-potato, Korean-Hawaiian, 64
    bird's nest, 64
    breadfruit chowder, Tahitian, 64
    champagne-almond, 65
    chicken, Japanese-Hawaiian, 65
    clam, Korean-Hawaiian, 65
    Cock-a-Leekie, Sydney, 66
    coconut, 64
        Bora Bora, 65
    cold
        fruit, South Pacific, 67
        melon, Polynesian, 71
        tomato, Australian, 72
    dried-pea, Pago Pago, 71
    egg-flower with cucumbers, 67
    Famous Korean-Hawaiian Wedding, 68
    fish, Filipino-Hawaiian, 66
    green, Tahitian, 66
    green-papaya chowder, Tahitian, 64
    haddock, New Zealand, 65
    kangaroo-tail, Australian, 66
    lentil, New Zealand, 67
    macadamia-nut, 71
    mutton, New Zealand, 67
    oyster, New Zealand, 71
    pumpkin-banana, 71
    seaweed, Hawaiian, 71
    shark's fin, 72
    shrimp-and-oyster bisque, 68
    Toheroa clam, New Zealand, 66
    turtle, Fiji, 68
    vichyssoise, New Caledonian, 72
    Wedding, with meat balls, 68
Soy
    marinade, 151
    See also Sauces, soy
Spinach
    in coconut milk, Fijian, 167
    salad, Victor's flaming, 80
Squab
    Chinese-Hawaiian, 114
    South Seas, 117
Squash flowers, Filipino-Hawaiian, 167

Squid
    general information on, 105
    baked, 105
    Filipino-Hawaiian, 55
    pan-fried, 105
    stuffed, 105
Steak-and-kidney pie, New Zealand, 125
Strawberries
    flaming, Polynesian, 201
    Romanoff, New Zealand, 196
Stuffing
    for duck or eggplant, dried-fruit, 117
    for duck or goose, 118
    for fowl
        fruit-and-rice, 117
        old-fashioned oyster, 118
    for turkey, Hawaiian macadamia-nut, 118
Sweet potatoes
    flaming, 167
    leaf salad, Filipino-Hawaiian, 79
    Luau, 166
Sweetbreads with apples, Australian, 140
Swordfish bake, Tahitian, 92

Tamales, old-fashioned, Filipino-Hawaiian, 177
Taro root, 167–68
Tea
    ice
        Australian, 207
        Hawaiian, 207
    punch, Hawaiian, 207
    rose-petal, 207
    rum, 207
Toad-in-the-Hole, Australian, 113
Trout, Honolulu, 92
Turkey
    barbecued, Polynesian, 146
    foil-wrapped Orientale, 114
    roast, Portuguese-Hawaiian, 117
    Wellington, New Zealand, 117
Turtle
    general information on, 106
    snapping-, fried, 106
    stew, 106

Veal
    in papaya Lilioukalani, 136
    Provençale Nouméa, 136

Water chestnuts, 160
    salad, 78
Watermelon, "Down Under," 57
Whale-Steak Chasseur, 95
Wild deer
    general information on, 136–37
    marinated, Molokai, 137
    stew, Molokai, 137
Wild duck, Chinese-Hawaiian, 112
Wild rice, 178
Wood goose, Australian, 113

Yorkshire pudding, roast beef and, 122